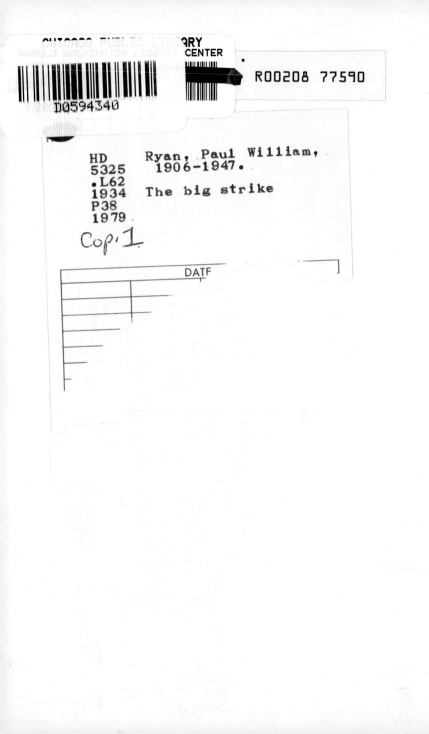

THE BIG STRIKE

THE BIG STRIKE

By Mike Quin

INTERNATIONAL PUBLISHERS, NEW YORK

Illustrations by Bits Hayden

Library of Congress Cataloging in Publication Data

Ryan, Paul William, 1906-1947.
  The big strike.

  Reprint of the 1949 ed. published by Olema
Pub. Co., Olema, Calif.
  1. Pacific Coast Longshoremen's Strike, 1934.
I. Title.
HD5325.L62 1934.P38   1979   331.89'281'3871640979461
ISBN 0-7178-0504-2   79-14101

To

NICK BORDOISE

HOWARD SPERRY

DICK PARKER

Stop in your tracks, you passer-by;
Uncover your doubting head.
The workingmen are on their way
To bury their murdered dead.

The men who sowed their strength in work,
And reaped a crop of lies
Are marching by. Oppression's doom
Is written in their eyes.

CONTENTS

[ix]

Ａ LTHOUGH IT WAS SENT THROUGH ME, Mike Quin's last letter was to his "Brothers, The Longshoremen and Warehousemen," the rank and file. He wrote it in May of 1947 when he knew he would not live to see his forty-second birthday. In it he reiterated his faith in working people and his love for them. And in return the workers loved Mike. They packed the memorial service where I tried to read his farewell message. I could hardly see the words and my voice broke on the last paragraph:

> When the next struggle comes, think of me as a kind of skinny guy in horn-rimmed glasses whose weapon was the typewriter, who fought with you side by side, and is with you in spirit with all his might.

The essence of Mike's spirit was his conviction (gained the hard way, by being a worker) that the real source of union power is its rank and file membership. This theme was a constant in his works—his books, columns, his radio scripts—which were sometimes serious, sometimes funny, and always dead-on.

This book of Mike's is about a general strike that demonstrated the might of the rank and file. Economists, lawyers, financial advisers, and even the officers they elected to lead them, while valuable and truly important skilled tools, ran second to the united strength of the workers. Rank and file strength is shown for what it is—indispensable. This principle remains eternally sound. Such was the message Mike passed on to all those who would aspire to working class leadership.

While he placed his faith and trust in the working class, Mike Quin understood that workers everywhere are only human and can and do make mistakes. In this connection, Mike himself would readily admit when he had been wrong. He did not consider it a show of weakness for him to say so. He used his faculty for self-criticism to help him grow, to change, and to change the world.

In the more than thirty years since his death, our struggles have continued, the ones to come already overlapping the ones we face today. In them we have missed Mike's agile mind and typewriter. We have missed his humor. However, we have always been aware of his support and his spirit that demanded that we stick to the tenet that the most important segment of the working class is the workers themselves.

And, though he was but one worker among many, Mike Quin's dedication and publications made a difference—a substantial difference—which continue to inspire us all. I said it then and I repeat it now, for it still holds true:

> The ILWU and the whole CIO on the West Coast would not be the organizations they are today had it not been for the contributions of Mike Quin.

New readers and re-readers of *The Big Strike* will know what I mean.

CHAPTER I
General Strike, A
Camera-Eye View

IN SAN FRANCISCO, JULY 1934, the laboring population laid down its tools in a General Strike.

An uncanny quiet settled over the acres of buildings. For all practical purposes not a wheel moved nor a lever budged. The din of commercial activity gave way to a murmur of voices in the streets.

Along the Embarcadero and in front of the National Guard Armory self-conscious-looking schoolboys wearing steel helmets and ill-fitting khaki uniforms paced up and down fingering heavy automatic rifles.

Highways leading out of the city bore a continuous stream of expensive cars carrying well-to-do refugees to distant sanctuaries. They were fleeing from bombs and rioting mobs.

There were no bombs.

There were no rioting mobs.

These existed only in the pages of the daily press which characterized the event as a Bolshevik revolution, and conjured up visions of tempestuous throngs sweeping, torch in hand, through the city streets.

Telephone and telegraph wires burned like an inflamed nervous system.

Unconvinced pedestrians bought copies of newspapers whose headlines exceeded the signing of the Armistice. These papers declared that the city was in control of communists who were threatening bloodshed and ruin. In residential sections some uninformed citizens were frightened out of their wits; they barricaded their doors and trembled in expectation of chaos.

But the people, in general, were unimpressed by headlines that screamed of communist violence. They knew better. They could look around and see for themselves that the General Strike was disciplined and orderly. Mobs and bombs had no part in it.

True, the city during preceding days had been shaken by violent industrial warfare. Major battles had been fought in the streets and innocent spectators as well as unarmed strikers had gone down before police gunfire. A general maritime strike had paralyzed all shipping up and down the Pacific Coast for more than two months; the merchant marine was tied up in the harbors like so many dead whales. The town bristled with bayonets and hospitals were jammed with the wounded. Clouds of tear and nausea gas had swept through business districts, penetrating windows and driving panic-stricken throngs from the buildings. Pedestrians running for shelter had been winged by stray bullets and crumpled to the pavement. The sounds of shouting, running crowds, pistol shots, screams, breaking glass, and wailing sirens had filled the streets.

All these things had happened before the General Strike; and still more violence was to come in the form of vigilante and police raids— buildings were to be wrecked and skulls fractured. It is not surprising that sections of the population expected almost anything to happen.

As a matter of fact, the streets were orderly and unalarming. No streetcars were running. Gasoline stations were closed and few automobiles were abroad. Children and adults on roller skates swayed up and down Market Street. Workingmen were out in holiday clothes, with celluloid buttons glistening on every coat lapel. Here and there a truck was tipped over and its merchandise scattered on the streets when business houses sought to move their goods with scab drivers; but these incidents were too few to make much impression on the population as a whole.

Saloons and liquor stores were closed "By order of the General Strike Committee."

Hastily scribbled signs and placards in the windows of most small shops and restaurants read: "CLOSED TILL THE BOYS WIN"; or "WE'RE WITH YOU FELLOWS. STICK IT OUT"; or "CLOSED TILL THE LONG-

Larger establishments simply stripped their windows of merchandise and pulled down the shades. The big department stores remained open but unpatronized.

Nineteen restaurants were allowed to remain open "By permission of the General Strike Committee." Each had its long line of waiting customers.

Outside the Labor Temple the street swarmed with union men anxiously awaiting snatches of news from within, where the General Strike Committee was in session.

All was not perfect harmony inside. Behind those doors two opposing points of view were battling it out within the committee. The newer and more determined union elements viewed the strike with confidence; they wanted to organize essential public services under control of the strikers in order that undue hardships be spared the public, so that the strike could hold out till the unions won their demands.

The older, more conservative union elements viewed the strike with alarm and were making every effort to loosen its grip.

Every few hours the newspapers issued blazing extras announcing: "BIG STRIKE BROKEN!"

The strike was not over, and there was no reason to suppose it was. But these extras served to create restlessness among the strikers, confusion among the general public, and a weakening of the solidarity behind the strike.

Demands of the striking unions were ignored in the vast chorus of prominent voices declaring that Moscow was trying to seize San Francisco as a colonial possession.

Gangs of vigilantes roamed the city smashing halls and homes where communists were known or supposed to gather. Over 450 persons were packed into a city jail built to accommodate 150.

This is a surprising spectacle for a civilized American city to present. There must be some logical explanation for it, even if the events themselves are a little mad.

General strikes on a small or partial scale had occurred before. In Seattle, just before the World War, a general strike of considerable proportions took place. But none of these strikes was on a scale with what happened in San Francisco.

We shall go back and follow the development of these happenings from the germinating seed to the full-grown tree heavily laden with the fruits of turmoil.

I N ORDER TO UNDERSTAND WHAT
happened in San Francisco it is useful to know something about the
city and its people, in the year 1934.

San Francisco is built upon a broad peninsula, swept by wind and
fog and prey to the most erratic weather conditions. It is washed on
its west shore by the waters of the Pacific and on the east by the
smooth waters of the bay. Sometimes within a single month it will
experience every imaginable variety of weather from the best to the
worst. Snow, however, almost never falls. When it does, the event is
celebrated as a novelty.

More than 600,000 people live here, only a little more than 200,000
of whom are women. Over 41,000 men are without possible mates.

Only half of the population works for wages. The rest are either
housewives, coupon clippers, or unemployed. Of the half that works,
50 per cent are white-collar workers and 50 per cent are laborers.

Sixty-one per cent of the population is either foreign-born or of direct foreign-born parentage. Of these, the foreign-born are in the majority, comprising one-third of the total population.

Considering direct foreign-born and one-generation-removed, there are more than 50,000 Irishmen, 48,000 British, 58,000 Italians, 45,000 Germans, 30,000 Scandinavians, and 13,000 Russians. There are 16,000 foreign-born Chinese and no figures at hand of American-born Chinese. Around 8,000 Negroes live in San Francisco.*

In the field of service, there are over 90,000 mechanics, laborers, and factory hands and 35,000 seamen, longshoremen, and others engaged in the transportation industries.

It takes 56,621 clerical workers to keep the books, look after the payrolls, add up the profits, subtract the losses, and service the city's ledgers generally.

More than 50,000 domestic and personal servants are required to make the beds, wait on table, wash the dishes, sweep the floors, and cook the meals.

Just 1,712 lawyers harangue the courts.

The whole city dances to the music of 2,398 musicians and says "Ah!" for 1,694 physicians.

There are 2,149 technical engineers.

A little over 18 per cent of the employed (61,581 persons) are engaged in merchandising.

Women comprise only a little over 25 per cent of all the working people. Nevertheless, 50 per cent of the clerical workers and 45 per cent of the professional people are women. They also comprise 38 per cent of the domestic and personal servants. In other occupations they are a small minority.

From a scenic standpoint San Francisco is abundantly blessed. Its harbors and panoramas are unexcelled. The heights of the city overlook the blue waters of the bay with the soft, rolling Marin hills and mountain peaks in the background. On a clear day the neighboring cities of Oakland, Alameda, and Berkeley can be seen spread out over the farthest shore. Ungainly ferryboats ply back and forth. Two giant bridges, the largest in the world, provide spectacular engineering feats.

At night the cities across the bay sparkle with a million lights. If a moon is out, the waters present a level area of silver light. In the

*By the middle of World War II the Negro population in the Bay Area was 60,000: San Francisco, 18,000; Oakland, 25,000; Richmond, 5,600; Vallejo, 11,000. Negro workers made their influence felt throughout the trade unions and the civic life of the community.

center the searchlight on the grim island fortress of Alcatraz Federal Prison blinks like an angry eye. Blue and green lights of anchored ships dot the harbor.

On foggy nights you stare into an impenetrable gray veil and the voice of the Alcatraz foghorn cries out in mournful tones. It has been described as the haunting wail of a thousand drowned sailors. It can be heard over a large part of the town, and the countless horns on vessels and docks join in a dismal wailing that might undermine the staunchest spirit.

Straight through the heart of the city cleaves a broad street, the backbone of the community. This is Market Street, with its four lanes of streetcar tracks and a continual seething of pedestrian and automobile traffic. It runs straight as a die and level over most of its course from historic Ferry Building to the foot of Twin Peaks.

Demonstrations and parades command more notice in San Francisco, perhaps, than in any other American city, for Market Street provides an imposing line of march running directly across the consciousness of the whole town.

The geometrical tangle of streets cutting into Market Street grew out of the city's earliest days. Lanes defined at the caprices of haphazard shack builders became permanent thoroughfares and are now asphalt gorges between the steep cliffs of skyscrapers.

The amazing pace of development may be reckoned from the fact that some of the men who hammered nails into the early sand-dune shacks are alive today amidst a towering maze of concrete and steel.

In earlier days Market Street comprised a social boundary. South of Market lived the vast and vigorous Irish population, together with all other laboring and unprosperous elements. North of Market was the domain of the well-to-do. Shipowners, wholesalers, financiers, and industrialists built their mansions on the north side.

In those days cable cars operated on Market Street, and the long slot through which they gripped the cable gave rise to the expression "North of the slot" and "South of the slot," which meant, literally, prosperous or poor, merchant or laborer.

San Francisco remains today a city of clearly defined social and industrial districts. The occupational cleavage of Market Street has survived inasmuch as the prosperous elements have not invaded the south side in their spreading of residences. Working people, however, have moved in on the north side and are entrenched in clearly defined areas, particularly in old mansions that the rich have abandoned and that have now been converted into rooming houses and flats. The majority of the Irish-American population is still concentrated "South of the slot," which exists as a powerful Roman Catholic stronghold.

The chaotic architecture of the city is spread over steep hills and deep valleys. Streets in many cases are so precipitous that automobiles cannot traverse them. Old-fashioned cable cars remain in operation over hills which electric cars cannot negotiate.

The waterfront runs diagonally to Market Street, jutting out to right and to left of the Ferry Building. Eighty-two huge docks capable of accommodating 250 vessels line the shore. A broad, cobblestoned street, gridded by the tracks of the state-owned Belt Line Railroad, runs the entire length of the front and is known as the Embarcadero, retaining its name from early Spanish days.

Here the most vital function of the city is performed amidst a constant din of commercial activity. Hissing, clanging locomotives shunt an endless flow of freight cars in and out the covered docks. Heavy-laden trucks thunder across the cobblestoned paving. Pedestrians swarm like ants through the dense traffic.

Across the Embarcadero from the docks is a long row of ramshackle, blistered buildings which house seamen's outfitting companies, pool rooms, cafeterias, saloons, tattooing parlors, cheap hotels, and cigar stores. In back of this dilapidated array loom the giant skyscrapers of the city, topped by gaudy signboards and electrical advertisements. The narrow alleys which chop into the Embarcadero to right and to left of Market Street lead into wholesale and warehouse districts, fruit, vegetable and poultry centers, and cheap hotel neighborhoods.

Market Street is lined with popular-priced shops, department stores, men's clothing establishments, markets, moving picture theaters, furniture stores, and cafeterias established on the ground floors of office buildings. The buildings themselves house the wildest variety of business ventures: novelty manufacturers, sales agencies, advertising companies, dancing schools, beauty parlors, attorneys, collection companies, small wholesalers, and all the myriad little negotiators and transactors who make up the froth of the petty commercial field.

South of Market Street, before you come to the vast working class residential areas, is an extensive warehouse and wholesale district, with a scattering of manufacturing enterprises and the railroad yards. Still farther south, beyond the residential areas, lies South San Francisco where the heaviest manufacturing is done, where the stockyards, tanneries, and packing houses are located. It is here the great highways lead into San Francisco from points south.

Fruit and vegetable wholesalers are concentrated just north of Market Street adjoining the waterfront. Here the sidewalks of narrow streets are piled high with sacks and crates of produce, cages of live fowl, and heaps of melons.

Bordering on this district is the city's imposing financial section. Montgomery and Sansome are the city's deepest streets. Comparatively narrow, they cleave between the walls of the tallest buildings in town, and are lined with banks, stock companies, brokerage houses, and insurance agencies.

This area is inhabited in the day by swarms of well-dressed, well-groomed people of college-educated appearance. In and out the shining corridors of palatial buildings, the greatest number of brief cases in town is carried. The Stock Exchange is located here, and the Chamber of Commerce and the Industrial Association. Offices are frequently sumptuous and seldom modest. The most up-to-date equipment and the most alert office staffs are the rule. Inside huge plate-glass windows, large green blackboards chalked with intricate stock quotations are illuminated by bright lights. Shirtsleeved and green-visored clerks toil constantly, erasing one figure and scribbling another. Well-dressed men fidget in mahogany chairs nearby, making frequent notes on pads of paper.

At night this area is dark and deserted save for one or two scattered lights high up in the buildings, indicating bookkeepers worrying overtime at their ledgers or janitors mopping up the lonely halls.

The fashionable shopping district, the legitimate theaters, palatial hotels, exclusive jewelry, furniture, and clothing stores are also located on the north side of Market.

About two miles up Market Street from the Ferry Building the administrative palaces of civic government stand in a granite cluster around a broad plaza. Here within the magnificently domed City Hall, which puts to shame the State Capitol, preside the Mayor and the Board of Supervisors. Other buildings flanking the square are the Federal Building, the State Building, the Opera House, the Civic Auditorium, and the Public Library.

A perpetual open forum seethes on the steps of the library where ragged men from "Skid Row," the extensive flophouse area south of Market, gather to air and exchange opinions, and frequently chalk astonishing predictions on the pavement.

The residential sections of the town provide a checkerboard of racial, national, financial, and vocational categories, for each district is as sharply defined as an autonomous republic.

Chinatown, on the north side of Market, occupies about seventeen crowded blocks on Stockton Street and Grant Avenue, extending all the way from the edge of the fashionable shopping district to North Beach. In this area the largest community of Chinese outside of China itself lives as completely within its own atmosphere as if it were a part of Peking. The architecture is Chinese. The language spoken is Chinese. They have their own schools, societies, newspapers, restaurants, and theaters, and even their own telephone exchange.

One step out of Chinatown and you are in North Beach, the Latin Quarter. Street scenes resemble Italian towns. The language spoken is predominantly Italian. Signboards and advertisements are worded in Italian. They too have their own newspapers, societies, and cultural life. Adjoining this area, and interwoven with it, are smaller French and Spanish settlements.

Another district farther uptown, and completely dissociated from Chinatown, is inhabited by Japanese, with their own signs, stores, clubs, and newspapers. Another area is set off for Negroes.

Racial areas are no less clearly defined than income groups. The enormous working-class residential section south of Market has been indicated. North of Market there are enormous areas of dirty, blistered wooden houses, former large homes now converted into cheap rooming houses and flats.

Another district consists mostly of run-down hotels and beer parlors where the city's most unscrupulous underworld elements congregate. It is to this area that police go directly when looking for hold-up men and racketeers.

A strip of choice land along the northern hills of the city overlooks a beautiful panorama of the bay and is given over exclusively to mansions and elegant apartment buildings. Carefully groomed lawns, marble lions, uniformed footmen, dazzling chandeliers, and shiny limousines are the order here.

The western side of the city contains Golden Gate Park, one of the largest in the world. Its wooded area is four blocks wide and fifty blocks long, extending in an oblong strip from the shore of the ocean to the center of the peninsula.

The park is flanked on either side by two huge and identical residential sections, the Richmond district and the Sunset district. Although numerous laboring people and a few of the wealthier class live in these two great areas, the overwhelming majority are white-collar workers, small businessmen and merchants, salesmen, agents and clerks.

Although to the eye these districts appear to be the most monotonous and least interesting in the city, from another standpoint they are fascinating. They comprise block after block, mile after mile of modest homes all very similar in design. It is not uncommon to see five or six blocks of stucco houses all cut from identically the same pattern. Regimentation and standardization are apparent here even to the naked eye. And yet these districts are the stronghold of the philosophy of rugged individualism.

It is here that socialism, or regimentation, or collectivism are the most greatly feared.

An investigation of the parlors of these dwellings reveals the same resemblance that their exteriors show to each other. The furnishings and decorations have been manufactured by mass production, turned out in huge quantities, advertised and sold to each and every household. Certain framed color prints by Maxfield Parrish and other magazine artists can be found, literally, in thousands of identical frames in thousands of identical parlors.

An examination of the books on the bookshelves and the magazines in the magazine racks reveals equal standardization. Living in identical surroundings and subject to the same influences, the minds of these people formulate uniform ideas, opinions, prejudices, and hopes.

The inhabitants of these regions shuttle back and forth between home and office on streetcars or in small autos, and their days are as alike as the houses in which they live. The essential businesses of life, as they understand them, are concerned with desks, files, inkpots, and telephones. Moving pictures and magazines have led them to regard themselves as the typical Americans. To a certain extent the conception has been nurtured in their minds that laborers are either foreigners or failures, and that such work is relegated to men who lacked the intelligence or initiative necessary to lift them into the white-collar world.

On the edge of Chinatown and North Beach is a grim, gray building —the Hall of Justice—where the city jail and police courts are housed. Surrounding it is an area of cheap hotels, beer halls, and houses of prostitution. Across the street is a burlesque show where nude dances are performed before audiences of sex-starved derelicts.

Many aspects of the maritime and general strikes will be incomprehensible without an understanding of the civic administration in office during the period and up to the present time. On this subject I will venture no opinion of my own. Edwin N. Atherton, a former U. S. Department of Justice agent, recently completed a thorough investigation of the matter at a cost of more than $60,000. I shall quote significant portions of his official report:

We found that there were approximately 135 regular old established locations in San Francisco where prostitution was carried on . . . 12 resorts, plus several others on different streets, were within a radius of three blocks of the Hall of Justice. There were five houses in one block on this street and it was not unusual, in several localities, to find two or more in one block. . . .

Houses of prostitution have been so plentiful in a section of the North Beach area that tenants in some buildings have been forced to put signs on their front doors announcing the fact that they are private residences. . . .

McDonough Brothers [an invisible government operating under the guise of bail bond brokers.—Q.] was discovered to be a fountainhead of corruption. . . . It has many tentacles reaching throughout the city government in the form of officials and employees in key positions to take care of almost any contingency. . . . The power of McDonough Brothers exerts itself over the Police Department in much the same manner. An officer who seeks to enforce the law honestly is regarded as a "snake in the grass" and no opportunity is overlooked to sabotage his career. On the contrary, an officer who is "right" with this firm can depend on a helping hand whenever he may need it. . . .

It might be well to pause here and point out that prostitution is against the law in San Francisco.

Continuing the Atherton report:

In the past persons intending to open a house of prostitution were usually required to pay an initial or opening fee, which varied in amount but frequently ran from $500 to $750. At the same time the regular monthly "payoff" was fixed and the time and manner of payment prescribed. These arrangements were usually made with some of the persons mentioned above and sometimes directly with police officers.

This main "payoff" was levied arbitrarily and distributed among the captain and sometimes other superior officers in the district, the special detail and the civilian interests, which jointly controlled this racket. In addition, the operators were also called upon to "take care" of the patrolman on the beat. They were permitted to make their own individual arrangements with these officers and the amounts usually ran from $10 per month upward, depending largely on the greediness of the officer. . . .

Another substantial form of prostitution is that provided by the vast number of "street walkers" or "hustlers" in San Francisco. The majority of these girls were compelled to pay the officers on whose beats they worked. If they failed to do so, they were harassed to the point of distraction. This class of prostitute comprised the most unfortunate and pitiful of any and the experiences of some of these women with police abuse and extortion were heartrending. . . .

We found that normally about 150 bookmaking establishments operated

[13]

in San Francisco. There were many more places where bets could be placed with agents but only the locations where handbooks were actually maintained were included in this figure. . . .

Bookmakers were compelled to pay the police for the privilege of doing business. . . .

Another lucrative prey for police extortion were the lotteries.

There were many public gambling houses which operated as chartered social clubs for members only. This was usually just a sham as identification was rarely, if ever, required. . . .

Slot machines contributed a large amount to the graft pool. . . .

The investigation reflects that a great many illegal abortions were performed in San Francisco...it can safely be said that they run into the thousands. . . . This is a racket, and a dangerous one, because extremely few licensed physicians and surgeons will perform an illegal abortion. Consequently, a majority of the illegal abortions are performed by men and women with no education or license to entitle them to practice medicine or surgery. . . .

According to persons who have engaged in this unlawful practice there was a definite and regular police "payoff" for protection. Two instances came to our attention wherein even inspectors of the State Board of Medical Examiners had been corrupted.

Some of the officers of the crime prevention detail of the Bureau of Inspectors had made it a practice to harass, or "roust" (to use the vernacular) panderers and other questionable characters in the so-called underworld until these worthies found it much more to their advantage to "pay off." The "$1,000 Vag" law, which enables the police to pick up a person for almost no reason, lends itself readily to "shake-downs."

During the course of this investigation we were informed that thieves and possessors of stolen goods obtained immunity by "paying off" to inspectors assigned to the duty of investigating burglaries and other forms of theft and of recovering stolen merchandise.

Graft was not entirely confined to unlawful activities. Their success in this field had emboldened officers and others to tackle legitimate business. For instance, a local citizen and substantial property holder gave us a statement. . . . He invested approximately $30,000 in a combination restaurant, bar and night club. Shortly after the place was opened and it began to appear that the venture would be a success, he was told that it was customary to make payments to the police. Owners of similar establishments in the same area informed him that they paid $75 per month to the special detail. In addition, he was told that "it would be to his interest" to give 10 per cent of the business to McDonough Brothers. . . . He was further advised that all police problems would be taken care of by this group and that necessary permits, which might otherwise be denied by the Police Commission, could be easily obtained.

It was intimated that, if a portion of the business were not assigned as suggested, the police would harass the patrons and management. . . .

Certain garages were given preference to the point of having a virtual monopoly on tow-car service in accident cases. . . .

We shall comment only briefly on petty graft. . . . However, it is practiced on a wide scale by police officers who, as a class, seem to feel they should be exempt from paying their way like other members of the community. They expect free meals, free drinks, passes to sporting events, theaters and other amusements, etc. It is said that a "smart" officer only pays when it is unavoidable. A typical case was recited by the wife of an officer, who informed us that her husband not only received groceries, liquors, household goods and supplies free of charge, but clothes and even free medical, dental and optician's services for himself and members of his family. They grant all sorts of favors and concessions for rewards in cash or presents of various kinds. . . .

During local political campaigns the Police Department was an organized and powerful electioneering force. Members of the department were not only responsible for many thousands of votes for the favored candidates and measures, but they aided materially in raising campaign funds. Proprietors of illegal businesses were canvassed and informed that contributions were expected. In many cases the amount of the contribution was arbitrarily fixed and the proprietor paid it as a special item separate and apart from their regular tribute.

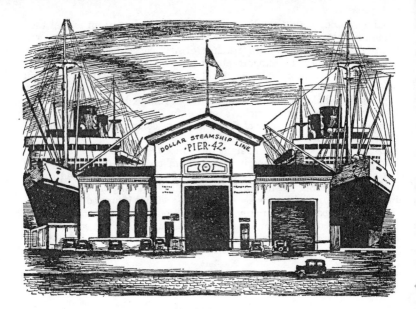

CHAPTER III
The Maritime Industry,
A Diagnosis

I T IS ALSO REASONABLE THAT IN order to comprehend the maritime strike you must know something about the industry involved.

Contrary to general opinion, the shipping industries of the United States are not private enterprises in the true sense of the word. They are largely financed by the government out of public funds, and the government has an ownership interest in the merchant fleets amounting, in some cases, to as much as 60 per cent.

Government subsidies have been a key factor in the development of Pacific maritime commerce to date, and they will be a determining factor in the future.

Out of this issue of federal aid to shipowners many important controversies have arisen which, at this writing, remain unsettled and present a problem the solution to which may not be evolved for a long time to come.

The nature of these controversies directly involves every phase of the shipping industry: shipbuilding, routes, schedules, freight rates, passenger fares, profits, wages, working conditions, and national defense.

Maritime commerce on the Pacific Coast divides into four classifications:

(1) *Coastwise.* Ocean traffic between United States ports on the Pacific Coast. This comprises about 65 per cent of Pacific shipping.

(2) *Intercoastal.* Traffic between ports of the United States on the East and West coasts. This amounts to about 11.9 per cent of Pacific shipping.

(3) *Non-contiguous.* Traffic between Pacific Coast ports and outlying U. S. possessions: Alaska, Hawaii, etc. (not including the Philippine Islands). This comprises 3.4 per cent of the total.

(4) *Foreign.* Traffic between U. S. ports on the Pacific Coast and foreign ports. This amounts to 19.7 per cent of the total.

In 1817 Congress enacted a law closing trade between United States ports to all except American-built, American-manned, American-owned ships flying the American flag.

Thus the first three classifications, embracing more than 80 per cent of all Pacific shipping, are protected by law, and American companies have an airtight monopoly. The question of subsidies does not, by right, involve any of these classifications, the whole intention being to enable American companies to compete with foreign lines in the overseas trade.

In actual practice, however, domestic shipping has shared many of the benefits of subsidies.

Prior to the World War the United States had the second largest merchant marine in the world, second only to that of Great Britain. Practically all of this fleet, however, was engaged in domestic shipping. In fact, the United States had only fifteen vessels in the overseas trade: six on the Atlantic and nine on the Pacific.

Lower construction and operating costs abroad made it impossible for American companies to compete with foreign lines.

This did not mean that no American-owned ships were engaging in foreign trade. It was the custom for American companies to build ships for this service in foreign yards, man them with foreign seamen, and sail them under foreign flags. At the outbreak of the war there were no less than two million tons of American-owned ships operating under foreign registry.

This practice has continued up to the present. Even today, when substantial subsidies are being paid by the government to equalize operating costs between American and foreign lines, a good 60 per cent of U. S. foreign trade is handled by foreign ships. Many companies that are being subsidized are, at the same time, operating huge fleets under foreign flags.

Typical examples are the Munson Line, which operates 67 ships under foreign registry; the United Fruit Company, operating 52 ships in this manner; and the International Mercantile Marine, operating 60 ships.

The American overseas merchant marine was at its peak in the clipper ship era. Since then the amount of American commerce transported on American ships has dropped from 89.7 per cent in 1830 to a mere 8.7 per cent in 1910. As a result of subsidies paid since the World War, the percentage has been raised to 34.7 in 1930, and 35.4 in 1933.

Several experimental efforts were made during this period to bolster the overseas merchant marine by government subsidy. But none of them was very effective. In most cases the bounty was too small to interest the shipping companies, and in one case a major bribery scandal resulted involving the Pacific Mail Steamship Company. It was not until the World War, which created an abnormal demand for merchant ships, both as cargo carriers and armed naval auxiliaries, that serious steps were taken.

The first problem arising from the war in Europe was that hundreds of cargo vessels were withdrawn from the American trade for service as naval auxiliaries. In addition to this, American owners operating under foreign flags were endangered by submarine warfare. Marine insurance companies either suspended all risks or asked prohibitive fees. To meet this situation Congress passed two bills, one permitting the immediate transfer of foreign ships to American registry, and another providing government insurance to replace private insurance. A third bill, calling for government ownership and operation of merchant vessels, was defeated.

Wartime traffic soon became so heavy that on September 7, 1916, Congress passed a bill creating a Shipping Board of five members, to be appointed by President Wilson, with authority for the construction, purchase, charter, and operation of merchant vessels.

Soon afterward America entered the war and a tremendous cry went up in the press to the effect that our merchant marine was incapable of handling the situation, even with the addition of many German vessels which had taken refuge in American ports and were seized as contraband.

The Shipping Board organized an Emergency Fleet Corporation and, with the approval of Congress, constructed 3,000 merchant vessels at a cost of $3,316,100,000 out of the public treasury. The total tonnage exceeded the entire merchant marine of the world prior to the war.

Publicists arguing for government subsidies still point to this tremendous wartime expense as an outlay that was "necessitated" for the reason that America had neglected her merchant marine prior to the war.

But more logical authorities doubt the "necessity." The truth is that the entire wartime task was carried out by the already existing merchant marine, and the Emergency Fleet Corporation's program was merely an abstract frenzy of ship construction.

Most of the vessels were built in the Hog Island yards, and the first one came sliding down the ways exactly one month after the Armistice was signed. This gigantic fleet was not built during the war, but after the war.

In 1919 some 3,579,826 tons of ships were launched. There was no conceivable need for them. They were never delivered, but simply tied up alongside each other in a sprawling boneyard.

But that is only part of the story. The building and launching continued all through 1920, 1921, and 1922 until 7,250,000 tons of steel ships and nearly 1,000,000 tons of wood and concrete vessels had been constructed.

This gigantic ghost fleet was launched and tied up in the form of a national problem and embarrassment.

Such a colossal blunder must have some explanation.

The most common and logical explanation is that the shipbuilding craze was whipped up and kept going by the publicity and political influence of the American Steamship Owners' Association and the National Council of Shipbuilders.

Now that the 3,000 vessels were built, the problem was what to do with them. The Republican administration then in office was vigorously opposed to government ownership and operation. The shipbuilders and owners were called into conference and a compromise plan was worked out. The majority of the vessels were scrapped and the remainder were turned over to private steamship companies to operate for the government under managing-operating agreements. The proposition was that the shipowners would operate the vessels in the foreign trade and the government would reimburse them for all their losses.

The losses soon became stupendous—so stupendous that the government decided to put an end to the proposition "at any cost."

In 1928 Congress passed the Jones-White bill which provided that private shipowners operating in the foreign trade should receive subsidies in the form of mail contracts to make up the differential between foreign and American operating costs. The avowed purpose of this bill was to maintain a high standard of living for American workingmen, and to develop an adequate merchant marine which could transport the greatest part of American commerce and be available as a naval auxiliary in time of war.

The first step in the new plan was to sell all government-owned vessels to the private companies for less than ten cents on the dollar, with liberal terms and plenty of time to pay.

In the second place, forty-four mail contracts involving annual payments by the government of approximately $30,000,000 were granted to private steamship companies.

In the third place, a $250,000,000 revolving fund was created out of which private shipowners could borrow money for the construction of new vessels at extremely low rates of interest. Many shipowners were able to borrow huge sums at rates of as little as a fraction of 1 per cent. Loans at this trivial cost were available for 75 per cent of the construction cost of any vessel the shipowners might wish to build.

The Dollar Line was able to borrow $10,575,000 partly at 1 per cent and partly at ¼ of 1 per cent.

It is estimated that ship construction loans of this kind have cost the public treasury in excess of $22,000,000 in interest losses up to the present time.

(These figures are all taken from government sources and particularly from the report and transcript of hearings of the Senate Committee to Investigate Aerial and Ocean Mail Contracts.)

It is interesting to examine some of the financial miracles that were made possible by the Jones-White Act.

The Dollar Lines, which employed Chinese labor on their ships at extremely low rates of pay, and had their ships overhauled in Chinese shipyards by coolie labor, were one of the heaviest beneficiaries of the bill. On October 2, 1922, the Dollar interests organized the Admiral Oriental Line with a cash capital investment of $500. They issued notes for capital stock in the amount of $499,500. On November 2, 1922, they began operating a service to the Orient using government-owned ships under a managing-operating agreement. Within three years and five months they chalked up net profits for themselves of $533,713.96 after having retired the notes they had issued for capital stock. Subsequently, without investing one penny more than the original $500, they purchased the entire fleet of ships from the government and made a net profit of $6,767,957.72 between 1922 and 1934.

R. Stanley Dollar, who negotiated the purchase of these and other ships from the government, received a total of $698,750 in commissions for successfully carrying out the transaction.

Almost one-third of the $30,000,000 a year expended in mail subsidies was awarded to Pacific Coast steamship companies, which entered into contracts netting them a bounty of $96,969,502 to be paid to them over a period of about ten years. The annual report of the Postmaster General for 1931 shows the following Pacific Coast companies to be beneficiaries of the ocean mail subsidies:

Name of Line	Sailing to	Voyages per year	Approximate total subsidy
FROM SAN FRANCISCO			
Oceanic S. S. Co.	Sydney	17	$9,863,436
Dollar Line	Manila	26	14,731,080
Dollar Line	Colombo	26	14,570,032
Pacific-Argentine-Brazil	Buenos Aires	18	3,005,323
Panama Mail	Puerto Colombia	26	7,132,570
United Fruit Co.	Puerto Armuellas	52	7,348,246
Oceanic & Oriental Navigation Co.	Saigon	—	4,014,516
Oceanic & Oriental Navigation Co.	Dairen	14-19	3,565,775
FROM SEATTLE			
Admiral Oriental	Manila	26	14,731,080
Gulf Pacific Mail	Tampico	12-24	3,393,130
FROM PORTLAND			
Admiral Oriental	Manila	24	4,341,518
States S. S. Co.	Dairen	12	2,053,632
Tacoma Oriental S. S. Co.	Manila, Dairen	24	3,933,519
FROM LOS ANGELES			
Oceanic & Oriental Navigation Co.	Auckland	12	1,711,545
Oceanic & Oriental Navigation Co.	Melbourne	12	2,109,600
FROM TACOMA			
Grace Line	Valparaiso	17	2,703,000
Total Approximate Payments for 10-Year Period			$96,969,502

Thus it is apparent that the Dollar Line and its subsidiary, the Admiral Oriental Line, gained nearly half the amount in subsidies that was paid to the Pacific Coast. Their contracts called for $48,373,710 within a ten-year period, or $4,837,371 per year.

From the years 1923 to 1932 inclusive, four officials of the Dollar Line—R. Stanley Dollar, J. Harold Dollar, Herbert Fleishhacker, and H. M. Lorber—received a total of $14,690,528 in salaries, bonuses, and profits.

Mr. R. Stanley Dollar alone draws $15,000 a year salary from the Admiral Oriental Line, $15,000 a year salary from the Dollar Line, and $6,000 a year salary from the Pacific Lighterage Corporation.

This Pacific Lighterage Corporation, which is owned by the Dollar interests, declared physical assets of $9,916.80 as of December 31, 1932. It derives most of its income from stevedoring services for the subsidized Dollar and Admiral Oriental Lines. Between the years 1929 and 1933 inclusive it chalked up profits amounting to $1,175,182.69.

Reflecting upon these profits, the Honorable Homer T. Bone stood up in Congress and declared:

The records of the Black Committee are so damning an indictment of this kind of business that at this time the bill constitutes a bold challenge thrown in the teeth of the hungry people of the nation. We made multimillionaires overnight under the Jones-White Act of 1928. Men in my section of the country became multi-millionaires almost overnight.*

Other examples of subsidy administration are no less startling. The Baltimore Mail Line was presented with $12,720,240, to be paid to them over a period of ten years. This sum is greater than the cost of all vessels in the line put together with the entire capitalization of the

*Shipowners, during and after World War II, fed so gluttonously at the public trough as to make the earlier figures seem like penny ante stuff. Here's a composite report of a number of Pacific Coast ship companies for 1946:

ASSETS

Current working assets	$344,358,919.70
Special funds and deposits (including capital reserve fund)	242,982,383.85
Investments	44,249,786.08
Property and equipment	265,549,583.77
Other assets, including pending claims on vessels lost or requisitioned	41,126,386.99
Total	$938,267,060.39

LIABILITIES

Current working liabilities	$132,584,093.43
Long-term debt, due after one year	70,831,893.25
Deferred credits and sundry operating reserves	32,043,483.26
Reserve for vessel replacement	57,346,399.75
Net worth (capital stock and surplus)	587,332,343.74
Total	$938,267,060.39

company, which amounts to $3,000,000. In addition to this, the government loaned the line $6,520,706 at 3 per cent interest payable in twenty years.

The good fortune that fell to the Export Steamship Company is nothing short of miraculous. First the government sold them eighteen steamships that had cost $42,000,000 to build, for 2 cents on the dollar. The full price the shipowners paid for the fleet was $1,071,431.

Between August 1928 and June 1929 these vessels transported exactly three pounds of mail, for which service the government paid them $234,980.

During 1931 they transported eight pounds of mail and received $125,820 per pound.

When Mr. Heberman, president of the Export Lines, returned from Washington where he had negotiated this deal, he turned in an expense account of $300,000.

The annual subsidies of $30,000,000 paid under the Jones-White Act to make up the differential between foreign and American operating costs, exceeded the total amount spent each year for wages, subsistence, maintenance, and repair on all vessels carrying the American flag over ocean mail routes.

By 1934 it became apparent that something had gone seriously astray with the Jones-White idea. Hundreds of millions of dollars had been poured out of the public treasury and had disappeared in the wind.

The most prominently emphasized purpose of the subsidies was to maintain a high standard of living for American workingmen and to provide jobs at good wages.

On this subject the Special Committee of the Senate to Investigate Air Mail and Ocean Mail Contracts reported (Report No. 898, Senate, 74th Congress, 1st Session):

The subsidy does not always reach its intended beneficiary.

While the clamor has always been made that our marine subsidy would provide funds for the payment to American seamen of wages set at a proper level, and substantially in excess of foreign wages, in many instances the proper wage scale has been cut and money transmitted to mail contractors in constructive trust for American seamen has been diverted by the contractors to their own private profits for exorbitant salaries and unearned bonuses. This practice and result are wholly indefensible.

Another expressed purpose was to provide America with a "merchant marine of the best-equipped and most suitable types of vessels sufficient to carry the greater portion of its commerce and serve as a naval and military auxiliary in time of war or national emergency."

Instead the American merchant marine had gone to seed and the U. S. Navy became alarmed at the prospect of having insufficient auxiliaries on which to depend in event of war. Seventy-eight per cent of the ships operating in the overseas trade were over thirteen years old. Practically all cargo ships were built according to prewar standards. Sixty per cent of our overseas commerce was still being transported on foreign vessels, and many of the subsidized lines were carrying extremely small cargoes—some of them merely cruising back and forth to collect the subsidies.

The Honorable Schuyler Otis Bland, representative from Virginia, chairman of the Congressional Committee on Merchant Marine and Fisheries, declared:

Do we want to preserve the American merchant marine—preserve it for national defense? It is departing from the seas and in a little while, with the age limit that is on it now, it will go. Our building must begin at an early date, or in seven years we shall find nothing but old tonnage in the merchant marine.

The Senate investigating committee reported:

The American Merchant Marine is neither adequate nor is it in any true sense privately owned. Responsibility for this country's failure to secure that which it sought and for which it was willing to expend and has expended hundreds of millions of dollars of taxpayers' money must lie at the door of three classes of people. First, this burden of costly failure rests upon the enactment of an ill-advised compromise law. Second, upon certain public officials who flagrantly betrayed their trust and maladministered those laws. Third, upon those individuals who, publicly posing as patriots, prostituted those laws for their private profit. . . .

Private ownership and operation of merchant and aerial transportation with government subsidy has resulted in a saturnalia of waste, inefficiency, unearned exorbitant salaries and bonuses, and other forms of so-called "compensation," corrupting expense accounts, exploitation of the public by the sale and manipulation of stocks, the "values" of which are largely based on the hope of profit from robbing the taxpayer, and a general transfer of energy and labor from operating business to "operating on" the taxpayer. Measured by results, the subsidy system, as operated, has been a sad, miserable, and corrupting failure. Many of its apologists have been shown to be those who have directly received financial profit, or those, who for various reasons, have been influenced by those who did directly profit from it. Not the least of these influences has been the millions of government dollars flowing through the hands of the immediate recipients, their associates, affiliates, subsidiaries, holding companies, and allies, into the treasuries of newspapers, magazines, and publicity agencies. Evidence before this committee has illustrated the existence and effect of these evil influences.

The Senate investigation discovered that shipowners had diverted a portion of the subsidies they received from the government, toward maintaining a powerful and costly pro-subsidy publicity agency through the American Steamship Owners' Association, and that one of the longest and strongest arms of this agency was the Hearst chain of newspapers.

The committee report stated:

The American Steamship Owners' Association in 1932 created a Committee on Shipping Information with a 6-month budget of $48,300 to be financed by an assessment on mail contractors at the rate of one-fifth of one per cent on the mail pay received from the Post Office Department during the fiscal year 1932. . . .

Between November 15, 1932, and July 13, 1933, the total expenditure of this committee averaged about $5,000 per month. The program which was carried out included news releases and popular illustrated articles, direct correspondence with newspaper editorial writers, radio, speakers before commercial organizations, congressional educational campaigns "disclosing interest of representative constituents in the merchant marine," and the publication of a book. The committee employed a director at a monthly salary of $800, an assistant director at a monthly salary of $300, four stenographers, and a "publicity agency."

The shipping interests have operated through many agencies without disclosing their activities to the general public. They have extended financial aid to numerous associations and organizations scattered over the United States some of whom innocently, and some of whom with their own knowledge and active cooperation, have been made the instrumentalities of insidious propaganda. . . .

The evidence shows that the Admiral Oriental Line of the Dollar interests had invested $20,000 in first-mortgage collateral trusts of Hearst Publications, Inc.

The ability of the organized steamship owners to influence public opinion and politics is well illustrated by an incident concerning General Pershing. I remember reading some years ago and being very much impressed by a widely publicized statement by General Pershing. It was voiced as an argument for subsidies, and read:

I feel that I can speak with some authority on this subject. At the head of our armies, 3,000 miles away, the responsibility rested upon me of upholding our country's honor and directing our part in the gigantic struggle which we had chosen to share with the Allies. Everything depended upon sea transportation. Our troops and most of our munitions, materials, and supplies had to come to us from home. Throughout the whole period there was scarcely a day when the danger of lack of sea transportation facilities was not present. It was a desperate race against time, in which we had to depend in a large measure upon our Allies for the necessary shipping, in spite of the fact that we were constantly suffering the severest losses by enemy submarines.

Two lessons stand out clearly from that experience. The first is the wisdom of the historical national policy of Great Britain in maintaining a strong merchant marine. But for her merchant fleet and her ability to replace losses rapidly, the U-boat campaign might well have been successful. The other lesson is the unwisdom of America and our risk of defeat because we had practically no ships on the high seas when we entered the war.

Because we had the second largest merchant marine in the world at that time, plus a large fleet transferred from foreign registry, and many vessels seized from Germany, this statement seemed most illogical to me as coming from General Pershing, whom I regarded as a man of some judgment and ability.

A portion of the stenographic transcript of the hearings of the Senate investigating committee clears up this point. The chairman was interrogating Mr. Thomas R. Shipp, one of the publicity agents of the American Steamship Owners' Association. He held in his hand a number of reports and documents obtained from the files of the association, with which he was confronting Shipp.

Chairman: (reading) "At Mr. Person's request, made contact with General Pershing who was in New York; wrote a statement for him which was later read in conference." [He refers to a U. S. Shipping Board conference.—Q.]

Shipp: I understand that the General did not make the speech we wrote for him.

Chairman: He did not?

Shipp: That is, he did not make any. He did not appear, but I think perhaps the speech was read, so we did not lose out altogether.

Early in 1935 President Roosevelt sent a message to Congress requesting that the Jones-White system of subsidies be terminated as soon as possible and a new form be devised to accomplish the same purposes. His message said, in part:

Reports which have been made to me by appropriate authorities in the executive branch of the government have shown that some American shipping companies have engaged in practices and abuses which should and must be ended. Some of these have to do with the improper operating of subsidiary companies, the payment of excessive salaries, the engaging in businesses not directly a part of shipping, and other abuses which have made for poor management, improper use of profits, and scattered efforts.

Several new bills were drawn up and one of them, the Copeland bill, was passed after sharp debate in Congress. This called for the termination of all existing mail contracts by June 1937, and provided for a new system of direct subsidies on the basis of a carefully calculated estimate of the exact differences between foreign and American operating costs.

It provided a $100,000,000 subsidy fund to be administered by a Federal Maritime Board appointed by the President. This board was invested with unusually broad authority covering wages, hours, conditions, and the right to probe into the ledgers of the shipowners.

Limitations were also placed on executive salaries and profits, and a system of continuous discharge books or "passports" was devised for seamen. The latter provision met with such opposition from organized labor that in 1937 it was revised. Seamen believed these books would enable employers to institute a blacklist against active union men.

The Copeland bill as a whole bucked a strong minority of opposition in Congress. One of the dissenting voices was that of Senator Burton K. Wheeler from Montana, who said:

While I am not a prophet nor the son of a prophet, if we do not have greater scandals in connection with this measure, if it shall become a law, than we have ever had in the history of the United States in connection with shipping, then I miss my guess, and I do not want to see this administration involved in the unparalleled scandals which we would have under this measure. . . .

We say that we are going to give a subsidy of the difference between the cost of operating an American ship and the cost of operating a foreign ship. What foreign ship are we going to base it upon? Are we going to base it upon the coolie labor of China, are we going to base it upon the coolie labor of Japan, or on what Great Britain pays, or on what Australia pays, or on what some South American country pays, or what are we going to base it on?

I say we have nothing whatsoever on which to base these payments except the wildest kind of judgment on the part of the Maritime Authority.

The Honorable Otha D. Wearin of Iowa declared:

The experience of the United States Government in the operation of the merchant marine under the 1928 act has been most disastrous. It has been disastrous from the standpoint of a lack of faith and evidently a lack of willingness on the part of the ship operators to cooperate with a program for the purpose of building up the American merchant marine. In the face of this fact we must also recollect that the Congress today is faced with the situation of having the same group of operators, the same interests that desired the 1928 act, and they have abused their privileges under the 1928 act, asking Congress for the legislation that is being proposed as a program for the advancement and development of an American merchant marine. We have no greater assurance today that they will keep faith with the American people any more under this act, if passed, than they did under the 1928 act.

It has been pointed out that the nonsubsidized lines have a monopoly protected by law.

Thus, without benefit of bounty, they have still managed to show imposing profits.

The Matson Navigation Company, one of the "Big Three" on the Pacific Coast (the others being the Dollar Lines and the American Hawaiian), has operated profitably for the past sixteen years, including the entire period of the depression. Cash dividends paid increased from $658,296 in 1920 to $1,545,856 in 1935, and showed a decided gain rather than a decline during the depression. From 1920 to 1935 they chalked up a net profit of close to $29,000,000, paid cash dividends of over $16,000,000, and stock dividends of over $27,000,000. In the same period they paid off their entire funded debt of about $5,000,000 and built up their net worth from $10,000,000 in 1920 to $39,000,000 in 1935.

The ledgers of the American Hawaiian Steamship Company showed some ups and downs during the depression, yet they paid dividends of $6,519,025 between the years 1930 to 1936 and are now enjoying a tremendous increase.

The McCormick Steamship Company operated at a good profit throughout the entire depression. In 1935 their net income was three times that of 1934. They paid off a large portion of their funded debt and have built up a surplus of over $600,000.

CHAPTER IV
Seamen, Longshoremen—
Their Life and Labor

R<small>EMOVE THE WORD "CARGO" FROM</small> the vocabulary of San Francisco and you strip it of its most essential expression. There is considerable manufacturing throughout the entire Bay Area, but this is not the backbone of the community's industrial life.

San Francisco, above all else, is a seaport, and it is from the handling and transportation of merchandise and products that it derives its existence as a metropolis. The majority of its population, either directly or indirectly, derives its income from transactions related to the movement of cargoes. Insurance companies, banks, real estate companies, wholesale firms, shops and other seemingly separate enterprises all directly or indirectly owe their existence to the movement of cargoes. Hospitals, schools, libraries, restaurants, theaters, hotels—all exist for the service or entertainment of a community devoted to a constant flow of boxes, barrels, bales, and materials.

The port of San Francisco alone (not counting facilities in the East

Bay cities) has 17 miles of berthing space; 82 docks with a cargo capacity of 1,930,000 tons, capable of accommodating 250 vessels at one time. It is a port of call for over 118 steamship lines, and approximately 7,000 ships arrive and depart yearly. Freight tonnage in and out of the Golden Gate during 1929 amounted to 31,391,558 tons.

It is amazing to consider that the men who lay hands on this cargo and make possible the fundamental life pulse of the community enjoy such a small share in its returns. And the seamen, whose hazardous profession is the cornerstone of the city's prosperity, comprise one of the lowest-paid classifications of labor in existence.

Warehousemen and teamsters shoulder all the burden between train and dock. Loading and unloading of the vessels is the work of the longshoremen and bargemen. Water transport is the responsibility of the seamen.

Yet the bulk of the enormous profits from this traffic is controlled by men who seldom lay eyes on the cargoes and never feel the weight of them.

The history of maritime labor in San Francisco is a tale of heroism and injustice. This needs little demonstration, for the bulk of all literature on the subject, either fiction or non-fiction, is in agreement on the point. A large percentage of the literature purporting to record the romance of the port of San Francisco consists of nothing more or less than accounts of how maritime workers were robbed, exploited, drugged, shanghaied, beaten, shot, stabbed, kicked about, and swindled. Famous old Barbary Coast itself was the locale of the snaring and fleecing of seamen turned into a major industry.

Brutality to seamen in San Francisco is a tradition. In the old days the common way of manning a vessel was to order the required number of men from a "crimp" who would dope a number of sailors and deliver them on board unconscious.

Even as late as 1934 the seafaring and longshore professions were regarded by most of the populace as a semi-underworld element. Men in sweat-soaked, often ragged garments who frequented the least desirable neighborhoods, they were looked upon as "misfits" and "failures."

In 1916 the longshoremen, organized in the Riggers' and Stevedores' Union, struck for higher wages and shorter hours. The bitterness of that conflict is best expressed by the millionaire shipowner, the late Robert Dollar, who stated publicly that sending ambulance loads of pickets to the hospital was the way to end the strike.

In order to break that strike the business interests in San Francisco organized a temporary "Law and Order Committee," which later became the Industrial Association.

They not only succeeded, but by the expenditure of $1,000,000 secured the enactment of an anti-picketing ordinance that greatly nullified the power of organized labor.

Three years later, in September 1919, the longshoremen walked out again, along with the seamen. The employers had been expecting this strike and were prepared for it. It was during the postwar hysteria and the issues of the strike were drowned in a flood of anti-radical propaganda. The strike was smashed, the men were badly demoralized, and the longshoremen were herded into a company-controlled union, the Longshoremen's Association of San Francisco and the Bay Region, which later became known as the "Blue Book Union," and remained in existence on the waterfront from 1919 to 1934.

Under employer patronage longshore work was reduced to casual labor. No regulation prevailed.

No hiring hall existed.

To obtain work, men got up before dawn, hovered about the waterfront or trudged from dock to dock. Sometimes a man would be three or four days or a week connecting with a job. Once at work, he might labor 24 to 36 hours at a stretch and there are cases on record of men who worked as long as 72 hours to a shift. The job might last one day, two days, or only a few hours. Then he'd have to look for another.

Competition for jobs was keen. Straw bosses did the hiring, and they were "little dukes" up and down the Embarcadero. They supplemented their incomes with bribes from men who in turn got preference of employment. It was a common thing to see men hanging around the waterfront saloons waiting for an opportunity to buy a drink for the hiring boss in order to toady favors.

In 1936 the San Francisco local of the International Longshoremen's Association published a small booklet called "The Maritime Crisis," in which an official description of pre-strike conditions is given:

Up to 1934, labor relations on the waterfront were not those of employer and employee, but of masters and slaves. The men were unorganized—except in a burlesque union, commonly known as the "Blue Book," which was actually controlled by the employers. Some men worked far beyond their strength in order to support themselves and their families; others were unable to get enough work to support themselves. Longshoremen were hired on the docks, and the Embarcadero was known as the "slave mart." Men hung around the docks all day, often in the rain, and then received two or three hours' work in the late afternoon—if they received anything. The speed-up system prevailed in order to avoid overtime payments. After a man had deposited a load, he was supposed to run back for the next load. Men dropped dead of heart failure under the strain, and others worked themselves to the point of continuous exhaustion.

But these were the "favored" few—men who were chosen first when jobs were given out and who were permitted to work from 24 to 36 hours without sleep. They were the men whom adversity had transformed into "yes men," the hat-in-hand "me too, boss" type of worker who curried favor with the employers' hiring agents, bought them drinks or bribed them with cash. In short, a small minority of men were privileged to work themselves to death while a majority were reduced to the level of casual labor.

In 1933, the average weekly wage of longshoremen at San Pedro—the only port in which such records were kept—was $10.45, while many of the shipowners were making large profits.

Employers constantly deny that any such conditions existed. Their side of the argument is published in another booklet, "The Pacific Coast Longshoremen's Strike of 1934," put out by the Waterfront Employers' Union on July 11, 1934:

Earnings dropped unavoidably during the depression following the year 1929; furthermore, there was no means provided in the old system of hiring to prevent the disparity of earnings referred to above.

On the whole, during this period of fourteen years, a satisfactory employment condition for longshoremen existed. During that period there were no disagreements and no strikes. On the contrary, there was a high degree of efficiency, and the men, generally speaking, were satisfied.

In contacting literally hundreds of longshoremen, I was never able to find one who was satisfied, or who did not reiterate the ILA argument.

In 1934, prior to the strike, wages were 85 cents per hour. At first this may sound fairly good. But it meant nothing in view of the fact that the task of obtaining work was greater than the work itself.

A. H. Peterson, representative of the San Pedro local of the ILA, in offering testimony before the President's National Longshoremen's Board on July 11, 1934, stated:

A dollar an hour [the strikers were asking for this wage.—Q.] looks like a lot of money to men working for 40 to 60 cents. The average man wonders what we do with all that money. In the first place, we don't get it. In the second place, even if we did, it must be remembered we put in at least 10 hours a week waiting around to see whether we will work that day or not, and other hours chasing around the piers.

It would be a vast and tangled task to work out a comparative scale showing the differences between wages of foreign and American seamen. Fluctuating money values, changing prices, and other considerations render vague any attempt. Postmaster General Farley, in a report to the President, said:

The rate of pay of American seamen is generally higher than that paid by foreign nations, but in view of the many benefits provided for foreign seamen, which are not received by American seamen, it is doubtful if the actual compensation received by the American seamen is greater than that received abroad.

However, we can flatly examine the wages of American seamen in dollars and cents and judge their merits.

AVERAGE WAGES OF SEAMEN ON U. S. VESSELS, SUMMER 1934
(FROM THE TABLES OF THE UNITED STATES DEPARTMENT OF LABOR, BUREAU OF LABOR STATISTICS)

Department and Occupation	Range			Average Monthly Wage Rate
DECK DEPARTMENT				
First Mates	$133	to	$250	$169
Second Mates	114	to	185	146
Third Mates	100	to	165	131
Fourth Mates	110	to	145	126
Boatswains	50	to	80	65
Carpenters	50	to	85	68
Able Seamen	40	to	63	53
Ordinary Seamen	25	to	49	36
ENGINEERS DEPARTMENT				
Chief Engineer	200	to	500	252
1st Asst. Engineer	133	to	275	170
2nd Asst. Engineer	114	to	185	147
Junior Engineers	75	to	120	94
Firemen	40	to	67	54
Oilers	45	to	72	62
Watertenders	50	to	72	61
Wipers	30	to	58	43
RADIO OPERATORS				
All Operators	60	to	135	98
STEWARDS DEPARTMENT				
Chief Stewards	90	to	350	126
2nd Stewards	70	to	165	96
Cooks	63	to	195	100
2nd Cooks	40	to	150	78
Messboys	25	to	42	35

The majority of seamen come under the lowest wage classifications. In the Deck Department, for example, able seamen and ordinary seamen make up the bulk of the crew.

The higher figures are for licensed officers. To become licensed officers these men must devote the best part of their lives to the sea. They must command fine skill and knowledge and pass rigid examinations. They shoulder tremendous responsibility. Yet their pay is scarcely higher than that of unskilled clerks ashore.

The average monthly wage of a cook is reported as $100. The skill and experience necessary to hold down a position of this kind requires a lifetime of devotion. The quality of work expected may be judged from the advertisements of steamship companies which proclaim the cuisines on their palatial liners to be as sumptuous as that of the most exclusive hotels ashore.

It is commonly believed that American seamen have been benefiting by the eight-hour day, which is practically universal throughout American industry. The truth is, however, that seamen in the Stewards Department, prior to the 1934 strike, worked fourteen and sixteen hours a day, including Sundays. Since the 1934 strike they have been working twelve hours a day, including Sundays.

The seamen in other departments have, theoretically, been enjoying an eight-hour day. In practice, however, it has worked out much differently. They have been required to work long hours overtime at all hours of the day and night, especially when the vessel is in its home port. The overtime is not paid for in cash, but in time off at a later date. The complaint of the seamen is that they are required to put in the overtime in the home port, where their wives, families, and friends live, and where they have very little time to visit with them in any case, and that when they receive the time off, they get it in some far-off desolate port where it is of very little value to them.

This grievance was adjusted after the ninety-nine-day strike of 1936-37.

The life of a seaman is, perhaps, less fitted to the needs of body and spirit than any other human occupation. The work itself is arduous and dangerous enough. But in addition to this, unnatural restrictions are imposed which make life exceptionally difficult.

For one thing, being on a ship at sea confined to the crew's quarters is not very different from being confined in prison. Under such circumstances good food and clean, comfortable quarters are the least a man could ask to make life endurable.

These fundamentals have been notably lacking on American ships.

Aside from designating a small amount of space on the least desirable decks for the seamen to frequent during their off hours, absolutely no recreational facilities have been made available. Seamen are men of imagination and varied interests, having a profound appetite for studies and hobbies. Nevertheless they have been obliged to makeshift in the most uncomfortable and crowded quarters, and, if they pursued their interests at all, they have had to do so under almost impossible conditions.

I sailed as a seaman for three years and know perfectly well what I am talking about.

On one ship more than forty men were jammed into a "glory hole" where the bunks were three deep, and hardly room between them to stand up to take off one's clothes. We were below decks, right on the waterline, so that unless it was clear weather the portholes had to be sealed tight and ventilation was nonexistent. The ship was at sea fifteen or twenty days at a stretch, and stayed in port only three or four days or a week at most. And during that time you had to put in your full hours, so shore leave was meager. On top of that, all forty men had to do all their washing and bathing out of a single fresh-water tap.

On liners seamen are barred from the passenger decks and familiarity with passengers is strictly forbidden, except in those instances when a traveler may wish to converse with a seaman as a diverting "slumming" experience. The crew eats an inferior grade of food in separate, bare dining rooms below decks and in every respect the men are treated as if they were an inferior grade of human being.

This class distinction dogs the seaman's life on shore as well as at sea. Like the longshoreman, he has in the past been regarded as a semi-underworld character—a failure who will never amount to much.

If the seaman wishes to maintain any practical link with shore life he has to quit his ship and go "on the beach" for a while until his funds give out. Otherwise the frenzied pace of modern shipping rushes him in and out of port so rapidly that he has little time for more than a glass of beer and a movie show before he sails again.

Modern electric winches, mechanized loading and unloading equipment, and oil for fuel instead of coal—all of these have speeded up dock service to such an extent that vessels, on many occasions, need put into port for only a few hours before they are ready to sail again. The effect this has had upon the personal lives of the seamen is disastrous. While they are sailing into harbor, before they have even approached the dock, a launchful of officials chugs out and comes aboard, and begins to make arrangements to sail again.

Shipowners never cease in their complaints about the turnover of their crews. But these things are the simple and logical explanation.

Few seamen marry, and those who do live in perpetual anxiety. They see their wives and families for only brief periods at long intervals, and their matrimonial ships sail almost inevitably toward psychological rocks.

Seamen have always had such slender prospects of ever making a decent living that mothers become alarmed if they hear that their daughters are associating with them. In some communities it is considered a disgrace for young women to have anything to do with seafaring men.

It is not surprising that many seamen drink heavily when they get ashore. The surprising thing is that they can adjust themselves to such an existence at all. Cut off from normal human relationships, subjected to long periods of confinement punctuated by brief, hectic spells of shore liberty, a man can hardly be expected to achieve an orderly personal existence.

For relations with women they are obliged to frequent prostitutes whether they like it or not. Hard work in the sea air and close confinement over long periods of time render chastity an absurd impossibility. Since the "Red Light" districts are regulated by no cleaner hand than graft, the seamen are prey to the tragedy of venereal disease.

The myths that seamen are universally roughnecks and hard characters, or that they are incompetents or failures, are as vicious as they are false. The efficiency and cleanliness of a modern steamship stand as an example of competence that few businessmen are able to achieve in their enterprises ashore. The seamen regard their profession with pride and sincerity, and would like to see it transformed into an occupation in which they might pursue satisfactory careers and at the same time lead sane existences.

The nature of the life they are forced to lead is by no means gentle. They are physically self-reliant and inured to hardship. This does not, however, make them the swaggering race of two-fisted bullies that imaginative fiction writers enjoy picturing.

In many respects they are more human and sensitive than their white-collared critics. They preserve the highest ideals regarding marriage, the home, and human relations. Friendship and ethics occupy the highest places in their esteem. The arts and sciences are of immense interest to them, and in no profession can you find so many men who lean toward creative work and strive in humble fashion to express this impulse. On political and social questions they are, as a rule, more sophisticated than the average man ashore.

As regards personal cleanliness, they certainly distinguish themselves. Forty or fifty men jammed into the confines of a "glory hole" or fo'c'sle could not possibly live in harmony without the highest degree of mutual consideration. Cleanliness under such circumstances is a collective necessity, since the sweaty, unwashed garments of a single man can smell up the whole place.

Traditions of hardship and travail have been romanticized by writers of seafaring fiction. The public has been conditioned to regard the sea as a necessarily murderous calling, and the seamen themselves as misfits and derelicts. The fact that it could be transformed easily into an inspiring and desirable profession has never, seemingly, occurred to writers of literature.

The seafaring fo'c'sle has become one of the treasured "hell holes" of romantic writers. Why seamen should occupy quarters any less comfortable than those of passengers, or why they should not eat food of equal quality is a matter of class discrimination and not material for the romantic pen.

Are the passengers any better than the seamen?

That is purely controversial—a matter of opinion. Ask any steward who has just finished cleaning the empty whisky bottles and filth of lechery out of a passenger's cabin and he will tell you that the opposite is the case.

CHAPTER V

*The Birth of the Maritime
Strike, How It Was Organized,
How It Was Called*

FROM 1919 TO 1934 THE EMPLOYERS
had their way on the waterfront, and they still refer to it as an era of
"peace and harmony." Any attempt to change this situation was
blocked by extreme difficulties.

The longshoremen were naturally in a better position than the
seamen to take the initial steps toward organizing a struggle. Most of
the seamen were away on ships all of the time and out of contact with
each other. A minority of them belonged to the International Seamen's Union, which was presided over by comfortable and not very
enthusiastic salaried officials; and a still smaller minority belonged to
the Marine Workers' Industrial Union. To all practical purposes, they
were unorganized.

The longshoremen had to contend with a company union blacklist,
and as soon as a man began taking any interest in organizing another
union, he was unable to find work on any dock. Although employers
persistently refused to grant preferential employment to any of the

later unions, they willingly entered into a "closed shop" agreement with their own subsidiary, the Blue Book. Preferential employment is not, strictly speaking, the closed shop, but in effect it amounts to the same thing.

The first step toward changing the situation occurred in the latter part of 1932 when a small mimeographed publication, the *Waterfront Worker*, began to appear on the docks and in places where longshoremen congregated. Humble in format and clumsily turned out, it hardly gave the impression of a powerful public influence.

Yet it was the first step in what was ultimately to develop into a general strike.

The contents of this little paper were devoted to arousing sentiment against the Blue Book and for the formation of a rank-and-file union. Its language was more expressive than elegant and as easily understandable as were the raw issues of life on the waterfront. It merely said what every longshoreman had long known to be a fact, and put into frank language the resentment that was smoldering in every dock worker's heart. Before long it attained a circulation of from 1,000 to 2,000 copies.

The publishers of the *Waterfront Worker* remained anonymous and the whereabouts of the mimeograph it was printed on was likewise a mystery. It came out at regular intervals, was passed from hand to hand by the men on the docks, and found an appreciative audience.

The employers were quick to brand it as communist propaganda. In this they were largely correct. The Communist Party was very active in San Francisco and a great many longshoremen and seamen were members. It had open headquarters in a converted store which faced on Civic Center, published a weekly newspaper, the *Western Worker*, conducted schools, open forums, and meetings, as well as frequent demonstrations and parades.

Over on Jackson Street, in a ramshackle hall not far from the Embarcadero, was the headquarters of the Marine Workers' Industrial Union. This was one of the pioneer organizations in the field of industrial unionism and in the struggle for rank-and-file control of unions generally. Its advanced policies and democratic innovations attracted the most radical maritime workers, but still it remained very much a minority group. Its membership was comparatively small. However, its agitation for progressive union principles, and the various moves which it initiated, made it a strong influence during the maritime strike. Not long after the strike it disbanded and its membership was absorbed into unions in the American Federation of Labor.

As a result of six months of agitational work through the *Waterfront Worker*, and by word of mouth along the docks, a strong sentiment was developed for the establishment of a local of the International Longshoremen's Association, an affiliate of the American Federation of Labor. About the middle of 1933 the movement began to take definite form. An initiative committee was organized which began to sign up men in the new union. Meanwhile similar steps were being taken in every port up and down the Pacific Coast, in some of which ILA locals already existed.

During this time passage of the National Recovery Act gave considerable impetus to the organizational move. The men took Section 7(a), which stated all workers had the right to join unions of their own choosing and bargain collectively, to mean literally what it said. Although recognizing the atmosphere of encouragement which the NRA lent, it is not correct to say that the organizational movement of the longshoremen is directly attributable to it. The men were at the end of their patience and would have organized the new union regardless.

It is more nearly correct to say that both the NRA and the organizational revolt of the longshoremen sprang from the same social causes, occurred simultaneously, and influenced each other.

Waterfront employers refused to recognize the ILA and would not hire any of its members. They pointed out the preferential hiring agreement with the Blue Book, and as rapidly as longshoremen signed up in the new union they were blacklisted. This brought enrollment virtually to a standstill, and it was necessary for a few men to "stick their necks out" and make a test case.

In September 1933 four ILA men were refused employment on the Matson Navigation Company docks where, in the past, they had been hired right along. A brief protest strike on the dock brought matters to a head. The men appealed the case to the Regional Labor Board, charging that it was a violation of Section 7(a) of the National Recovery Act, which specified they had a right to belong to an organization of their own choosing. The board sustained their charges and ordered the employers to reinstate the men. It ruled also that employers could not discriminate against members of the International Longshoremen's Association.

This effectively broke the deadlock and longshoremen swarmed into the new union so rapidly that very soon practically all the dock workers on the Pacific Coast were signed up.

The Blue Book was drained of its membership so thoroughly that soon it became little more than an office with a telephone number.

The next problem was how to utilize the new union to obtain better conditions. The employers refused to recognize the ILA or negotiate any agreement with it. The reasons stated were that they had no assurance that the new union represented a majority of the men, and furthermore, they were already bound by an agreement with the Blue Book.

After numerous fruitless efforts to open negotiations the men began to talk strike.

On December 10, 1933, the employers unexpectedly raised wages from 75 to 85 cents an hour, with $1.25 per hour for overtime. This was some improvement, but did not touch at all on the main grievances. The men were complaining not so much about wages as the haphazard system of hiring, the speed-up, and the uneven distribution of work. They still could not tell from one week to another how much they would be earning or whether or not they would work at all. They still had to spend more time hanging around looking for a job than they did working on it. Even as regards wages the 85-cent scale fell short. The general sentiment of the men was for a dollar an hour. It was estimated that at this wage, and with the help of a union-controlled hiring hall, they could equalize the work for all longshoremen so as to assure each man a regular wage of about $30 a week.

As a first step toward gaining recognition of their union the men called a coast-wide rank-and-file convention. By "rank and file" it was meant that the delegates were to be working longshoremen elected right off the docks in all Pacific Coast ports. Long years of experience had ingrained the workers with a deep mistrust of salaried union officials, who more often were the favored appointees of higher A. F. of L. bodies than elected representatives of the men. One of the things that characterized the subsequent strike and the history of the Pacific Coast maritime unions from that time forward was the insistence on complete democracy in all matters.

The rank-and-file convention took place in San Francisco in February 1934 with accredited delegates representing 14,000 longshoremen in the various ports. The first order of business was the drafting of demands for a uniform West Coast agreement with a uniform expiration date.

The demands agreed upon were brief and to the point. They asked for an hourly wage of one dollar, a thirty-hour week, a six-hour day, and regulation of all hiring through the union hall. The hiring hall issue was regarded as the basic demand without which the other demands would be useless. The convention went resolutely on record against arbitration.

A delegation of twenty men was elected to go directly from the convention to present the demands to the shipowners. The shipowners called them a "bunch of communists" and refused to deal with them. They intimated, however, that they might be willing to discuss matters with the conservative, salaried union officials, but would have nothing whatever to do with rank-and-file delegations.

When this report was carried back to the convention the men decided that if the employers had not acceded to their demands by March 23, 1934, the longshoremen in every port on the coast would walk out on strike. It was decided also that a ballot be taken immediately in all ports to confirm the strike decision.

Mr. George Creel, Regional Labor Director of California, advised employers to enter into negotiations with the officials of the ILA. On March 5 such negotiations were opened.

Employers flatly turned down the demands outlined by the rank-and-file convention and entered into a long series of conferences with union officials.

Reasons stated for turning down the demands were that each port must negotiate its own separate agreement, and that the men were asking for a closed shop which, in their opinion, was contrary to the provisions of the National Recovery Act.

In the meantime the strike ballot was completed in all ports with the result that a 99 per cent majority of the 14,000 coast longshoremen voted to walk out on March 23 if the demands were rejected.

While employers and union officials engaged in totally unproductive negotiations, the men on the docks proceeded with arrangements for the strike. In San Francisco they elected a rank-and-file strike committee of 25 men right off the docks, and similar preparations were afoot in other ports.

Next to the employers the reactionary, salaried officials displayed more anxiety over the prospect of a walkout than anyone else. They consistently opposed it and made every effort to delay action. Lee Holman, president of the San Francisco local of the ILA, who later turned out to be a racketeer and was expelled from the union, was in continual conflict with the activities of the rank and file.

On the evening of March 22, close to the zero hour for the strike, Regional Labor Board Director George Creel telegraphed to President Roosevelt urging him to intervene. William J. Lewis, president of the entire West Coast ILA, also telegraphed to Joseph P. Ryan, international president of the union, saying, "The sentiment of the men is so strong that a strike cannot be averted unless the President intervenes."

Response from the President was swift. A telegram arrived from Roosevelt appealing to the men to call off the strike and give the government an opportunity to mediate.

Lewis, who received the telegram, called off the strike immediately without referring the matter to the rank and file, and announced that negotiations would continue.

President Roosevelt appointed a mediation board consisting of Charles A. Reynolds of Seattle, Henry F. Grady of San Francisco, and J. L. Leonard of Los Angeles. These gentlemen were the Regional Labor Board directors of their various cities.

Hearings before the mediation board began on March 28 in the Merchants' Exchange Building in San Francisco. At first they were open to the public and the longshoremen thronged in daily to witness the proceedings. But on April 1 it was decided to hold the remainder of the meetings behind closed doors.

On April 3, when the hearings had been concluded and the board had made its recommendations, the employers submitted a proposed "agreement" which William J. Lewis and other ILA officials promptly accepted. (See Appendix 1.) Newspapers announced that an agreement had been arrived at which was "satisfactory to the men." Actually the men knew nothing of the contents of this agreement until Lewis appeared before a membership meeting of the ILA on April 9 and waved it at them.

Employers had sought to prepare the ground for the April 3 agreement by publishing two full-page, paid advertisements in all the local newspapers during March, trying to convince both the longshoremen and the general public that the demands of the rank-and-file convention were "impossible." (See Appendixes 2 and 3.)

Although the April 3 document recognized the ILA and agreed to enter into collective bargaining with it, in reality it was no agreement at all. It stated simply that both sides would enter into negotiations and outlined the objectives that the negotiations would try to achieve.

By this time the longshoremen were so exasperated with negotiations that the mere mention of the word created resentment.

When Lewis appeared before the union meeting with the agreement in his hand, he sensed the dissatisfaction of the men and tried to pass the whole thing off as a joke. He waved the paper at them and said, "Well, here's the damned thing I sold you out for."

The men were in no mood for joking. Their attitude took his words literally and he was assailed with a rapid fire of questions from the floor.

"Is the 'damned thing' even in writing?" asked one longshoreman.

"No," replied Lewis. "It is a gentlemen's agreement."

A roar of ridicule shook the hall.

Then a thin, sharp-featured longshoreman stood up and subjected the agreement to a scorching analysis. This was Harry Bridges, an Australian-born dock worker who had been elected to the rank-and-file committee, and who was to become one of the outstanding labor leaders in America.

Despite widespread dissatisfaction with the so-called agreement, the men decided to extend their patience a little longer. They submitted to still another series of negotiations and sat back to await results.

By April 29 no tangible results were forthcoming, even though the negotiators had been locked in almost continuous confab ever since April 9. The men had reached the end of their patience. At the union meeting that night one official after another took the floor and tried to explain away the difficulties. Finally Harry Bridges stood up and described the whole rigmarole as a trick to lead the demands of the men into a wilderness of negotiations and lose them. He pointed out that the demands were simple and clear-cut, and that months of alleged negotiations could have no purpose other than stalling for time in order to place the men at a disadvantage.

On one occasion Lewis, his face blazing with rage, leaped to his feet and pointed a finger at Bridges. "God damn you!" he screamed.

Before he could say anything more, loud protests from the floor silenced him. He was forced to sit down and allow Bridges to continue. At the conclusion of his talk the men voted to give the employers until May 7 to arrive at some decision. If the demands were not granted by that time, a strike would be called.

On the following day the employers received a brief communication addressed to Mr. T. G. Plant, president of the Waterfront Employers' Union—later called the Waterfront Employers' Association.

Dear Sir:

The following motion was unanimously concurred in by Local 38-79, International Longshoremen's Association, at a special called meeting held Sunday, April 29, 1934.

Motion: Regularly moved and seconded and carried, that unless something definite shall have been arrived at by the joint committee of five and five and the committee of two and two, by Monday Evening Eight p.m. May 7, 1934, negotiations shall be discontinued.

During the ensuing week the negotiations committee failed to accomplish anything. The San Francisco local of the ILA, at a meeting attended by 1,500 men, voted unanimously to strike on the morning of Wednesday, May 9. Simultaneous votes were being taken in all other ports with overwhelming decisions to strike.

Joseph P. Ryan, international president of the ILA, dispatched a flock of telegrams from his New York office urging other ports to disregard the San Francisco local and not go on strike. Previously he had reiterated the shipowners' charge that the San Francisco longshoremen were a "bunch of communists."

Another telegram arrived from Washington, this time not from President Roosevelt but from Senator Robert F. Wagner, chairman of the National Labor Board, urging that the strike be called off once more and that the mediation board be given an opportunity to reconsider the matter.

It was ineffective.

On May 8 the employers inserted another full-page advertisement in all papers, and on May 9 T. G. Plant issued a public statement:

The plea of the National Labor Board to the longshoremen not to go out on strike has apparently gone unheeded.

The basic agreement which the International Longshoremen's Association entered into only a month ago to exhaust the resources of mediation on all matters before resorting to a strike has been broken over wages. Force is resorted to instead.

The Waterfront Employers' Union of San Francisco have avoided recruiting any men in advance of the actual strike in the effort to avoid widening the breach as it developed through Monday and Tuesday. It now becomes necessary to load ships with new men and recruiting will begin at once. The recruiting office has been opened at 23 Main Street; the Police Department has given assurance that protection will be provided the men hired.

Those regularly employed longshoremen who have reported for work as usual this morning will be given complete protection and lodged on their respective docks so that they need not go through the picket lines if these form.

A month and a half before, on March 20, T. G. Plant had been quoted in newspapers as saying, "There are thousands of men now unemployed who will be glad to get the jobs." On March 22 the same papers quoted him as saying that he had already recruited 2,500 strikebreakers.

On May 9 at 8 p.m. the longshoremen went out on strike in San Francisco, Seattle, Tacoma, Portland, San Pedro, San Diego, Stockton, Bellingham, Aberdeen, Gray's Harbor, Astoria, and all other Pacific

Coast ports. The walkout was practically 100 per cent effective, and by May 11 all the waterfronts were tied up over 1,900 miles of coast-line.

The strike committee of the International Longshoremen's Association issued a statement:

Longshoremen on the Pacific Coast are on strike—striking for better conditions, a shorter day and a living wage; also for recognition of their union. This strike is called, not in defiance of the government, but the opposite. It is called to get all the things that the government, itself, has advocated and after every means available under the NRA for an amicable settlement has been exhausted.

The Longshoremen of the Pacific Coast have already granted the National Labor Board and the employers 45 days to settle their grievances, but the employers have refused at all times to grant the demands of the ILA.

The Longshoremen take this means of asking the fullest cooperation of all labor, of all industry, to help win labor's biggest struggle on the Pacific Coast.

The following item appeared in the *Western Worker:*

The Communist Party in all sections along the Coast immediately wired to all units for the speediest mobilization of every available force into strike activity. "No Scab" leaflets are already covering many points. There is to be a thorough canvass of all neighborhoods for solidarity with the strikers.

CHAPTER VI
The Strike Begins,
The Strike Spreads

SAN FRANCISCO'S EMBARCADERO
quickly took on the aspect of a zone of war. The heavy steel folding gates of the pier were drawn shut, and electrified barbed wire guarded the entrances. Police guards were stationed in front of all docks. Additional police cruised the waterfront in radio patrol cars, on motorcycle and horseback. Lookouts with field telephones were stationed at high vantage points.

The longshoremen were evident in a giant picket line of 1,000 men parading two abreast up and down the sidewalk in front of the docks with an American flag at the head of their column.

Display advertisements appeared in all papers:

LONGSHOREMEN WANTED
EXPERIENCE DESIRABLE BUT NOT NECESSARY

Apply Navy Landing Pier, foot of Howard Street, San Francisco
85c an Hour Straight Time — $1.25 an Hour Overtime

STRIKE CONDITIONS PREVAIL
WATERFRONT EMPLOYERS' UNION
By J. W. Petersen

When strikebreakers were hired they were escorted under police guard to the docks and quartered aboard the liner "Diana Dollar," the famous "scab ship" of the strike. Here they were confined in a state of siege—meals, laundry, entertainment, and even banking facilities being provided for them free of charge.

At first scab hiring was carried on at the offices of the Waterfront Employers' Union, and the police threw a cordon around the building. The longshoremen also flung a picket line around the building and several minor clashes occurred. Scabs were afraid to apply at this address so, on the advice of the Police Department, the employers moved their hiring office to Pier 14 (Navy landing pier) where it remained for the duration of the strike.

Although Thomas G. Plant had announced prior to the walkout that he had plenty of men all ready to go to work the minute the longshoremen struck, no such army of strikebreakers ever appeared. Greatest hope of the employers rested in the unemployed who, they believed, would grab at the chance to get any kind of work. But even before the strike began, communist organizations had saturated the poorer neighborhoods with leaflets urging them to support organized labor and refuse to scab.

Some professional strikebreakers were imported from distant cities, but these men had no appetite or ability for work. Their specialty was gangsterism and slugging, not stevedoring.

On May 11 the employers ran another advertisement in the newspapers and addressed it to the longshoremen. It read, in part:

We want to pay you as good wages as the industry can afford. We always have paid top wages—and hope to keep it up.

Recovery is not yet here—it is only on the way. You are hurting, not helping, to bring it back for yourselves, for us, and for San Francisco.

It is an ill-advised strike.

Be reasonable!

The teamsters, who lived and worked in close contact with the longshoremen, knew the situation on the docks and had a strong bond of sympathy with the strikers. They were united by a thousand personal friendships. To them the longshoremen were neighbors and pals, and they did not relish the idea of cooperating with the scabs on the docks. On May 13 they assembled in general membership meeting and voted overwhelmingly to boycott the waterfront. Michael Casey, president of the Teamster's Union, and other conservative, salaried officials, strove energetically to block such action, even trying to substitute a motion to the effect that merchandise would be trucked to the pierheads but not onto the docks. This was emphatically rejected in favor of not moving anything at all to or from the Embarcadero. Following the meeting, hundreds of teamsters marched to the waterfront and paraded with the longshoremen in a demonstration of solidarity.

The following day Oakland teamsters voted similar action, and a day later Seattle teamsters followed suit.

This left only one link of transportation functioning between the docks and the warehouses: the state-owned Belt Line Railroad whose employees were civil service and bound by a "yellow dog" contract whereby if they took any strike action they would lose pension privileges and seniority.

The next question was, how would the strike affect the seamen? Ships were beginning to accumulate at the piers and the seamen for the first time since 1919 had an opportunity to get together in large numbers. The officials of the International Seamen's Union, an affiliate of the American Federation of Labor, had no more appetite for a strike than did the salaried officials of the longshoremen or teamsters. They waited nervously to see what might happen. The Marine Workers' Industrial Union stepped forward and began calling the seamen off the ships, not only in sympathy with the longshoremen, but for demands of their own. The crews of thirteen ships walked off in the first few days of the strike and took their places in the picket lines side by side with the longshoremen.

On May 14 the Boilermakers and Machinists Union declared a boycott against all ships worked by scabs, and the Los Angeles teamsters voted sympathetic action similar to that in other ports.

By this time the shipowners' pretense of carrying on "business as usual" began to sag. Passenger and freight lines were abandoning services and canceling sailings.

Within a few days the officials of the International Seamen's Union perceived that if they did not take action the Marine Workers' Industrial Union would be seizing their laurels. On May 15 and 16 strikes were declared by the Sailors' Union, the Marine Firemen, Oilers, Watertenders and Wipers, and the Marine Cooks and Stewards—all affiliates of the ISU. Meanwhile the Ferryboatmen's Union, the Masters, Mates and Pilots, and the Marine Engineers Beneficial Association began demanding pay increases and improvements without declaring any strike.

The Belt Line Railroad continued to operate, but under the severest difficulties. Strikers parked their cars across the tracks, sat down in the path of the locomotives, and the train crews were only too glad to

[49]

make the most of these incidents as an excuse for delays and interruptions of service. Under pressure of their "yellow dog" contracts they went through the motions of work with no enthusiasm and considerable discontent.

Employers, meanwhile, were flooding the press with martyred expressions of their own virtue and clamored for the government to intervene. In Seattle they abandoned every pretense of continuing operations, and Mayor John F. Dore made formal demands for state and federal troops to maintain order. His requests went unheeded by authorities.

The federal government ordered Assistant Secretary of Labor Edward F. McGrady to proceed at once to San Francisco by plane. Newspapers heralded his arrival as the coming of a sure and immediate settlement. Meanwhile employers were making every effort to summon Joseph P. Ryan, international president of the ILA. Ryan, however, was busily engaged preventing the spread of the strike to East Coast docks and could not come immediately.

The paralyzing effect of the strike on industry was creeping inland and newspapers were whipping hysteria to a frenzy. Lumber mills in the Northwest were shutting down, grain shipments were halted, and numerous other industries were affected by lack of essential raw materials which were tied up on ships.

In Los Angeles the strikers had a special problem since the docks were not concentrated in one area, but were scattered at considerable distance. Picketing was difficult and employers took full advantage of the situation. On May 15 the first serious clash occurred there when pickets surrounded a stockade where scabs were quartered, and sought to enter the enclosure. Police fired into their ranks, killing one and injuring scores.

The killing of young Dick Parker created tremendous resentment up and down the coast. He was given an impressive funeral in San Pedro at which more than 5,000 strikers and sympathizers attended and paraded through the streets.

In the early days of the strike employers had sought to isolate the Negroes from the whites and play them against each other to their mutual disadvantage. Bosses who would never hire Negroes except for the most menial jobs now made special, and relatively unsuccessful, efforts to recruit Negroes as scabs.

Smaller clashes between pickets and strikebreakers were almost daily occurrences in every port. When Edward F. McGrady arrived from Washington guns were blazing on the Oakland waterfront across the bay from San Francisco. Negro strikebreakers fired on an automobile full of pickets which had drawn up in front of their agency. Three union men were seriously wounded.

The strike committee, however, was alert to the danger of such a pitfall. Strict precautions were taken against racial animosity. Negroes were welcomed into the union, marched side by side with the whites on picket lines, and were elected to committees. Absolutely no discrimination was tolerated within union ranks. As a consequence, although clashes did occur between Negroes and whites, they were in no sense of the word "race riots." To the contrary, the strike established a degree of equality and understanding between Negro and white dock workers that persists to this day as an unbreakable bond of solidarity.

When McGrady landed from his plane in San Francisco he went into immediate conference with the President's baffled mediation board, and with representatives of employers and unions. Newspapers announced that he was taking matters in hand and that a settlement was imminent.

By this time some ninety-four vessels were tied up in San Francisco alone, and thousands of tons of cargo, much of it perishable, was congested on the docks.

In Seattle an additional controversy had broken out over transportation of commodities to Alaska. This territory was completely isolated by the walkout. Furthermore, the salmon season was just beginning and the cannery companies were without means of supplying their far northern posts. After much bickering the longshoremen agreed to load one vessel with essential supplies for the residents of Alaska. Eventually a separate and tentative agreement was entered into with the Alaska Steamship Company to relieve the situation.

McGrady's first act toward arriving at a settlement was to dispatch telegrams, through the mediation board, to all employers and unions requesting that negotiation committees representing both sides be empowered to arrive at a full settlement which, when signed, would be binding on both sides.

This request was not viewed with favor by the longshoremen. In the first place, they had little confidence in the reactionary, salaried union officials who were handling negotiations. In the second place, they saw no reason why they should bind themselves to a proposition the nature of which no man could predict at that moment. In the third place, the seamen also were now involved in the strike, and if the longshoremen should sign an agreement without considering them it would be tantamount to "leaving them out on a limb." Without the support of the longshoremen the seamen could have little hope of gaining their demands.

On the evening of May 19 the longshoremen met in general membership meeting to consider McGrady's request. All aspects of the situation were discussed and Harry Bridges, chairman of the rank-and-file strike committee, advised strenuously against agreeing to any proposition sight unseen and against signing a separate agreement that would kick the props out from under the seamen.

As a result of this meeting the most important resolution of the strike was passed by unanimous vote. The longshoremen ruled that any proposition arrived at through negotiations must be referred back to the rank and file for approval before it could be decided on. They resolved further that the longshoremen would not go back to work until the seamen also received some settlement of their grievances.

McGrady was infuriated when he heard news of the decision. "Communists are throwing a monkey wrench into the situation," he declared. "San Francisco ought to be informed of the growth of the hold of the Red element on the situation. There is an element among the longshoremen that lives on strike and does not want a settlement."

This was a surprising reaction to the simple and sensible request of the men for democracy in arriving at an agreement. Much of McGrady's rage, and that of the employers, was caused by the fact that communist newspapers and leaflets distributed thickly over the waterfront that morning had urged exactly the precautions which the men ultimately adopted in their resolutions.

Later on McGrady embellished his comments by stating:

A strong radical element within the ranks of the longshoremen seems to want no settlement of this strike. I have observed that Communists, through direct action and pleas made in the widely circulated Communist newspaper here, are trying to induce the strikers to remain out despite our efforts to arbitrate.

We are very far away from a settlement. On Friday we believed the Executive Committee of the ILA had power to act for the strikers along the entire coast. But that same night the rank and file of the strikers stripped them of that authority. The Executive Committee appears to me to be helpless to do anything with the men they represent, or to combat the radical element in the Longshoremen's Union.

McGrady almost hit the nail on the head. The executive committee was not supposed to "do anything with the men they represent." It was supposed to represent them and nothing more. McGrady's "do anything with" phrase amply sustained whatever mistrust the men already had for their salaried officials.

The employers were quick to pick up the spark of McGrady's anger and fan it into a blaze. J. W. Mailliard, Jr., president of the San Francisco Chamber of Commerce, issued an inflammatory statement which the newspapers eagerly published under banner headlines: "STRIKE OUT OF HAND! *Reds Lead Dock Strike, City Warned! Situation Hopeless, Says Mediator.*"

When McGrady saw the extras he realized that his statements were far out of proportion to what had happened. He tried to throw water on the blaze by issuing a retraction.

"As long as both the strikers and shipping men are willing to sit down around a table and talk things over, it is far from hopeless," he said. "I'm here to bring peace, if possible—and I'm convinced it is possible."

But it was too late to throw cups of water on the inferno. The "red herring" had been unleashed and was running wild, all up and down the coast and far inland.

The full text of Mailliard's sensational statement read:

The San Francisco waterfront strike is out of hand. It is not a conflict between employer and employee—between capital and labor—it is a conflict which is rapidly spreading between American principles and un-American radicalism. As president of the San Francisco Chamber of Commerce, it is now my duty to warn every businessman in this community that the welfare of business and industry and the entire public is at stake in the outcome of this crisis.

The so-called longshoremen's strike has spread since the morning of May 9 to include sympathetic walkouts by unions that presented no demands. On April 3, the workers and employers were in complete agreement on every point but wages and hours, and the President of the United States had set up machinery by which these differences would have been amicably and promptly settled through mediation.

The longshoremen are now represented by spokesmen who are not representatives of American labor and who do not desire a settlement of their strike, but who desire a complete paralysis of shipping and industry and who are responsible for the violence and bloodshed which is typical of their tribe.

The Assistant Secretary of Labor, sent here from Washington, in a last effort to terminate the strike, has indicated that the situation is hopeless and that all negotiations have failed.

There can be no hope for industrial peace until communistic agitators are removed as the official spokesmen of labor and American leaders are chosen to settle their differences along American lines.

Two days later Roger D. Lapham, president of the American

[53]

Hawaiian Steamship Company, in a speech before the Los Angeles Advertising Club, declared the strike leaders were "communists out and out," and that "they don't want the strike settled. They want to break down the walls of government."

The strike committee immediately issued an answering statement which appeared in all papers:

Regardless of who the Chamber of Commerce says is running the strike, the fact remains that the longshoremen are striking only for what the NRA provides for them, that is: Recognition of their union, a shorter week, and an increase in the hour-rate of pay to compensate for the shorter week.

All leaders of the ILA are conservative American Federation of Labor men. It was to be expected that the Chamber of Commerce would inject a political angle into this controversy. If a very small number of longshoremen are interested in Communism, that is their privilege. Neverthelesss, it is a fact that a great majority of the striking longshoremen are adherents of conservative political parties.

Regardless of their political affiliations, all of them are agreed upon one thing: Conditions such as have prevailed along the waterfront will not be tolerated in the future.

The Chamber of Commerce, in allying itself with the shipowners, is now playing its trump card by attempting to draw a "red herring" across the trail. Longshoremen are interested in recovery from the depression. To attain this, the purchasing power of longshoremen must be increased. Apparently the shipowners do not see this obvious route to recovery as recommended by President Roosevelt.

The Communist Party published a reply in the *Western Worker:*

What does the Chamber of Commerce, speaking for the shipowners, want? They want the old-line A. F. of L. method for conducting and settling a strike. The paid officials get into star-chamber conferences with them and "close the deal." That the workers be divided and each section be defeated separately by the united bosses.

But although the ILA is an A. F. of L. union, the workers insist on making it serve their own interest. They have broken down craft lines, and realize the power of organization. That only united action and settlement of all marine workers will guarantee a living to the workers, and that an agreement will not remain on paper.

In the midst of the excitement of charges and countercharges, two more unions walked out on strike—the Masters, Mates and Pilots, and the Marine Engineers' Beneficial Association. The strikers' side of the case now encompassed the entire maritime profession.

On which side did the weight of public opinion rest? As yet there had been no test of sentiment. The strike occupied the headlines of all papers and dominated the conversation of millions. Effects of the tie-up reached far inland and there was not a man, woman, or child whose life was not touched.

This much could be observed. The longshoremen depended upon public contributions to carry on their fight. Thousands of dollars were pouring in from every direction—from unions, organizations, and individuals up and down the coast. Small farmers were sending truckloads of produce to the strikers' relief kitchen. Organizations all over the countryside were holding public meetings and inviting the longshoremen to send speakers to explain their cause.

In Seattle Mayor Dore became exasperated with the rigmarole of negotiations and proclaimed that he was going to "open the port." Everyone knew what this meant: dispersing the picket lines by force and an attempt to operate the industry with scabs under police protection. The phrase "open the port" became a common one with employers from then on, and the implied threat of violence was always clear.

Alarmed at the turmoil that might result from such a move, McGrady wired Dore, "I strongly recommend that you take no action at this time. The government is negotiating. Both sides are seated around the table here attempting to reach an amicable settlement. I trust you will allow the government to continue its effort."

Dore took one look at the message and said, "Who is this man McGrady that he should be trying to run our business for us? We are not going to paralyze our business and industry to make things easier for him."

Employers in San Francisco were marking time and awaiting the arrival of Joseph P. Ryan, international president of the ILA, who was now on his way from New York in a plane. The mediation board had meanwhile submitted a proposal for government operation of a hiring hall. The men rejected the idea and the employers themselves were not very enthusiastic about it, so matters were allowed to drag pending the arrival of Ryan.

What magic Ryan had under his hat to solve the deadlock was never explained. It was just taken for granted by employers, mediators, and the press that his arrival presaged a settlement, just as they had assumed that McGrady would bring with him some charm to make the men abandon their demands and go back to work.

On May 24 Ryan stepped jauntily from his plane in San Francisco and said, "The recognition of the ILA by the employers in collective bargaining is the most important, the only vital point at issue. Once the employers do this we can begin to talk about wages and working conditions. Until they do this, I can see no hope for peace."

This was an extraordinarily uninformed statement coming from the international president of the longshoremen. How could Ryan have been ignorant of the fact that employers had already agreed to recognition of the union and collective bargaining and that neither of these things were points at issue at all? In fact, collective bargaining had been going on now for two months. Even the pilot of the plane must have been aware of that.

Nevertheless employers were overjoyed at his statement and hailed it as a "ray of hope." It was immediately apparent that they were now going to settle things, not with the longshoremen but with Joseph P. Ryan. In case the longshoremen might have any idea of protesting this amicable course, J. W. Mailliard, Jr., issued an ominous statement to the press:

We do not wish to make a statement pending the outcome of negotiations with Mr. Ryan and his group, following which we will open up the port of San Francisco to commerce.

This was not the shipowners speaking, but the organized business interests of San Francisco represented in the Chamber of Commerce, of which Mailliard was president.

The stage having been set, employers now went into a series of conferences with the international president of the ILA. On May 26, after having discussed matters at length with the shipowners but without even consulting the longshoremen, Ryan declared, "We are making progress. If we were hopelessly deadlocked, there would be no necessity of meeting further. We are all smiling and optimistic." Later the same day he said, "We don't give a hoot for the closed shop. All we are interested in is recognition and preference." He stated also that the longshoremen would not go back on any union which struck in sympathy with them, but that they would not stay out in support of unions which struck with their own demands.

This was a curiously contradictory statement. In the first place, practically all the other unions had raised demands of their own. In the second place, if they had not there would be no sense in discussing remaining out on strike with them. Boiled down to its essence the statement meant that the longshoremen would sign a separate agreement, and to hell with the seamen.

Ryan was so entirely out of gear with the situation that he apparently did not know that the longshoremen had held a meeting that very morning in which they reaffirmed their determination not to return to work until all the other unions on strike had been considered, and furthermore, that they would not go back unless they had a closed shop and a union-controlled hiring hall.

During that meeting Harry Bridges said, "Settlement for mere recognition may mean a lot to national heads of the International Longshoremen's Association who get fat salaries; but the workers are going to hold out for nothing less than a closed shop."

That afternoon another union, Oakland Local No. 6 of the Association of Certified Welders, walked out in sympathy strike with the maritime workers.

Having simplified the situation to his own satisfaction, Ryan did not waste much time in coming to an agreement with the employers. On May 28 the settlement was drawn up under Ryan's supervision and was signed readily by the salaried officials of the union. (See Appendix 4.) It included a clause which signified the employers' willingness to bargain collectively, but failed to recognize the ILA as sole bargaining agent. It provided an employer-controlled hiring hall and spent considerable phraseology establishing the employers' right to hire union or non-union workers according to their pleasure.

Ryan proclaimed the document a victory and newspapers announced that to all intents and purposes the strike was over.

McGrady said, "Never in many years of labor work have I seen a finer spirit than was displayed at the meetings which led to this agreement. There was a spirit of cooperation and give and take which I have never seen equaled. I believe the agreement is the basis for an equitable settlement of the differences of employers and employees."

Beyond all doubt the harmony which prevailed over this meeting was warm and complete. But at the very moment these gentlemen were signing the document the Embarcadero presented a different scene.

Ever since the first day of the walkout the strikers had paraded their giant picket line of 1,000 men up and down the sidewalk in front of the docks. The orderly procession marching behind the American flag was a daily spectacle and went a long way toward impressing everyone who saw it with the discipline, unity, and strength of the union men.

True, there was an ordinance in San Francisco prohibiting picketing. But it was generally regarded by authorities as impractical and had never been enforced stringently, especially in major strikes like this one. Throughout the whole period of the maritime strike to date no effort had been made to enforce it, nor had anyone given the slightest indication that such an effort would be made.

Yet at precisely the same time that Ryan and other officials were putting through their settlement, the police, without any warning, decided to enforce the defunct and almost forgotten anti-picketing law. When the giant picket line reached Pier 18 and swung over to the sidewalk to continue their customary parade, they were met by a heavy detail of police on foot and horse who sought to drive them away from the pavement.

John Schomacher, who was leading the parade, was the first to meet the onslaught and he answered back with his fists. He was a big man, over six feet tall, and gave a good account of himself, pulling two policemen from their horses before he was beaten to the ground. The police applied their clubs freely and the pickets responded with their knuckles. In an instant the Embarcadero was converted into a battlefield. Huge reserves of police appeared suddenly and began flailing with their clubs. The strikers stood their ground, felled officers with their fists and pulled them from their horses.

When the police drew back and released a barrage of tear gas, the strikers retreated across the street to a vacant lot and replied with a hail of bricks.

The battle spread over a wide area, bricks flying, fists thwacking, clubs swinging, and tear-gas shells whistling through the air. As the men drew back to their union hall on Mission and Steuart streets, the police opened fire, shooting one man in the back and wounding many.

A few minutes after the incident the Hearst *Call-Bulletin* was out on the streets with a very generalized description of the clash and an account of how Harry Bridges, who was leading the parade, was clubbed down by police.

Harry Bridges was nowhere near the scene. He is a slightly built man and no one could mistake the towering bulk of Schomacher for Bridges.*

Later on the Hearst *San Francisco Examiner* reported:

Gas bombs exploded; a sawed-off shotgun roared; clubs smashed against heads, and cobblestones flew along San Francisco's waterfront yesterday as police and strikers clashed in the fiercest battle yet produced by the coast-wide maritime strike.

The *Chronicle* said:

In a terrific surge of violence climaxing the twentieth day of the longshoremen's strike, nearly 1,000 striking stevedores staged a bloody pitched

*Schomaker has since joined the drive to "get Bridges."

battle with police yesterday afternoon on the San Francisco waterfront. Casualties were many as officers and strikers battled savagely at close quarters.

With the strikers still in a threatening and ugly mood, Chief Quinn took personal command at the waterfront last night. His first move was to issue this significant order:

"Henceforth all pickets must remain on the town side of the Embarcadero, across the width of the Embarcadero from the piers."

Under command of Lieutenant Joseph Mignola, a squad of police armed with sawed-off shotguns fired into the ranks of a group of strikers who were attempting to cover their advance on Pier 18 under a barrage of bricks and cobblestones.... Six asserted participants in the fracas were arrested on charges of "participating in a riot."

... Splotches of blood appeared on scores of faces. Police suffered heavily from the barrage of bricks and stones. Their own clubs wreaked equal damage.... Lieutenant Mignola gave his men orders to fire. The officers drew pistols and fired over the heads of the strikers.

When the barrage continued they leveled their sawed-off shotguns and fired directly into the line.

Lieutenant Mignola afterward stated to the press:

If the strikers come back for more, you'll find some of them in the morgue after the next time.

The police were on duty and instructed to stop all rioting. These strikers —more than 600 of them, I would say—began a rush on Pier 20.

They began throwing bricks and cobblestones, and when I saw several policemen struck I shouted to them to fire their pistols into the air and use their clubs freely if they were in danger. Then I ordered some of the boys with shotguns to fire into the crowd....

We weren't out to hurt anybody seriously, but those men were looking for trouble and they found it. If they come back, I'll not take any chances of their injuring policemen. If bricks start floating at us again, somebody will wind up in the morgue, and I don't think it will be any of us.

Captain Arthur DeGuire, commanding the Harbor District, also made a public report:

There was an indication of trouble when the strikers formed their parade yesterday about as usual. They started with a large escort of police, in the same orderly manner that has marked the other parades.

But when the parade was approximately opposite Pier 18, the marchers broke up into a mob. Besides the officers on foot, there were several police cars with inspectors on the scene.

The strikers became a howling mob. They began to surround the police cars and tried to drag the inspectors out. From then on it was a case of everybody for himself.

At this time I don't know whether anyone issued orders to use tear bombs. If anybody did, it would have been Lieutenant Joseph Mignola, who was in the center of it.

But these officers were all police-trained and no orders were necessary. In a situation like that, with the mob trying to pull the inspectors from their machines, the officers as a matter of training would use tear bombs to disperse the mob.

Further, the mob seemed to be led by communists. A lot of the banners carried in the parade had signs about "down with this" and "down with that." And when the fight started, the paraders ripped the banners from the poles and used the poles as clubs.

When the mounted officers arrived it was a general melee. Any officer was justified in doing what was done in this riot.

But as later events proved, these two officers found themselves unable to justify manifold indecencies and corruptions. At this moment they were the heroes of the day and were hailed by newspapers and leading citizens as brave defenders of the public good. Their contradictory and ridiculous stories were accepted as the official truth about the waterfront conflict.

However, sometime later both Lieutenant Joseph Mignola and Captain Arthur DeGuire were discovered to be in league with the underworld. Their complicity with the prostitution shakedown and other criminal grafts resulted in their being removed from the force and dismissed in disgrace. The fact that they both are not in the penitentiary is accountable to—well, read the summary of the Atherton investigation back in Chapter II. I am not making any statements that are not already proved, so I shall refrain from drawing any conclusions of my own.

The International Longshoremen's Association delivered a protest to the Board of Supervisors in which they stated their version of the affair:

For no reason whatsoever the mounted police this afternoon rode into the parade and attempted to disperse it. The attack was carried out by the police with tear gas, drawn guns and revolvers. Several men were shot, and many clubbed and beaten to the ground, and, even after they were lying unconscious on the sidewalks, were kicked and beaten by the police.

Inasmuch as the strikers carried no weapons of any kind, unless the staffs of the American flag and the ILA banner carried at the head of the parade could be called weapons, and were violating no laws or ordinances, but peacefully parading, we insist that as one of the heads of the city administration, you take some immediate action to stop this unwarranted incitement to riot.

The Board of Supervisors immediately authorized Mayor Angelo J. Rossi to appoint a committee of five to investigate. However, the Mayor refrained from making the appointments and the investigation was never made.

On the day of the attack many newsboys ignored the contents of the papers they were selling, which accused the strikers of fomenting a riot, and shouted: "Read all about it! They're murdering pickets on the waterfront! Read how they slaughter strikers!"

In the midst of all these events the Ryan settlement was unfurled. It was examined by the rank-and-file strike committee and they decided it wasn't even worth discussing. They issued a statement:

Reports in the newspapers that the strike is settled are absolutely untrue. The strike has just started and will probably involve other unions which have no connection with the maritime industry. The possibility of a general strike along the Pacific Coast is almost a certainty.

The *Western Worker* came out with a front-page editorial flaying Ryan's proposal as a betrayal, and urging the longshoremen to stand by the seamen until justice had been won by all. During the strike the *Western Worker* printed a special supplement called the "Baby Western" which carried the official bulletins of the strike committee and was distributed among the men. On the occasion of the Ryan proposal they got out a special "Baby Western" and distributed 4,000 copies along the waterfront.

The proposal was to be submitted to a ballot vote of the entire membership on the Pacific Coast. The San Francisco strike committee, however, called a special membership meeting in Eagles Hall on May 29 to consider the proposition. Ryan appeared and tried to argue the virtues of his settlement. He evoked nothing but boos and a hail of "razzberries."

Spokesmen of the rank-and-file strike committee met warm ovations of applause. Harry Bridges characterized the Ryan agreement as "a mere attempt of the employers to sound out the weak spots in the ILA organization."

The meeting rejected the proposal by unanimous vote.

The union officials from Northwest ports, who had affixed their signatures to the Ryan agreement, saw which way the wind was blowing and trimmed their sails accordingly. They declared that after giving the matter more sober thought, they had reversed their attitude, and recommended that the strikers reject the proposal.

Assistant Secretary of Labor McGrady said, "If the proposal is rejected the employers are bound to take the offensive and bloodshed and violence will result." He knew what he was talking about.

Realizing that he was merely shouting into the wind so far as San Francisco was concerned, Ryan boarded a plane and flew to Portland with the hope of swinging the northwestern ports to his deal and isolating San Francisco. He declared upon arrival, "San Francisco opposed the peaceful settlement and it is up to the locals of the Northwest to vote down San Francisco and save that local from itself." Why did he put the emphasis on "peaceful settlement"?

Portland turned thumbs down on him and refused even to take a secret ballot on the proposition, which was rejected by an almost unanimous vote of acclamation.

Considerably rebuffed, Ryan also trimmed his sails to suit the breeze and announced: "I have a different slant on it now and the issue has resolved itself entirely into a question of full recognition of the union. I don't blame the strikers if they reject the peace offer."

This statement was just as much askew and out of gear as anything else Ryan had said. There was still the matter of loyalty to the seamen, and the issue of the hiring hall.

Ryan now devoted his efforts, with no success whatsoever, toward bringing about separate agreements with the separate steamship companies for separate ports. This also was directly contrary to the purpose of the strikers, which was for a uniform West Coast agreement with a uniform expiration date.

CHAPTER VII
*The Memorial Day Attack,
The First Parade, San
Francisco Newspapers*

Police Lieutenant Mignola, who had threatened "you will find some of them in the morgue after next time," did not wait long to demonstrate what he meant. Already the phrase "Clubs are trumps" was popular among officers on the waterfront. And only two days following the battle at Pier 18 this uniformed accomplice of the San Francisco underworld unleashed one of the bloodiest attacks of the entire strike.

May 30 was Memorial Day, which is usually given over to military parades and services commemorating the dead who had fallen in America's wars. It had also been chosen by young people in liberal, radical, and anti-war organizations throughout the country as National Youth Day. On this occasion anti-war meetings and demonstrations were held all over America by students and young people generally. Although numerous youth organizations, particularly from high schools and universities, took part in these annual demonstrations, the Young Communist League was usually prominent among them.

The open-air meeting this year was to be held on the Embarcadero, as it had been the year before. It was also intended that, in view of the strike, it would combine anti-war speeches with expressions of student and youth solidarity with the unions. Although given no publicity in the daily papers, it had been circularized widely by leaflets and invitations. It was strictly a young people's occasion and no adults were in attendance other than strikers who were naturally in the locality and looked on with interest.

As the hour approached for the meeting to begin, it was noted that hundreds of policemen had been concentrated in the vicinity. A request for a permit to parade had been denied, and the scene looked ominous. It was decided to call off the meeting.

Later on a committee representing twenty-two organizations and church groups, under the chairmanship of Reverend Alfred C. Fiske, Ph.D., held a thorough investigation of the incident, taking testimony from all available witnesses. They described the scene:

On one corner a crowd of 250 youths and girls stood irresolute and confused. It was May 30, the National Youth Day, a day of speeches against war and fascism, but something was wrong, there were no speeches. The crowd waited.

Presently a young man mounted on the shoulders of a comrade. It was his duty to tell the assemblage why they could have no meeting like that of former years on the same day and place. The young man was supported in his precarious position by a young girl. The speaker began the message, "Comrades and fellow workers—"

Instantly the police were down on them with clubs and saps. They swarmed in a blue-coated mob over the handful of youths, some of whom were no more than children, laying open skulls right and left with their heavy riot sticks.

So overwhelming in numbers were the police that escape was almost impossible. Sixty-five young boys and girls went down with broken heads. Kids in corduroys crouched on the sidewalk trying to shield themselves while police beat at them with blackjacks and nightsticks. Longshoremen who had been watching from the sidelines were so enraged at the spectacle they leaped into the melee and began felling policemen with their fists.

Some of the young people broke through the lines and tried to run. They were pursued into alleys off the Embarcadero and clubbed to the pavement.

Since the crowd presented every variety of dress, some being students from universities and high schools and others being young workers, the police were unable to discern between who had come to attend the demonstration and who were merely pedestrians. Consequently a large number of mere bystanders were clubbed down.

A talented young local sculptor, Peter Macchiarini, was thrown into the police patrol bleeding from the ears with a fractured skull. Despite the entreaties of other prisoners that he was dying, he was thrown in a cell and not removed to a hospital until many hours later, when his cellmates gave evidence that if something were not done about him they would shake the bars off the cage and scream the roof off the jail.

It was many months before Pete's head mended, and when he was able to get around again he had to face trial on charges of rioting.

One young student described his experience:

I left Berkeley with my wife to go to San Francisco. We got off the ferry and started to walk up Market. When we got to Steuart, I saw some mounted police crossing the street. There was a crowd there, and suddenly a big man pointed at me and said, "Here's a dirty kike son-of-a-bitch!" He grabbed at me and struck me on the back of the head with something. I started to run, but one of them grabbed my arm and started beating me. As he held my arm, he kept shouting for me to run. I naturally couldn't because he was holding me. I twisted away and ran into another group. They slugged me and one of them hit me in the mouth with a blackjack. It cut my lips very badly and broke off two teeth.

In the meantime, they struck at my wife and called her a "bitch." She dodged them and managed to get away somehow. [Testimony from the report of Rev. Fiske's committee.]

Mr. J. D. Jordan testified:

I was at the corner of Embarcadero and Mission when I saw a crowd of people at the corner of Steuart and Mission. I started to walk toward them intending to see what it was all about. As I approached I noticed I was followed by a large number of men who were obviously plainclothesmen. As they overtook me, one of them started swearing at me in the vilest manner I have ever heard. There must have been at least ten of them who jumped upon me and started beating me. Not all of them could hit me at once and they seemed to go crazy with rage. I only had time to think that they were tearing me to pieces.... They knocked me down and I got to my feet, blood streaming down my face and clothes.

The worst slugging took place in the street right outside the headquarters of the ILA. Many longshoremen witnessed it from the windows in the second story, and one of them testified:

I was in the hall on Wednesday, and I want to tell you people right now that I have seen violence and brutality in many forms all over the world.

I've been a seaman and you get to see plenty of things like that. But I want to say that I have never seen anything like that attack upon those kids last Wednesday. It was nothing but murder.

We were locked in the hall, but we saw plenty from the window. Those cops just slugged and beat everybody they could reach. Nobody had a chance. They seemed to go crazy and we just about went crazy watching them.

Other typical bits of testimony were:

Q. What is your name?
A. Leonard Pressel.
Q. How old are you?
A. I'm fifteen, going on sixteen.
Q. Leonard, what are you doing here in San Francisco? I mean, what and why are you here, are you working, etc.?
A. I'm not working. I'm just—
Q. You are on the bum, so to speak?
A. Yes.
Q. Why did you leave home?
A. Well, I couldn't get work and no money for school.
Q. Now, Leonard, tell us what happened to you on Wednesday when you were thrown in jail.
A. I was walking up Howard near Second Street when a big car full of men drew up and some of them jumped out. One of them shouted at me and they started running towards me. I didn't know what it was all about. They grabbed me and one hit me over the head with a club. It knocked me down, but two more grabbed me and held me up and I got hit again. I broke away from them and started running and I ran right into another bunch. One of them grabbed my arm and hit me in the back of the head while another one hit me in front. I don't remember much then except them hitting me. I had blood all over my face and I could feel it running down the back of my neck. They left me for a moment and I finally got up again. This time, another bunch that had come up got me and hit me real hard. I was taken to the jail, but I don't remember much.

And again, from Miss Frances Rabin:

My sister Alice was run up on the sidewalk by a policeman who hit her over the head wth his club and knocked her down. I ran behind a machine. Another policeman on foot ran to where my sister was lying on the sidewalk and was going to hit her again when I screamed—and he came over after me. I kept on screaming and he let her alone and wanted to hit me.

I picked up my sister and took her to a store at 36 Steuart Street. Three boys in there gave us some water and towels.

While all this was going on, Mayor Rossi was out in the National Cemetery at the Presidio orating:

We are thus drawn together in a contemplation of the great glories, the lofty deeds and the weighty sacrifices which have been the foundation of our national life.... The impressive scene we have just witnessed, the silent ranks of veterans who have assembled to honor those who died in the service of God and their country, should leave in our hearts a spirit of thankfulness that the memory of their valor is not forgotten.

It seemed to me today as I looked into the resolute faces ... that nothing ill can befall a country whose citizens accept their patriotic duty in so cheerful and steadfast a spirit ... if we enshrine in our hearts the devotion we owe them, we will have little time to harbor thoughts of revolution, of the destruction of governmental fabric and running after false Gods.

The *Examiner* rushed into print with a blaring extra: "17 MAIMED IN S. F. RED BATTLE."

The story read:

Fierce rioting marked San Francisco's observance of Memorial Day yesterday as more than 250 Communists clashed with 100 policemen in a series of skirmishes that raged over the area bounded by the Embarcadero, Second Street, Market and Howard.

The *San Francisco News* read:

Clubs flailing, police broke up a possible demonstration of striking longshoremen on lower Market Street today, injuring one unidentified 16-year-old girl and sending 24 men to the hospital wth head injuries.

Trouble started, according to witnesses, when a party of longshoremen began a march, either toward the waterfront or up Market Street—the destination was indefinite.

The *Chronicle* said:

Two hundred and fifty communists and police staged a bloody battle yesterday afternoon near the Embarcadero—the second major riot to mark the longshoremen's strike this week.

Nineteen persons were treated at hospitals as a result and two youths were reported to have been shot and subsequently spirited away in the ensuing confusion. Scores of others were injured.

Lieutenant Mignola was credited in all papers as commander of police forces on the occasion.

The strikers immediately dispatched a telegram to Acting Governor Frank Merriam and issued the same as a public statement:

Local 38-79 of the International Longshoremen's Association vigorously protests the insane brutality of San Francisco police in clubbing children and aged women into insensibility and in clubbing peaceful picketers and innocent bystanders. We recognize this unprovoked attack as an attempt to intimidate the longshoremen and we demand the right to arm in self-defense. As acting governor of this state we hold you personally responsible for future violence on the San Francisco waterfront.

By this time the strike dominated the minds of the whole population. San Francisco was living and breathing strike. Everyone was discussing it. Everyone was trying to understand it. Everyone had something to say about it and something to ask about it. Homes, restaurants, and public places became virtual open forums, and people were rapidly taking sides. Bitter disagreements were splitting homes and friendships; at the same time new bonds of sympathy and common viewpoint were being forged—bringing people together, creating new ties.

Despite garbled accounts in the press, the public was able to get an impression of what had taken place, if not a specific picture. And that impression was a bad one, so far as the employers and the civic administration were concerned.

On the following evening the International Labor Defense held a mass protest meeting in California Hall. Every available seat and all standing room was packed, and overflow crowds jammed the sidewalk outside. More than a score of young people with bandaged heads occupied chairs on the platform. Eyewitnesses described the events of the day before, and the crowd was addressed by speakers representing the striking unions, various local organizations, and the Communist Party.

Two days later, on Sunday, the first big public demonstration occurred. Five thousand persons assembled on the Embarcadero, marched up Market Street to Civic Center, and protested against police brutality on the very doorstep of City Hall. Clerks, professional people, and students were in the ranks of the marchers, as well as trade unionists from practically every craft in the city. It was an ominous procession, for these people had come in a spirit of defiance. Three days before, 250 school children had attempted to hold a demonstration on the waterfront and many had been clubbed into insensibility. Now 5,000 people gathered on the very same spot with the attitude, "Club us if you dare!"

No one dared.

As a result the demonstration assembled in perfect order and proceeded to the Civic Center without incident, a living example in itself of who had been responsible for the violence and disorder of preceding days.

Newspapers said:

Assertedly "in protest of police brutality," the parade in San Francisco formed at Steuart and Mission streets. It was led by a dozen small children of striking stevedores, followed by a hundred women. . . .

In silence broken only by the sound of marching feet and occasional cheers, the paraders wended their way up Steuart to Market Street, and thence to the Civic Center, where the crowd formed in orderly fashion about loudspeakers to listen quietly to the remarks of their representatives.

Although practically every newspaper in San Francisco threw its weight with the employers, the heaviest logic was on the side of the men. The strike comprised a dispute within the maritime industry. The strikers' side comprised a united front of virtually every man or boy who performed any practical function within that industry, from the captains of ships right on down to the lowest in rank, including the men on the docks. It was difficult to convince anyone that these men who spent their whole lives in carrying on one of the most difficult and complex services in industry, were an undisciplined and dangerous "mob."

Of the four daily papers in San Francisco, three supported the employers quite frankly. The circulation of these papers, especially in the months immediately following the strike, sagged alarmingly, whereas the fourth paper, the one that sought to maintain an appearance of impartiality, experienced a tremendous increase.

Two of the frankly pro-employer papers, the *Examiner* and the *Call-Bulletin*, are owned by William Randolph Hearst, and San Francisco is the cradle and stronghold of the Hearst publication enterprises, which have always been strongly implicated in local politics.

The other pro-employer sheet was the *San Francisco Chronicle*, an independently owned paper in which the Fleishhacker shipping interests have a heavy investment.

The fourth paper, the *San Francisco News*, of the Scripps-Howard chain, had its largest circulation in working-class districts. As a consequence it followed a sick and troubled course throughout the strike. Its circulation depended on labor and its advertising depended on the employers.

No newspapermen were regarded with any favor by the strikers, who frequently excluded them from their meetings. But Hearst representatives in particular got the worst treatment and were booted out whenever discovered. It was impossible for Hearst men to get any information from the unions. This venom was not directed against the reporters themselves as individuals but against the Hearst organization. Many of the Hearst newsmen were strongly sympathetic to the unions and turned in as straight accounts as they could. But they had no control over what might happen to these stories in going through the editorial mill.

All waterfront unions and large numbers of uptown unions have strict boycott rules against Hearst papers, and any member found purchasing one or having a copy in his possession is subject to heavy fine. Following the strike, the heaviest boycott fell upon the two Hearst papers which dwindled to such trivial circulation that they sent armies of house-to-house solicitors ringing doorbells all over town offering to pay people to subscribe.

The Dollar Steamship Company has a financial investment in the Hearst publications.

The *Chronicle* too might have suffered more, only that, alarmed by the fate of the Hearst press, they revised their editorial policy and began making a bid for the "liberal" circulation which the *News* was reaping so successfully. Ever since the strike the *Chronicle* has been bending over backward in an effort to conciliate the laboring population and gain the reputation of being a "common man's" paper.

I MMEDIATELY AFTER THE Memorial Day battle, Assistant Secretary of Labor McGrady boarded a plane and flew back to Washington. Things were getting too much for him. Negotiations were deadlocked and he had already expressed his knowledge that employers were about to open up an "offensive." Indeed plenty of evidence to this effect had already bloodstained the cobbles of the Embarcadero.

On the day before his departure the International Seamen's Union held a membership meeting of all crafts and adopted a resolution similar to the one already passed by the longshoremen, that they would "stand by our agreement with the Pacific Coast District Unions of the International Longshoremen's Association, also on strike for better conditions, and will not return to work until those demands are met."

The ports of the Pacific Coast were sewed up tight, with the exception of a trivial amount of cargo trickling through Los Angeles. Within the San Francisco docks a scattering of incompetent scabs toyed hopelessly with a mountain of congested merchandise. Slings slipped or broke and crates smashed open. Hands were skinned and bones fractured.

It takes years of experience to know how to stow cargo in a hold so that it will not shift at sea and capsize the vessel. Anyone foolish enough to put to sea on a ship loaded by scabs might as well go canoeing with an epileptic.

The affectation of carrying on business with such slipshod and indifferent riffraff as scabs proved so expensive and impractical that two years later, during the famous ninety-nine-day strike of 1936-37, employers did not bother to make such an effort.

It was generally concluded that McGrady had gone to Washington to lay the whole predicament before President Roosevelt. Dean Henry Francis Grady, chairman of the President's mediation board in San Francisco, telephoned ahead of McGrady to the National Labor Board in Washington saying that he saw no immediate hope of a settlement. Then he sat down and penned a lengthy statement to the effect that, in spite of the fact that the Ryan proposal of May 28 had been turned down by a 99 per cent majority vote of the longshoremen, he, Dean Grady, considered it fair and was still of that opinion. In conclusion he pleaded for federal legislation which would give mediation boards mandatory powers to enforce the acceptance of agreements which they believed fair.

Longshoremen, meanwhile, were receiving assurances from foreign ports that dock workers in other nations would refuse to unload any cargo that was loaded by scabs on the Pacific Coast. From New Zealand came word that the "watersiders," as the longshoremen called themselves there, were in full support of the strike. Similar sympathetic action was reported from Canada, and from the Central Union of Transport Workers in Amsterdam and Rotterdam.

Joseph P. Ryan, having failed to put over his proposition in the Northwest, was back in San Francisco and attended a membership meeting on June 4 at which he tried to persuade the men to negotiate separate agreements with the various ports and companies. He met with complete rebuff.

The idea of separate agreements was rejected for the reason that it would chop up the membership into countless small units, all bound by conflicting agreements not to support each other.

Employers were now concentrating on the state and federal governments, urging them to intervene or pass legislation that would force the longshoremen to accept the proposition of May 28 or some similar agreement. On June 5 a meeting was held with Acting Governor Frank Merriam which no union representatives were invited to attend.

Newspapers also were extolling the virtues of the May 28 deal and urging its enforcement. The 99 per cent vote by which the longshoremen had rejected it was disregarded as meaningless. They pointed out how well pleased they, the editors, were with the proposal, how well pleased Dean Francis Grady was, how well pleased the employers were, how well pleased Joseph Ryan and Edward McGrady were, and then argued that this collective pleasure constituted proof positive that the proposal was fair.

About this time Lee Holman, the ousted president of the San Francisco local of the ILA, turned up again and began organizing an independent union. He decried the ILA as a Red organization and proclaimed himself the champion of the "real American longshoremen." He was an adventurer with an abnormal appetite for publicity and, together with the assemblage of hooligans which he tried to pass off as a "union," he made such a nuisance of himself that ultimately he even got in the way of the police and was arrested for carrying concealed weapons.

Everyone who had even the slightest contact with the waterfront knew what manner of man Holman was and that his "phony" union didn't amount to a row of beans. It was a combination of cheap publicity stunt and revenge gesture. Once before Holman had pretended to pan gold in Golden Gate Park in order to get his picture in the paper. He was roundly despised the length of the waterfront, to the extent that he didn't even dare show his face. Nevertheless newspapers pretended to take him seriously, announced a "split" in the ranks of the longshoremen, and made the most of him to create confusion in the public mind.

Meanwhile, back in Washington, McGrady was making poor headway with his plea for intervention. It would be difficult to imagine anything more unpopular than taking an agreement which had been rejected by a 99 per cent vote of the men and forcing it down their throats. The Administration wanted no such unholy anecdote hanging over its head in the next election. President Roosevelt merely referred the matter back to the mediation board, and the mediation board, clutching at a straw, revived the idea of government supervision of hiring halls.

This suggestion had been brought up before without any success. Employers were not very enthusiastic about it and labor was emphatically against it. It hung in the air for a little while and then blew away like smoke. Nobody suggested granting the demands of the men.

The last hope of government intervention having faded, the employers began laying plans to "open the port."

As far back as May 13 thirty prominent industrial heads had met in conference to discuss such a program of action. As a result of that conference J. W. Mailliard, Jr., president of the Chamber of Commerce, and John F. Forbes, president of the San Francisco Industrial Association, dispatched telegrams to prominent business leaders calling them to a meeting which was held on May 21 in Room 237 of the Merchants' Exchange Building. The sixty men who showed up were addressed by Roger Lapham, president of the American Hawaiian Steamship Company. A committee of action consisting of seven members was elected, which immediately conferred with representatives of shipping interests in all ports, and also with Dean Henry Francis Grady and Assistant Secretary of Labor McGrady. (This was probably where McGrady got his information that the employers were planning an offensive.)

Another meeting was called on June 1, attended by between forty and fifty employers from various industries; and still another on June 5, attended by one hundred men. These were the councils of war which planned the events to follow. It was decided that henceforth authority for dealing with the strike would be vested in the Industrial Association, instead of in the shipowners. This meant that the strikers were no longer pitted against the shipowners alone but must reckon with a united front of all moneyed interests.

These meetings were conducted in secrecy and did not become known until a much later date, and then to only a small number of people. While they were going on, another development occurred which evidenced that labor was tightening its ranks.

Although the teamsters, in compliance with their resolution passed early in the strike, were refusing to truck merchandise to and from the docks, the employers, in connivance with the salaried officials of the Teamsters' Union, had devised a scheme to get around the blockade.

Freight was being moved out of the docks by means of the Belt Line Railroad, which was still in operation. The boxcars were shunted onto remote industrial sidings in another part of town and then unloaded onto trucks.

For some time this plan worked successfully. The union officials were fully aware of what was going on but the rank and file knew nothing about it. Eventually, through sympathetic railroad men or other sources, the suspicion of the strikers was aroused. They worked out a method of tracing all freight cars from the moment they left the Embarcadero to the time they reached their destinations. The whole procedure was discovered and exposed by the longshoremen to the rank and file of the Teamsters' Union. At the next membership meeting on June 7 the teamsters raised a storm of protest against their officials and passed a resolution banning the handling of any freight whatsoever that had been touched by scabs on the docks, no matter whether it was unloaded from freight cars or out-of-the-way sidings or in any other manner. Thereafter longshoremen and teamsters cooperated in checking up on every freight car, and the leak was completely plugged up.

This meant that the waterfront was sealed up airtight. Not an ounce of cargo could enter or leave it. Merchandise could be loaded in boxcars and sent out on the Belt Line Railroad but no matter how far away they were sent, the strikers traced them and the teamsters refused to unload them.

An additional tightening of union ranks occurred on June 8 when all the engineers on the tugboats walked out in sympathy strike. Since the aid of tugs is essential in docking vessels, this meant that no ships could be moved from their present docks, and what few vessels were still arriving must drop anchor out in the bay and await the end of the strike before they could be moved up to the piers.

Information was received by the strike committee that various offices of the Citizens' Emergency Relief Committee throughout the city were urging unemployed men to go down on the docks to scab. Immediate protest was made to the Board of Supervisors. An investigation was made and orders were issued by the Relief Committee prohibiting any agency or official from advising clients to take work under strike conditions, or allowing the solicitation of strikebreakers to be carried out on the premises.

Through sympathetic members of the unemployed the strikers were able to keep close check on relief offices, and all efforts of the employers to recruit scabs from these sources were blocked.

Also, at this stage the International Longshoremen's Association, San Francisco Local 38-79, began what has since become famous as its "march inland." They started organizing the warehousemen as an auxiliary of the ILA.

Rumors that the Industrial Association was about to "open the port" by force mingled with rumors of a general strike which would close down the entire city until the strikers' demands were complied with. The ILA had already sent letters to all unions to sound out general strike sentiment.

Dean Grady, chairman of the mediation board, had winged off to Washington in a plane to renew his plea for compulsory arbitration. Meanwhile the employers sounded a new note by announcing willingness to accept government control of hiring halls. The unions rejected the idea and stood firm for democratic control of their own hiring hall.

Joseph P. Ryan was up in the Northwest trying to argue the longshoremen there into accepting a government-controlled hiring hall. He declared that the San Francisco local was "out of hand" and that he intended to try to negotiate separate agreements for the Northwest and then "force the San Francisco employers and strikers to accept them." He was expending a great deal of language but no one was paying any attention to him. A short while later, when he realized the total ineffectiveness of his effort, he again changed the tack of his sails to suit the breeze and proclaimed that nothing could be done in the north and any settlement at all would have to come from San Francisco.

O N JUNE 12 THE ORGANIZED employers of the city began to enact a carefully rehearsed drama for the benefit of the public. J. W. Mailliard, Jr., president of the Chamber of Commerce, addressed an open letter to John F. Forbes, president of the Industrial Association, declaring that the strike was in the hands of radicals, and urging the Industrial Association to take command of the situation. Newspapers featured the letter as a headline development.

In view of the fact that invitations to the conference which planned this maneuver had been sent out over the signatures of Mailliard and Forbes, the gesture was more than a little ambiguous.

The letter read:

As president of the San Francisco Chamber of Commerce the duty is laid upon me of formally bringing to your attention the facts of an intolerable situation which has developed in San Francisco as the result of a strike called on May 9, 1934, on the waterfront by the International Longshoremen's Association. Some weeks ago, in an open, published statement, I called attention to the fact that the strike was out of hand; that control of the longshoremen's local union had been wrested from responsible San Francisco leadership by an irresponsible group of radicals who do not want a settlement.

This irresponsible group is still in control. It has all but paralyzed the port activities of this community and is now engaged in a conspiracy to promote a general strike of San Francisco union workers in the various trades and crafts.

Something must be done immediately to end this condition; to stop the heavy daily losses to our merchants, businessmen and workers already amounting to millions and to give back to the people of this community the use of our waterfront.

To permit representatives of the President of the United States to bring about a fair agreement and resumption of trade and commerce the businessmen of San Francisco have waited patiently for more than a month under a penalty of staggering losses. Such a settlement was worked out by the government mediators and accepted by both employers and union leaders.

The local unit of the Longshoremen's Union repudiated this agreement. The President's personal representative returned to Washington and reported that he had failed.

The strike has cost San Francisco to date millions of dollars. Today not a truck is moving on the waterfront. Approximately $40,000,000 worth of merchandise lies on the docks, in warehouses and in the holds of 96 ships, stalled here by the strike. Freight entering the port for the first month of the strike was less by 600,000 tons, worth another $40,000,000 than in the month preceding the calling of the strike. Meantime, shipping that belongs to San Francisco is being diverted to Los Angeles where the port has been kept open.

There are no trucks moving on the waterfront because those in control of the Longshoremen's Union have intimidated by threats of violence not only bona fide union teamsters and warehouse workers who have no quarrel with their employers, but have made like threats against the families of such workers. Many of these teamsters have been thrown out of jobs entirely. The jobs of many thousands of additional workers will be jeopardized if the strike continues.

The time has now come for the citizens of San Francisco to settle this strike which has been carried beyond an ordinary and legal dispute between employers and workers to a point where it has become a conspiracy against the community. The people of this city cannot be left longer at the mercy of a handful of radicals who are leading the strike, and who are paralyzing our industry, our commerce, our present and future as a great seaport and our very security.

Therefore, as president of the San Francisco Chamber of Commerce, I am requesting you, as president of the Industrial Association of San Francisco, to place this letter before your Board of Directors, and that the Industrial Association of San Francisco immediately assume the responsibility of determining a method of ending this intolerable condition.

The reply from Forbes was not delayed an instant, for it was decided and rehearsed at the same time and by the same men who had drawn up the Mailliard letter. (See Appendix 5 for complete document.) It read, in part:

The Industrial Association accepts the responsibility which you ask it to assume. . . . We have been alive to the situation. . . . We have deferred any action because of the request of the President's personal representative, Assistant Secretary of Labor Edward F. McGrady. . . . We agree with you, however, that the time has now come when San Francisco must protect itself from what you describe as an intolerable situation. . . .The various settlements which have been proposed have not only been accepted by the representatives of the men and then repudiated because of the capricious and arbitrary attitude of the local leaders but were urged for acceptance by the Pacific Coast representatives of the federal government. . . .Only efficient police cooperation has prevented further violence. . . . This is no local industrial dispute. Already its effects have worked back into the great valleys of the state where the year's crops are being prepared for harvest and shipment. The possibility of moving these fruits of the land to market is seriously threatened. Nor is this all. Our difficulty here is beginning to assume national and even international proportions. Rumblings have been heard of refusals to handle our cargoes not only on our eastern seaboard but in foreign ports as well. Ships now departing from Pacific Coast points are threatened with complete tie-ups when they touch foreign shores. . . . Sailors, cooks, stewards, and other maritime workers are on strike in sympathy. You point out that workers who have no quarrel with their employers have been forced into unemployment.

In assuming the responsibility for solving this situation the Industrial Association still hopes that an immediate and amicable settlement can be reached. In any event, however, the Association intends to take whatever lawful steps are necessary to protect the economic interests of this community and to restore to the people of San Francisco that security to which they are entitled.

In these words the Industrial Association, at the request of the Chamber of Commerce, openly assumed the role of government in San Francisco—and San Francisco didn't like the idea any too well.

I shall not dwell upon the many interesting points of these documents, most of which the reader will catch with his own eyes. But it is well to note that the seamen, who were on strike for their own demands, were described as being out "in sympathy." Thenceforth it was the consistent policy of the employers to ignore the seamen and refer to the issue solely as a longshoremen's strike, and this was one of the most important points in later developments.

Simultaneous with the publication of this exchange of letters, Acting Governor Merriam, with whom the employers had conferred privately in preceding weeks, issued a challenging proclamation. Most papers published this statement side by side with Mailliard's letter and under a single heading. It read, in part:

Among us a horde of irresponsible, professional agitators, mostly aliens, are trafficking shamelessly in the agonies of these stressful times. They are seeking revolution, not reform; to make conditions worse, not better.

These public enemies deliberately provoke demonstrations and incite alarms at a time when peace and civil tranquillity are the supreme requisites in our battle for national recovery; a battle calling for all the energies of our people.

Their alien creed of violence and sabotage strikes venomously at the heart of constitutional democracy.

The International Longshoremen's Association immediately replied with a statement in the form of a letter to Mayor Rossi, pointing out that the recent 99 per cent vote of the longshoremen rejecting the proposal of the shipowners and supporting the stand of the strike committee amply refuted the charges of the Chamber of Commerce and the Industrial Association. They concluded:

We, the longshoremen of San Francisco, demand that you settle this strike at once by giving the true facts to the public. We ask that you stop this small group of ship operators from tying up the commerce in the port of San Francisco rather than grant recognition to our union and give us the right to conduct a decent hiring hall for our members.

At this moment Joseph P. Ryan turned up in town again and laid a new proposal before the Mayor. As usual he evolved the idea without once consulting the strikers.

Newspapers, however, ran banner headlines predicting that the strike would be over before night.

Since the proposal included preferential hiring of union men, the shipowners flatly rejected it. They insisted they be allowed to hire union or non-union workers at will.

The first official act of the Industrial Association, in its role as self-appointed government, was to call a conference in its offices attended by all officers, directors, and members, and by Joseph P. Ryan, Michael Casey, president of the San Francisco Teamsters' Union, J. P. McLaughlin, its secretary, and Dave Beck, president of the Teamsters' Union of Seattle.

Ryan's congeniality with the employers has already been shown. The three teamster officials were the very men who had recently cooperated with the shipowners in bootlegging cargo through the picket lines by means of the Belt Line Railroad.

The first question employers asked of Ryan was whether or not, if an agreement could be worked out which was satisfactory to him, he could guarantee that the longshoremen would accept it. Ryan assured them this was the case.

Everybody in the room knew it was not the case but this was beside the point. So far as Ryan was concerned, he was operating in a vacuum and his opinion in the matter was so much empty wind. Already he had drawn up and agreed to numerous agreements, both here and in the Northwest, and the strikers had torn them up and laughed in his face.

The teamster officials were now asked whether or not, if an agreement were drawn up satisfactory to Ryan, they could guarantee that the teamsters would go back to work on the Embarcadero.

They assured very definitely that this was the case.

Even the slightest amount of common sense is sufficient to convince anyone that all this was nonsense. Nevertheless the assemblage accepted these assurances as fact, even though they knew better than anyone else that it was all damned foolishness.

The general plan was to have Ryan sign an agreement, whereupon all newspapers would announce that the strike was over. The teamsters would begin hauling on and off the docks, and the longshoremen would be stampeded back to work. The seamen would be left helpless and would return to their posts meekly.

It is difficult to believe that very many of those in the room really believed such a preposterous and unrealistic plan would work.

Following the conference in the Industrial Association offices, a series of meetings was held in the City Hall with Mayor Rossi. Shortly thereafter it was announced that to simplify matters all negotiations would be narrowed down to the "two principals." Ryan and Thomas G. Plant, president of the Waterfront Employers' Union, retired to the overstuffed comfort of the latter's residence to settle matters in private.

Outside in the streets the propaganda barrage was being laid down thickly. Close on the heels of Acting Governor Merriam's declaration of war against the "Reds," Seattle's Mayor Charles L. Smith announced that he was taking command of the police forces, swearing in additional deputies, and preparing to "open the port" by force. Mayor Carson of Portland issued a similar proclamation, and the Tacoma Citizen's Committee, an organization comparable to the San Francisco Industrial Association, announced that it was "going to open the port of Tacoma if a settlement of the longshoremen's strike is not forthcoming."

[81]

The San Francisco Industrial Association addressed a long public telegram to President Roosevelt which read, in part:

Unless settlement is effected within the next few days of longshoremen's strike now tying up shipping in San Francisco and other Pacific Coast ports efforts will be made to start movement of cargoes to and from docks and it appears inevitable that an industrial conflict of character too serious to contemplate will be the outcome. This telegram is being sent to you in the belief that only through your direct intervention can this impending tragedy be averted.

Telegrams to the same effect were dispatched to Secretary of Labor Perkins, Assistant Secretary of Labor McGrady—now back in Washington—Acting Governor Frank Merriam, and to the two senators and twenty representatives of the State of California in Congress.

All of these communications were given prominent display in the press, together with optimistic reports of the "splendid progress of negotiations."

Newspapers were providing something like an orchestral accompaniment to the drama, churning opinion to the highest pitch of excitement preparatory to the "springing" of the agreement.

An additional threat was hung over the heads of the strikers when Lee Holman announced that he had conferred with Joseph Ryan and had been assured that if the local ILA did not accept the forthcoming agreement, Ryan would withdraw their American Federation of Labor charter and give it to Holman and his new union. Ryan was also quoted as saying that an outfit similar to Holman's was being prepared in Portland.

Later on Ryan denied having made these statements. Nevertheless they were given wide publicity in the press at the time.

In the meantime the strikers were by no means idle. They were taking preliminary steps toward uniting all maritime unions in a Pacific Coast federation that would present a solid front to the shipowners in all negotiations. This goal, however, was not realized until some time after the strike.

Ever since the battle at Pier 18 on May 28 the pickets had been driven from in front of the docks to the sidewalk across the street. The strike committee now sought to obtain an injunction against Chief of Police Quinn to prevent further interference with peaceful picketing. The petition was heard in several courts but no final action was ever taken.

United action by the city's employers immediately strengthened the issue of united action by labor. The International Association of

Machinists took the initiative in sending out a General Strike Call to all other unions. Wives, daughters, and sisters of the strikers, who had been organized into a Women's Auxiliary, were busily handing out leaflets headed: "FORWARD TO A GENERAL STRIKE!"

By the time Ryan and Plant emerged from the latter's home with an agreement all worked out, the city had been whipped to a foam of excitement. The document was first turned over to the Industrial Association for scrutiny by its various officials. (See Appendix 6.) To all intents and purposes, Ryan might just as well have been asleep under the table while Plant drew up the agreement with a free hand. Aside from a difference in phrasing, the only way it differed from the agreement of May 28 was that instead of providing that employers pay the full expenses of the hiring hall, expenses were to be shared half and half by employers and the union. Furthermore, a clause was added prohibiting the ILA from taking any sympathy action in support of other unions. Other variations were minor. To the longshoremen it was a restrictive and undesirable agreement.

After the document had been examined and approved by the Industrial Association, a meeting was called in the office of the Mayor. It was now June 16. Those present were: Ryan; Plant; Mayor Rossi; John F. Forbes, president of the Industrial Association; Colbert Coldwell and Albert E. Boynton, also of the Industrial Association; the members of the President's mediation board; William J. Lewis, president of the Pacific Coast District of the ILA; A. H. Peterson and J. J. Finnegan of the ILA executive committee; Michael Casey; John P. McLaughlin; and Dave Beck of the Teamsters' Union.

The conference lasted four hours, at the end of which time Ryan and Casey were called upon to repeat their assurances that if this document were signed the longshoremen and teamsters would return to work immediately. They both emphatically assured that such was the case. With no more ado the assembled officials solemnly affixed their signatures.

In addition to the signatures of waterfront employers and ILA officials, a special clause was appended reading: "We guarantee the observance of this agreement by the International Longshoremen's Association membership." This "guarantee" was signed by Casey, McLaughlin, Beck, the mediation board, and Mayor Rossi.

Everyone in the room at the time was perfectly aware that the strikers had decided by democratic vote that no agreement could be signed until it had been submitted to the men for approval, and that no agreement would be signed in any case unless the grievances of the seamen were considered also. No one in that room had either the authority or the power to sign or guarantee anything.

No sooner was the last signature affixed than the newspapers loosed a torrent of prearranged propaganda. Paul Eliel, director of the Industrial Relations Department of the Industrial Association, in that organization's official record of the strike, describes the strategy as follows:

In an effort to force a speedy termination of the maritime difficulties the Industrial Association had, for some days preceding, contacted with publishers of the principal newspapers in the San Francisco Bay Area pointing out to them the serious effects of the strike on the entire community and urging that some common action should be undertaken by the metropolitan press. These conferences resulted in an understanding being reached between the publishers of the papers that simultaneous editorials would appear on the morning of June 16 all directed toward the general idea of an early settlement of the strike difficulties. This agreement was carried out and most of the papers published on their front pages the editorial material which they had prepared.

Newspapers assumed the role of speaking for the public and hinted at dire action by an outraged populace if the longshoremen refused to accept the agreement and return to work. The only paper that took a contrary stand was the *Western Worker*, which described the document as a "sell-out" and told the men to pitch it in the wastebasket.

Much of the plan depended upon stampeding the men back to work before any balloting on the issue could be attempted. Extras were already on the streets announcing the strike was ended. June 16 was a Saturday. Joseph Ryan told the press, "Under any circumstances the longshoremen go back to work Monday. There is no question but that they will approve and ratify it. When I talk to them tomorrow and explain it, they will ratify it."

Michael Casey, president of the Teamsters' Union, said, "Our men will return to work Monday morning regardless of what action is taken by the longshoremen at their Sunday meeting. No ratification by our membership is required."

Dave Beck, president of the Seattle teamsters, declared that the strike was over and he was flying home immediately.

On the following afternoon at 2 p.m., Eagles Hall on Golden Gate Avenue was packed to the rafters with 3,000 longshoremen who were shouting their disapproval of the agreement even before the meeting opened. Several speakers had taken the floor and flayed the proposition before Ryan arrived, half an hour late. He was greeted by a storm of boos and profanity that shook the building. When he tried to address them the interruptions were so frequent that it was more like a conversation with the entire union than a speech. On several occasions his remarks were drowned in laughter.

Soon the cries of "Throw him out!" and other, unprintable, suggestions flew so thick and fast that he was forced to sit down. Since his entry into the hall he had been called every insulting name in the vocabularies of several languages, but the favorite epithets were "fink" and "faker."

Under his very nose they turned down the agreement by a unanimous vote.

Harry Bridges asked him why he had not reported the progress of negotiations to the membership, and why he had not conferred with the men at any time. Since he failed to give any sensible answer, the men, by another unanimous vote, severed all salaried officials from negotiations and decided to elect a negotiations committee out of their own ranks. It was agreed that a Joint Strike Committee should be elected consisting of five representatives from each union on strike, and that out of this body a committee should be elected to contact the employers and open negotiations.

Ryan got up again and begged for three minutes to explain himself. He was greeted by such an uproar of derision that the chairman had difficulty quieting the house.

"I was only trying to avoid trouble," he pleaded, "and if I had known such unity existed between the seamen and longshoremen I would never have signed the agreement."

The whole assemblage burst into laughter. "Go back where you came from!" they shouted. "You're a fink. You're a faker. We didn't come to listen to you."

On the same day longshoremen in Portland, San Diego, and Tacoma rejected the agreement by almost unanimous votes. In San Pedro the vote was close, 638 to 584 for rejection. This had been the weakest port on the coast and the one that had encountered the severest difficulties in carrying on effective picketing. It was also noted for its "beef squads," "sluggings," and "dumpings" whereby salaried officials kept the rank and file "in line" by a species of gangsterism.

Observing the reception Ryan got, Michael Casey quickly backed down from his positive assertion that he would "order the teamsters back to work." William J. Lewis, president of the West Coast ILA, voiced the opinion, "I do not believe the teamsters will haul scab cargo, no matter who orders them to."

Ivan F. Cox, secretary of the San Francisco local of the ILA, issued a statement in which he said, "Sufficient confidence has been expressed to us by members of the local Teamsters' Union, unofficially, to assure that even though they should be ordered to return to work, they will still maintain their stand not to move freight to and from the docks."

Ralph Mallen, chairman of the publicity committee of the ILA, stated:

The public should understand that it is not the officials that are on strike, and it is not the officials that would have to go back to work under these so-called agreements. The officials say that this is the best agreement that they could get—and that it was pretty fair. The men themselves, after studying the agreement, found it to be not an agreement between employer and employee, but merely an employer's agreement....

It should be understood that the longshoremen have broken no agreement as no agreement was ever entered into by the longshoremen and employers. International President Ryan had no power to sign any agreement, but merely assumed that power.

On the following day—Monday, June 18—the signatories and witnesses to the agreement again met in the office of the Mayor where Ryan told them that the union had been captured by communists and was completely out of control.

Thomas G. Plant, president of the Waterfront Employers' Union, immediately issued a public statement in the form of an open letter to the Industrial Association (Appendix 7) which read, in part:

This agreement was in no way contingent upon ratification by the union membership.... We have now been informed that the members of the International Longshoremen's Association have refused to abide by the agreement signed by their International President but plan to continue the strike until the demands of other unions have been satisfied and to cause a general strike if possible.

The Waterfront Employers' Union has no power or jurisdiction to discuss or negotiate demands of sailors and other marine workers...the longshoremen's strike must be settled without reference to the demands of sailors.... This immediate repudiation of an agreement made in good faith is convincing evidence that the control of the Longshoremen's Association is dominated by the radical element and Communists whose purpose is not to promote industrial peace, rather their avowed purpose is to provoke class hatred and bloodshed and to undermine the government. Further evidence of this is afforded by the fact that a majority of the committee of five selected at the longshoremen's meeting on Sunday have been active in the affairs of Communist organizations.

It was now apparent that the employers' propaganda mill had gone out of gear somehow, and had no effectiveness in swaying the opinions of men on the waterfront. Nor could all the city, state, and federal officials on the Pacific Coast, chanting like a Greek chorus to the tune of the Industrial Association, avail to persuade the strikers to abandon their demands and return to work.

Evidence that a strong general strike sentiment was developing began to appear on every hand. Many unions, including the machinists, window washers, waiters, bookbinders, garment workers, and the Oakland teamsters had scheduled general strike votes for dates around the 19th and 20th of June.

The strike committee obtained the use of the Civic Auditorium, the largest assembly hall in town, for the evening of June 19, and invited the general public to come and hear the strikers' side of the case.

Failure of the Ryan-Plant agreement, however, was not as much of a surprise to the Industrial Association as they pretended. In their official report Mr. Eliel stated:

For some days prior to this the Industrial Association had been intensively engaged on a program looking toward the movement of freight by trucks from the docks. Preliminaries looking toward this end had consisted of rental of warehouses, purchase of trucks and other necessary equipment and the establishment of a temporary organization with the cooperation of warehousemen and truck operators.

Such preparations would have been unnecessary if the reopening of normal operations was expected following the signing of the Ryan-Plant agreement. This "temporary organization" referred to had nothing to do with normal operations. It was a plan to start trucking on and off the docks with scab drivers in defiance of both longshoremen and teamsters.

On the afternoon of June 18, 150 of the city's largest employers held a council of war in the Merchants' Exchange Building and decided to go ahead with the Industrial Association's plan for "opening the port." A final ultimatum was sent to President Roosevelt in the form of a long telegram (Appendix 8) which read, in part:

We understand there is evidence in hands of Department of Labor that Communists have captured control of the Longshoremen's Unions with no intention of strike settlement. We have reached crisis threatening destruction of property and serious loss of life in various ports on Pacific Coast unless you act to compel performance on the part of Longshoremen's Unions of the agreement signed by their International President.

This was signed by John F. Forbes, president of the Industrial Association.

Mayor Rossi, on the same day, issued an urgent plea for the long-shoremen to return to their jobs.

Mayor Carson of Portland announced to the press:

The port will be opened. The city government stands ready to use every force at hand to resume business. Patience is no longer a virtue and I am damned tired of it. The police have their instructions as to what to do and I prophesy they will do it. Beat-up gangs and other rowdies will find the going tough if they try their tactics when our people resume work.

The phrase "our people" was a common one used by employers throughout the strike. Usually it was expressed, "our loyal employees," or "the loyal employees who did not go out on strike."

The truth is that these men were "scabs" in the full sense of the word, and complete strangers to the waterfront. One of these scabs, Theodore Durein, subsequently published an article about his experiences during the strike (*Reader's Digest*, January 1937). In it he said:

... the strikebreakers were mostly pasty-faced clerks, house-to-house sales-men, college students and a motley array of unemployed who had never shouldered anything heavier than a BVD strap before in their lives.... Some of the scabs were hard nuts, imported strikebreakers from Los Angeles and Chicago.

Employers in Los Angeles issued a statement:

Since the union has repudiated its leaders up and down the coast the employers feel justified in carrying this fight to a finish and have called off all negotiations.

So far as the strikers were concerned, negotiations were just about to begin. They elected their Joint Strike Committee and their negotiations committee and called upon the Mayor. The Mayor told them to present their basic demands in writing, which they did in the following document:

1. All strikebreakers to be discharged.

2. Employers hereby recognize the fact that the Longshoremen of San Francisco are members of the ILA and will recognize the ILA as representing the longshoremen.

3. The employers agree to hire members of the ILA and agree to hire no non-union men until the supply of ILA men is exhausted. Subject to reasonable time for dispatching.

4. The employers agree not to discriminate against any man for his activity in the ILA or for his activities during the strike.

5. The ILA shall establish a hiring hall, operated and paid for by the ILA and the employers agree to place their orders for gangs of longshore-

men at this hall. The ILA agrees to furnish longshoremen whenever required by the employer.

6. If the above is agreed to, the demands regarding hours, and wages may be submitted to arbitration.

7. Gang committees shall be set up in each gang to try men for drunkenness, pilfering or shirking of work.

8. This agreement shall be declared invalid if either party to this agreement does not live up to the terms of this agreement.

Soon afterward the other unions presented similar documents outlining their demands. It was made clear that none of the unions on strike would return to work until all of their grievances had been settled.

The Masters, Mates and Pilots wanted an increase in wages on a classified scale, recognition of the union, provision that deck officers should not work as longshoremen except in emergencies, and adequate expenses for officers while in port.

The Marine Engineers' Beneficial Association wanted an eighthour day, a five-day week, union recognition, and wage increases on a classified scale.

Although the sailors, the stewards, and the unlicensed engine-room workers had separate unions, they were all member organizations of a parent body, the International Seamen's Union, affiliated with the American Federation of Labor.

The Sailor's Union of the Pacific wanted a $65-a-month minimum wage and 65 cents an hour overtime for deep water ships; a $75-a-month minimum wage and 75 cents an hour overtime on coastwise vessels; an eight-hour-day; a forty-four-hour week in port; and recognition of the union.

The Marine Firemen's, Oilers, Watertenders and Wipers Association wanted an increase in the number of men in their crews, and otherwise the same basic demands as the Sailors' Union.

The Marine Cooks and Stewards wanted an increase in wages on a classified scale, an eight-hour day at sea, a forty-four-hour week in port, and forty specified improvements in working conditions.

To this, Thomas G. Plant, speaking for the employers, replied in a letter to Harry Bridges, chairman of the Joint Marine Strike Committee (Appendix 9), stating:

We think it should be apparent to anyone that a small group of vessel operators, whose offices are located in San Francisco, agents of foreign steamship companies whose vessels trade here and of contracting stevedores who have nothing whatever to do with the management of vessels, can't possibly have any authority or jurisdiction with respect to a matter which is so far-reaching in its scope.

The letter again pointed out the Ryan-Plant agreement of June 16, urged the men to accept it, and ignored the request for reopening of negotiations.

The strikers were unconvinced. They concluded that if the employers could so thoroughly coordinate their efforts toward breaking the strike, they could easily cooperate toward settling it. Harry Bridges said, "It's up to the employers. We found a way to get together and agree on what we wanted. There is no reason why all the employers can't do the same thing."

While the strike committee persisted in its efforts to draw the employers into negotiations, the Industrial Association went ahead with its plans for "opening the port." Meanwhile Attorney General Cummings handed down a ruling that shipowners were under no legal compulsion to organize for the purpose of collective bargaining.

CHAPTER X
The Public Talks Back, The
Industrial Association Declares War

THE PUBLIC MASS MEETING
held by the strike committee on June 19 enabled the Industrial Association to gauge the results of its publicity campaign of preceding weeks.

Every available bit of space in the Civic Auditorium was jammed with people long before the meeting opened. The hall seated 10,000, but the crowds filled all possible standing room and swelled the attendance to a much higher figure. It was conservatively estimated that about 40 per cent of those present were strikers and the rest were public spectators. Choruses throughout the giant, rumbling audience could be heard singing, "We'll hang scabby Ryan from a sour apple tree."

Harry Bridges, chairman of the Joint Marine Strike Committee, was greeted by a tumultuous ovation. He began in a calm, methodical manner to review the events to date and to explain the attitude of the men. Midway in his speech Mayor Rossi made a dramatic entrance surrounded by a guard of uniformed police. His appearance roused a deafening roar of booing and hissing. The chairman had difficulty restraining the uncomplimentary noise in order that the meeting could proceed.

When the Mayor got up to speak he touched off another uproar of derision, more overwhelming than before. He left before the meeting was over, and as he stalked out surrounded by blue uniforms he was followed by a third outbreak of booing which echoed in his ears as far as the street.

Members of the Joint Marine Strike Committee took the floor one after another and explained the cause of the men. When mention of a general strike was made, applause shook the great hall in a mighty din.

Three important resolutions were passed. One called upon President Roosevelt to force the shipowners to grant union demands; another called for a sympathetic strike of Atlantic Coast maritime workers; and the third laid all guilt for the tie-up on the shoulders of the employers.

A telegram was dispatched to Ryan, who was now in Portland trying to push through a separate agreement for the Northwest, asking him to call out the East Coast longshoremen in sympathy. He replied that he had no intentions of taking any such action.

The next day San Francisco longshoremen advanced their "march inland" by starting to sign up workers on the Sacramento River lines as an auxiliary of the ILA.

On June 21 another huge breaker rolled in on the Industrial Association's propaganda surf when all newspapers published prearranged editorials on their front pages demanding in the name of the "general public" that the strikers accept the Ryan-Plant agreement of June 16.

To date, employers had consistently refused to meet with the newly elected negotiations committee of the strikers. In a letter to Mayor Rossi, Thomas G. Plant explained:

... I must withdraw from further conferences on such demands, since it would only result in delay and confusion in settlement of the longshoremen's strike.

The strike was always referred to in such communications as a "longshoremen's strike," and the concern of the seamen was consistently ignored.

Secretary of Labor (Madame) Perkins telegraphed from Washington to Thomas G. Plant, urging:

Will you submit the one point still in dispute between the employers and employees in the longshoremen industry namely the control of the hiring halls to arbitration by an arbitrator of the United States Department of Labor? . . . I give you my full assurance that the persons appointed to act for the Department of Labor will be fair, honorable and practical and that the decision will be in the public interest.

Thomas G. Plant replied:

On Saturday the Waterfront Employers' Union . . . entered into an agreement with the International Longshoremen's Association through its International President J. P. Ryan.

As proof of its complete fairness, the observance of the agreement by the longshoremen was guaranteed by Mayor Rossi [here followed the long list of officials who signed the agreement.—Q.]. . . . On Sunday the agreement was repudiated at a mass meeting of longshoremen, dominated by Communists, on the grounds that it did not provide for settlement of demands of various other unions technically on strike. . . . It is apparent that the demands of seafaring unions can only be taken up with individual companies.

We believe that the responsible labor leadership here and the responsible membership in labor unions are entirely convinced of the fairness of the contract entered into and the press of San Francisco today all carry leading editorials requesting the men to return to work under its terms. . . .

We welcome your participation in the solution of these difficulties and in view of the institution of the agreement on Saturday we suggest that you join in the request that the men return to work at once. . . . The most important thing at first is that commerce be started and that the men return to work, and we again repeat our earnest request that you ask the men to do this at once under the terms of the existing agreement. (Complete message in Appendix 10.)

Despite these and other entreaties, Madame Perkins refused to make any such recommendation, a circumstance that greatly annoyed and embarrassed the employers.

In connection with this incident, Michael Casey, employer-minded president of the Teamster's Union, was summoned to the offices of the Industrial Association and asked to communicate with William Green, president of the American Federation of Labor, urging him to contact Madame Perkins and request her to take the action desired.

Casey obligingly telephoned to Green from the offices of the Industrial Association and received assurances that the request would be made. But apparently the word of Green had little effect on Madame Perkins, for she still refused to take such a stand.

It is interesting in this connection to quote from the Industrial Association's official record of the strike, compiled by Paul Eliel:

. . . the Association requested Michael Casey to call at the office and discuss this problem with members of the Association's staff. Mr. Casey, with

[93]

whom the Association has for many years had relations of the friendliest kind, immediately responded to the request. The entire situation was discussed and it was finally suggested to Mr. Casey that the most practical method for securing adequate presentation of the facts and difficulties to the Secretary of Labor would be for him to communicate directly with William Green, president of the American Federation of Labor at Washington, and ask him in turn to lay the facts before the Secretary of Labor. Mr. Casey agreed to these suggestions and the long distance call for Mr. Green was put in over the Industrial Association wire. . . . Mr. Green agreed to get in touch with the Secretary of Labor at the earliest opportunity to lay the facts before her as they had been outlined by Mr. Casey and advise Mr. Casey of the results. On the following day Mr. Casey informed the Association that Mr. Green had contacted with the Secretary of Labor and discussed the situation with her and that Mr. Green felt sure that there would at least be no further misunderstanding in the Secretary's mind as to the basic problems which confronted San Francisco.

The strikers also received a telegram from Madame Perkins, identical in wording to that sent the employers. The Joint Marine Strike Committee replied:

Reports by shipowners that longshoremen insist on original demands absolutely false. Longshoremen have conceded many points including hours and wages but shipowners have not conceded one single point and are prolonging strike by insisting on controlling hiring halls where active unionists and strikers would be blacklisted. Our counter proposal follows.

The rest was a repetition of the basic demands as outlined to Mayor Rossi.

On June 21 a new incident occurred which effectively sealed the last pinhole in the coastwise tie-up, with the exception of the small amount of cargo that was still dribbling through Los Angeles. Earlier in the strike Seattle unions had partially lifted the ban on Alaska ships in order not to inflict undue hardship on that isolated community. But on this date Mayor Smith of Seattle threw a police cordon around the dock, thus forcing union men to work under guard as if they were scabs. The strike committee immediately revoked the permit and issued a statement:

Throughout the conferences which have preceded the consent to allow Alaska shipping to resume, the committee was impressed with the idea in return for our consent that the Mayor and the city would assume a neutral attitude.

Now the police have taken control of Pier 40. They were not called there to prevent rioting or to save lives. There has been no property damage. We have served notice on Mayor Smith that we feel that the spirit of his agreement with us has been violated.

From that time on the ban was replaced on Alaska cargo and all longshoremen working under permit were withdrawn.

By this time the idea of a general strike in San Francisco had entered the minds and conversation of union men to such an extent that conservative officials of the Labor Council were seriously alarmed. The Labor Council, comprising delegates from all the unions in the city, was to labor, in a certain sense, what the Chamber of Commerce and the Industrial Association were to employers. The organized employers of the city had already taken command of the whole strike situation, but so far the Labor Council had not budged.

The reason for this was that the top officials of the council consisted of men like Joseph P. Ryan and Michael Casey who were more congenial to the interests of the employers than to the unions. They vigorously opposed all mention of a general strike and even passed an anti-communist resolution which, in effect, sided with the employers in their oft-repeated charge that the rank-and-file committeemen of the waterfront unions were "irresponsible" and that Joseph P. Ryan was the bona fide representative. The resolution conformed exactly with the statements previously issued by J. W. Mailliard, Jr., Thomas G. Plant, and others. It was passed by a vote of 129 to 22 in the council, which at the time was under the complete dominance of the conservative faction. It read:

Whereas, Communist propagandists have taken advantage of the Water Front strike to issue numerous, scurrilous attacks upon the unions affiliated with the American Federation of Labor, and upon the duly elected officers of said unions, and

Whereas, the anonymous slander of the A. F. of L. unions and the officials thereof has had a tendency to weaken the morale of the strikers and to confuse the minds of trade unionists not familiar with the tactics of communistic character assassins, and

Whereas, at the mass meeting of Water Front strikers held in the Civic Auditorium, Tuesday, June 19, the chairman introduced a spokesman for a notorious Communist organization, thereby creating the altogether erroneous impression that the unions involved have made common cause with the Communists; therefore be it

Resolved, by the San Francisco Labor Council, in regular meeting assembled on Friday, June 22, that we repudiate all Communist organizations, especially the so-called Marine Workers' Industrial Union, and denounce their efforts to inject themselves into an Industrial conflict for the sole purpose of making converts to communism, further be it

Resolved, that San Francisco Labor Council strongly advises the International Longshoremen's Association, its members and representatives, to disavow all connections with the communistic element on the waterfront.

Communist newspapers and leaflets had for many weeks been decrying Joseph P. Ryan, Michael Casey, and their intimates as "fakers" and "sell-out artists," warning the strikers against their dealings. Now, with the rise of general strike sentiment, these same publications were beginning to raise warnings against Edward Vandeleur, president of the Labor Council, John A. O'Connell, secretary of the council, and others in the top officialdom. This was what the resolution referred to when it scored "scurrilous attacks" by the "communistic character assassins."

The "spokesman for a notorious communist organization," who was said to have been introduced at the mass meeting, was Harry Jackson of the Marine Workers' Industrial Union.

It was known beforehand that many delegates came to the council meeting prepared to introduce and fight for a resolution endorsing a general strike movement. This would, more or less, have put the conservatives "on the spot" before the labor unions generally. Although they were already committed against general strike action, they dared not oppose it beyond a certain point or else they would find themselves isolated in the lap of the Industrial Association and pitted against the very forces they were supposed to lead and represent.

Before any mention of a general strike could be brought up, the anti-communist resolution was introduced which, despite the minority of opposition present, precipitated a tumultuous discussion that lasted most of the evening and forced the general strike issue into obscurity.

Delegates from striking unions, including Harry Bridges, vigorously opposed the resolution, and newspapers quickly made use of the fact in their propaganda. The truth was that they opposed it solely on the grounds that it was detrimental to the cause of the strikers. But in view of the ambiguous wording of the proposition, anyone who cared to do so could interpret their opposition as an espousal of communism. Their position was such that if they argued for the resolution, they were playing into the hands of the Industrial Association, and if they argued against it, they would be, apparently, professing communism. They were caught between the red herring and the deep blue sea.

Furthermore, the maritime unions were committed to the principle that all members would have absolute freedom of religious or political belief and that no man would be discriminated against on such grounds. To them it was the old gag all over again: "Have you stopped beating your wife? Answer yes or no."

E. B. O'Grady, president of the Masters, Mates and Pilots, described it as a "kick in the face for the unions just when they need help."

One delegate from the striking unions firmly supported the resolution. He was Paul Scharrenberg, president of the Sailors' Union of the Pacific. A year later Scharrenberg was expelled from the union, not for this act but for numerous anti-union activities, among them a public statement that he had made that a war with Japan would be a fine thing because it would make jobs and tend to raise wages.

By the time the subject of a general strike came up, the assemblage had been drenched with discussion on the anti-Red resolution and was waterlogged with words. They wanted to go home.

John P. McLaughlin, secretary of the Teamsters' Union, however, had enough breath left to say that his union was firmly opposed to a general strike, and he advised all other unions to take a similar stand.

Meanwhile the Industrial Association was rapidly completing its plan to "open the port." On the day after the Labor Council meeting a conference took place between officials of the Industrial Association and the Police Department, following which Chief of Police Quinn issued a statement to the press:

We shall do everything possible to handle the situation. If necessary every available police officer in San Francisco will be detailed to the waterfront to give the necessary protection.

Theodore J. Roche, president of the Police Commission, said:

The police have had no hand in laying these plans. They have merely been notified that the Industrial Association and a group of men working to end the strike, are about to pursue certain plans and have asked for our protection.

Mayor Rossi said:

Plans are now being evolved to open the port of San Francisco at the earliest possible moment. To do this would require the cooperation of the state and municipal police authorities.

How close this cooperation was between employers and the Police Department is reflected in a confidential letter written on June 21 by Thomas G. Plant, president of the Waterfront Employers' Union, to Eugene Mills, president of the Marine Service Bureau, a similar organization of shipowners in San Pedro. The letter was later purloined by a person sympathetic to the strikers and turned over to the International Longshoremen's Association. It read:

Our membership at today's meeting expressed themselves very forcibly on the subject of expense at San Pedro.

A statement which was studied indicated an average expense of approximately $7,000 per day to June 11th, after taking out the cost of preparing the housing ship.

No balance sheet is furnished giving information as to the cost position —how the money is being supplied, who has paid in, who has not, who has made advances, who is in arrears, or like pertinent facts.

The item of guards, cost and boarding, amounting to about $100,000 is one we think should be borne by the city. Here, the police in ample numbers are supplied without cost, and the only guards employed are those needed on the housing ships. Each company has extra guards or watchmen, the cost being borne by the individual line.

We have suggested through our various agents that you put into effect the same system followed here, whereby the individual employers pay the men a daily allowance for board and lodging, which is in turn paid to the Pursers on the Housing Ship. This provides necessary revenue for running expenses on the ships and serves to restrain employers from ordering more men than they actually need.

A method must be adopted without delay to provide an income in the form of tonnage assessments and board and lodging assessments, so that you will all pay as you go, otherwise your costs will be inequitably distributed.

The committee also feels that some plan should be devised for charging the individual lines for crew members furnished though the M. & M. A. recommendation on this point is desired.

An immediate survey should be made by a committee to determine if any safe reductions can be put into effect and a report should be prepared as quickly as possible.

Among other things, this clearly refuted the employers' claim that they were not organized to deal as a body and that separate agreements must be entered into for the various ports and companies.

The close relationship of the police, the city government, and the conservative officials in the Labor Council with the plans of the Industrial Association is revealed by Mr. Paul Eliel, who states in the Association's official record:

While the public was not kept advised through the press or by the Association as to the latter's plans for the movement of freight the Association kept the leaders of the organized labor world in San Francisco thoroughly in touch with its plans and conferred with them almost daily relative to its program. As soon as it had been definitely decided that a movement must be undertaken to restore normal freight movements to and from the waterfront and across the streets of San Francisco the Association called in Messrs. Casey and McLaughlin, representing the Teamster's Union and told them of its decision. Almost daily, thereafter, either in personal conversations in the offices of the Association, or by telephone, these men were advised of the successive steps which the Association had undertaken: when warehouses were leased they were informed to this effect. When trucks were purchased they were advised of this. When non-union men were engaged to drive the trucks and act as warehousemen they were informed of this also. In fact, these officers of the Teamsters' Union were more thoroughly in touch with what the Industrial Association proposed to do than was anyone except the high officials of the city and the officers and staff of the Association itself.

As already indicated, as early as June 7th, it had been stated to Messrs. Casey and McLaughlin that unless the boycott of the waterfront by the teamsters was withdrawn, the community sooner or later would insist on hauling freight in some other fashion. At this time it was suggested by a representative of the Association that it might be possible to work out some sort of plan under which the operations of the Association's trucks, if and when this plan was inaugurated, would not jeopardize the agreement between the Teamsters' Union and the Draymen's Association of San Francisco which had maintained peaceful conditions in San Francisco in the teaming trade for more than a third of a century. These suggestions were renewed when the Association began actively to consider plans for opening the port and positive and definite assurances were given to representatives of the Teamsters' Union that when the Association undertook to move trucks over the streets of San Francisco with non-union men it would be understood that it was an emergency operation only, that it would only be continued for so long a time as the emergency might continue and that the moment normal trucking operations, through customary channels, were resumed, the Association would disband and terminate its trucking operations entirely.

While it is not known that this information was conveyed to others by Messrs. Casey and McLaughlin, it is reasonable to suppose that at least some of the more responsible labor officials in San Francisco in organizations other than the Teamsters were advised of the position taken by the Association. It is almost certain, in any event, that John A. O'Connell, secretary of the San Francisco Labor Council, and a member of the Teamsters' Union, had been advised of these discussions by the other officials of the teamsters' organization.

Governor Merriam issued an official statement to the effect that he was prepared to call out the National Guard, if necessary, to support the employers' intended efforts to open the port. Instructions were sent out to all National Guard commanders to prepare their troops for mobilization.

At this tense moment Assistant Secretary of Labor McGrady arrived back from Washington and again began calling conferences.

On June 26 a committee from the Industrial Association, headed by Leland W. Cutler, called on Mayor Rossi and announced they were now ready to "open the port" immediately.

The Mayor pleaded, "I beg of you, gentlemen, not to do it. Give us another 24 hours and an opportunity to get the men back to work. Give Mr. McGrady an opportunity to work out his plans, under which he first will ask the men to go back to work while the President appoints a board to give them a square deal."

It will seem strange that the Mayor should plead in this manner, especially since the plans of the Industrial Association depended 100 per cent on the cooperation of the Police Department, which was under the authority of the Mayor. But this is one of the phenomena of San Francisco politics which can best be understood by reading the summary of the Atherton report in Chapter II.

In any event, the Association postponed its intended offensive and issued a public statement to that effect.

Late that evening it was announced that President Roosevelt, in response to private communications from Governor Merriam and Mayor Rossi, had appointed a National Longshoremen's Board to take the situation in hand. Appointees of this board were: Archbishop Edward J. Hanna, of the Catholic Diocese in San Francisco; O. K. Cushing, an attorney; and Edward F. McGrady, Assistant Secretary of Labor. This pushed the previous mediation board appointed by the President out of the picture (where it had already drifted of its own accord) and simply duplicated a gesture which had been made a month or so before.

Newspapers breathed a journalistic sigh of relief in headlines, editorials, news stories, and feature articles. The strike, in their opinion, was as good as over. No one, surely, would oppose any decision these presidentially appointed authorities would devise. The fact that the previous presidentially appointed mediation board had been buried in obscurity was not taken into consideration.

McGrady, as a first move, informed the strikers that the employers were dissatisfied with the present membership of the International Longshoremen's Association, and with its leadership. He declared that a thorough examination and combing over of the membership would have to be accomplished by paid investigators and experts, and that steps must be taken to determine whom the strikers wanted to represent them. His exact words were:

From the employers has come the charge that the ranks of the ILA here and in other Pacific ports have been stacked with men who are not really longshoremen and have never worked at this craft. Equally from the ranks of the men has come the charge that "ringers" have been thrust into waterfront employment with instructions to vote for any measures favored by the shipping men.

Therefore the first task of the board will be to determine who are the longshoremen and who they want to act as their spokesman. We will undoubtedly employ paid investigators and experts to determine this point and we will subpoena records of the employers and of the union, one to be checked against the other to determine who the real longshoremen are.

If McGrady had carefully studied what would antagonize the men the most, he couldn't have done any better. No more unsavory or undiplomatic overture to the strikers could be imagined than this. They had just finished repudiating Joseph P. Ryan so emphatically that no one could be in doubt on that point. They had expressed their mistrust of the reactionary, salaried union officials by taking all negotiations out of their hands by a unanimous vote. They had elected representatives out of their own ranks and the employers had refused to meet with them. So far as they were concerned, McGrady's plan was an effort to ignore their democratically elected Joint Marine Strike Committee and place matters once more in the hands of the discredited top officials.

About this time another character appeared on the stage, Andrew Furuseth, the "old man of the sea," eighty-year-old president of the International Seamen's Union, who arrived by plane and proposed that everything be settled by arbitration.

Newspapers were energetically cooperating in the campaign to discredit the Joint Marine Strike Committee, and made wide use of a statement issued by Joseph P. Ryan on June 27 attacking Harry Bridges, chairman of the committee. Ryan said:

The leader of the local strike committee has refused to go along with the majority.

A policy was decided on by the Executive Committee of the International Longshoremen's Association on the Pacific Coast, and, under the rules of the Association should be adopted. But the local strike leader has refused to agree to it. Bridges won't go along with anything, but sticks to his original demands. It is my opinion that the time has come for modification.

Bridges doesn't want this strike settled and it is my firm belief he is acting for the Communists.

The fact that Ryan's first proposal had been turned down by a 99 per cent majority vote of the men, and that when he presented his second proposal he was booed out of the hall and stripped of all powers of negotiation by a unanimous vote of the rank and file, did not abash him.

In reply to Ryan's attack, the Joint Marine Strike Committee, consisting of five elected representatives from each striking union, met and passed two unanimous resolutions. One accorded a vote of confidence to Bridges; the other called a conference for June 30 to which every union in the city was invited to send representatives to discuss plans for a general strike.

Normally any move toward a general strike would be handled through the Labor Council. But the strike committee knew that it could wait forever before the conservative officials of that body would take such action. It knew that if a general strike were to be called it would have to be through the pressure of an extraordinary conference.

On June 29 the strike committee did bring the question of a general strike before the Labor Council, but received only sparse encouragement. The president of the Butchers' Union said that if the Industrial Association followed through with its threat to "open the port" all workers in meat jobbing houses would strike in protest. However, the majority of union representatives were noncommittal. Officials of the teamsters took a firm stand against any such move and advised all other unions to do the same.

Meanwhile the Industrial Association issued another public statement to the effect that, at the request of Archbishop Hanna, they were again postponing their "opening of the port" from June 29 to 1 p.m. on July 2.

Employers persistently refused to negotiate with the Joint Marine Strike Committee and feigned confusion over the issue. They declared to the President's Longshoremen's Board that since all their attempted settlements with Ryan and the salaried officials had failed, they were at a loss to know who represented the men or with whom to deal.

Realizing that a showdown was imminent, the strike committee issued instructions:

All pickets will hold themselves prepared to mobilize in front of docks on short notice. This move is necessary as an attempt may be made to open the docks momentarily.

The President's board issued a request that all strikers return to work by midnight July 5, and that all issues be submitted to unconditional arbitration beginning July 6. The communication was worded:

Because of the acuteness of the situation, the board requests that you reply not later than Thursday, July 5, midnight.

The Industrial Association again postponed its threatened offensive from 3 p.m. on July 2 to noon of July 3, exactly 60 hours in advance of the mediation board's arbitration deadline.

There was no further postponement.

Employers "turned on the heat" at exactly 1:27 p.m., Tuesday, July 3, 1934.

CHAPTER XI
The Offensive Opens, A Day Of Industrial Warfare

ALL DAY MONDAY THE ATMOSPHERE was tense on the Embarcadero. Pickets stirred restlessly the entire length of the front, their eyes alert for any indications of a surprise move.

At 6 p.m. five empty trucks rumbled onto the Embarcadero surrounded by an escort of police radio cars. They disappeared into Pier 38 of the McCormick Steamship Company, and instantly a mobilization of over 1,000 pickets arrived on the spot.

"The men who drove those trucks are not on the pier," said Police Captain DeGuire. "They were taken off on a launch. If you don't believe it, send two men in with me."

Two men were delegated to go in and look around. They reported that the trucks were standing empty in the deserted dock and that no effort was being made to load them. Satisfied that no attempt would be made to start trucking till the next morning, the crowd dispersed.

Newspaper headlines on the morning of July 3, 1934, heralded the "opening of the port."

Chief of Police Quinn issued a warning:

Stay away from the waterfront unless you have business there.

The Police Department will have its hands full on Tuesday preventing violence on the waterfront. We do not want any innocent bystanders hurt.

He announced that 200 additional men were being added to the waterfront force, bringing the total to 700, and that new supplies of tear gas and riot guns were being handed out.

A more fascinating advertisement could not be conceived. The hills overlooking the Embarcadero on Tuesday were black with thousands who turned out to witness the battle. Hundreds of persons put on their old clothes and joined the ranks of the pickets, swelling their numbers to unprecedented strength.

Although huge numbers of pickets had been on hand since daybreak, no effort was made to interfere with them until about 11 a.m. at which time police began moving in on foot, horseback, and in radio patrol cars. All activity was concentrated around Pier 38 where the trucks were located.

Pickets were forced back gradually and a wide area cleared in front of the pier. A long row of empty boxcars was strung across the width of the Embarcadero on the south side of the pier and left standing on the tracks of the state-owned Belt Line Railroad. This effectively blocked off that end of the street. The north end was barricaded by a string of patrol cars, bristling with revolvers, riot guns, and clubs.

At 1:27 the steel rolling doors of Pier 38 lifted and the five dilapidated old trucks rolled out preceded by eight radio patrol cars. Only one truck bore a license plate, and that was of ancient vintage. The trucks were destined for a warehouse only a short distance away, which had been rented especially for the occasion.

A deafening roar went up from the pickets.

Standing on the running board of a patrol car at the head of the caravan, Police Captain Thomas M. Hoertkorn flourished a revolver and shouted, "The port is open!"

With single accord the great mass of pickets surged forward. The Embarcadero became a vast tangle of fighting men. Bricks flew and clubs battered skulls. The police opened fire with revolvers and riot guns. Clouds of tear gas swept the picket lines and sent the men choking in retreat. Mounted police were dragged from their saddles and beaten to the pavement.

Nearby streets were filled with office and factory workers who poured red-eyed and gasping from the buildings into which tear gas had drifted.

The cobblestones of the Embarcadero were littered with fallen men. Bright puddles of blood colored the gray expanse.

Squads of police who looked like Martian monsters in their special helmets and gas masks led the way, flinging gas bombs ahead of them. Regularly uniformed police on foot and horseback followed in their wake.

Chief Quinn arrived in an automobile just in time to receive a brick through the windshield.

The *San Francisco Examiner* described part of the battle:

After the first riots the strikers gathered slowly at Second and Townsend streets. From that distance they shouted epithets at police and truck drivers. Suddenly Captain Hoertkorn drove up, behind his several loads of policemen.

"Let 'em have it, boys!" shouted Hoertkorn.

The Captain pulled his revolver, fired several shots in the air, and advanced with drawn club. The policemen followed him and they waded into the crowd with flailing clubs and fists. The crowd retreated slowly, many with heads bleeding from police clubs.

At short range the police discharged gas shells from their revolvers into the crowd. As they fell back they threw hand grenades of gas and shot other grenades from gas guns. The gang made a halt at Second and Brannan streets. There, several strikers picked up gas grenades before they could explode and hurled them back at police.

Dense crowds lined every rooftop and leaned from every window in the neighborhood. The gas seeped into these buildings, and tearful spectators wiped their eyes.

Nonpartisan winds picked up the clouds of gas and waltzed them all over the Embarcadero, strangling pickets, bystanders, and police alike. Bricks and stray bullets crashed through plate-glass windows of restaurants, followed by vagrant clouds of gas which brought customers and waiters running out with tears streaming down their faces.

A vast gallery of thousands stared aghast from the hillsides. Soon they would scatter to all parts of the city, bringing home tales of warfare and bloodshed that would galvanize the whole community into action.

Overhead two airplanes filled with spectators circled around and swooped low over the battlefield.

The fighting continued for four hours. Finally, overcome by gas, the pickets retreated up side streets and alleys, battling every inch of the way.

Scattered fighting continued throughout the afternoon, during which Captain Hoertkorn again distinguished himself. The *Examiner* described it:

Another truck loaded with empty cartons was attacked by the mob as it was passing Third and Townsend streets. Captain Hoertkorn dispersed this mob single-handed. He fired several shots from his revolver over the heads of the crowd and then laid about him with his club.

A stray bullet crashed through the window of a bank at Third and Townsend streets, wounding a teller over the left eye.

The sirens of ambulances screamed up and down Market Street all day long, carrying a stream of wounded from the scene of conflict.

Newsboys cried their extras: "READ ABOUT THE BLOODY MASSACRE! THEY'RE TURNING THE WATERFRONT INTO A SLAUGHTERHOUSE!"

Captain Hoertkorn was proclaimed "the hero of the day," and his numerous exploits were lauded in the papers.

Two years later he was discovered to be a henchman of the underworld. As a result of the vice-graft investigation he was expelled from the force in disgrace, along with Lieutenant Mignola, Captain DeGuire, and thirteen other officers, many of whom were active in the 1934 battles. In addition to this, five other officers were indicted by the Grand Jury for criminal offenses. Specific evidence was lacking to indict others, but a shadow of implied guilt fell over the entire Police Department.

Five trucks were operated throughout the day, making eighteen trips between the docks and the warehouse while police battled pickets. The trucking had no commercial significance whatsoever. The warehouse was just a dummy and the insignificant amount of cargo moved into it was just as far away from its destination as it had been on the dock. The whole purpose was to scatter the picket lines and score a moral victory over the strikers, which was calculated to dishearten their cause.

The Industrial Association ran a display advertisement in all newspapers:

THE PORT IS OPEN

Notice to the Public:

Beginning yesterday, July 3, the Industrial Association of San Francisco is moving goods to and from the waterfront.

We will continue to do this only until such time as our citizens are at full liberty to move their own goods without interference. The moment that normal trucking operations are resumed through regular channels we will discontinue this emergency service.

We rely upon the full protection of the authorities in this peaceful undertaking. The men employed to move our goods are unarmed. They ride the trucks alone. They are instructed to provoke no disturbance.

Merchants desiring to avail themselves of this service should advise us promptly.

Our action is taken without prejudice to present negotiations for a settlement of the longshoremen's strike and other associated difficulties, still under consideration by the National Longshoremen's Board appointed by the President of the United States.

In our desire that these negotiations succeed, and that the strikes be settled, we have cooperated with all concerned to the best of our ability and we shall continue to do so.

Five times we were asked to delay in moving goods to and from the waterfront, and five times, in deference to the authorities, we withheld action.

These strike negotiations must no longer be confused with the right of our citizens to move goods to and from the waterfront. The right has been in abeyance for 56 days at an estimated loss of nearly one million dollars a day, accompanied by rioting, assaults, arson and violence of all sorts.

This situation is no longer tolerable. The San Francisco waterfront is public property exactly as Market Street is public property, and all citizens are entitled to use it without interference in the lawful conduct of business, whether or not a strike is in progress.

The port of San Francisco is now open to the business of San Francisco.

The word "arson" was inserted gratuitously. There had been no arson.

In the course of the afternoon five different trucks were tipped over in the streets by pickets. The Industrial Association disclaimed any connection with them, stating that the strikers had mistaken them for scab carriers.

Newspapers reported twenty-five men sent to the hospital, including nine policemen. Strikers had taken the most of their casualties to private homes to avoid arrest. The number of less serious injuries was beyond estimation.

The next day was the Fourth of July. In honor of the day the Industrial Association announced trucking operations would cease, but would resume promptly again at midnight. At the close of July 3 they sent a message of appreciation to Mayor Rossi:

We wish to take this means of thanking you personally at this time for all you have done in connection with our trouble on the waterfront and for the remarkable cooperation you have given us through the Police Department and other public agencies.

A similar message was sent to Chief Quinn:

It is impossible for me to express in words the admiration and gratitude which you and your force have earned as a result of the trucking operations which were inaugurated this afternoon.

Both messages went out over the signature of John F. Forbes, president of the Industrial Association.

Action of the state-owned Belt Line Railroad in providing boxcars to block off the Embarcadero caused an unexpected development. The strike committee served notice that henceforth no more freight cars would be allowed to move in or out of the piers.

Train crews of the Belt Line deserted their posts and refused to continue work. P. W. Meherin, president of the State Board of Harbor Commissioners, flourished their "yellow dog" contract in their faces and said, "Do you realize that if you walk off, you will be striking against the state and may lose your jobs?"

They walked off anyhow. The Industrial Association said they were afraid of violence. The strikers said it was a sympathy walkout.

Efforts to obtain new crews from other railroad lines failed when officials of these companies declared their unwillingness to face possible trouble with the railroad brotherhoods. Finally, on midnight of July Fourth, an attempt was made to operate the line with crews of untrained scabs. They succeeded in shunting some fourteen freight cars onto the Matson dock where they were unloaded. But on the return trip the pickets, who were more familiar with the workings of the line than the scabs, threw a switch and derailed several cars.

Governor Merriam issued a proclamation from Sacramento declaring any further attempts to interfere with the Belt Line Railroad would result in his calling out the National Guard, and he notified Adjutant General Howard to prepare his troops for mobilization.

"Strikers having refused to arbitrate must take the consequences," said the Governor.

Upon receiving the Governor's message Adjutant General Howard told the press that when the guardsmen moved in they would not monkey with tear gas, but would use vomiting gas, the worst nonfatal gas in existence. This type, the general explained, causes violent nausea and a splitting headache and incapacitates the victim for at least two days.

In the midst of this situation, William Green, president of the American Federation of Labor, issued a statement from Washington supporting the stand against communists taken by the San Francisco Labor Council and endorsing the anti-Red resolution which had been passed. Newspapers played it up as further evidence of the "irresponsibility" of the Joint Marine Strike Committee.

The Fourth passed as a nervous truce amidst the crackling of thousands of firecrackers. It was a day of intense conversation in which events of the preceding day passed from mouth to ear all over the city. The strike even projected itself into Independence Day exercises in the Civic Auditorium, where Mayor Rossi stated in his speech:

The insidious poison which is seeping into the veins of our civil and religious life and imperiling the most sacred ideal of the home is Communism. . . .

It relegates man to the hopeless status of a machine, repudiating the soul, denying and blaspheming the source of all good. It would utterly destroy every reliance we have on the most noble aims of mankind.

It is observed the Communists are making rapid headway because they are united. They know what they want; they have will and direction.

This has been abundantly demonstrated by activities of some of their members in the strike which has paralyzed the business of San Francisco's port for fifty-six days, ending only Tuesday.

But nothing was ended, no one believed it was.

The city was restless and tense. Despite the constant bursting of firecrackers there was no holiday spirit. It was a lull before the storm. And San Francisco felt itself in the grip of a desperate situation. Not since the earthquake of 1906 had there been such a state of alarm and expectancy.

The city was angry.

The city was thinking.

And a great decision was shaping.

Thousands of people lay awake far into the night, rolling over events in their minds, weighing the worth of words, and speculating on the morrow.

It was the eve of "Bloody Thursday."

CHAPTER XII
"Bloody Thursday!"

O N THURSDAY MORNING FIGHTING
on the Embarcadero began as punctually as if the combatants had
punched a time clock, stuck their cards in a rack, and turned to. There
were no preliminaries this time. They just took up where they left off.

Newspapers announced that the "opening of the port" would be
resumed promptly at 8 a.m. Spectators had come early to "get a seat."
Teeming thousands covered the hillsides. Enterprising vendors moved
about hawking chocolate bars, chewing gum, and cigarets. Since last
Tuesday picket lines had swollen to unheard of proportions. Many
high school and college boys, unknown to their parents, had put on
old clothes and gone down to fight with the union men. Hundreds of
workingmen started for work, then changed their minds and went
down to the picket lines.

Approximately 800 police were on duty hefting brand new riot
sticks, extra long and extra heavy. Others carried sawed-off shotguns
and riot guns. The "Martian monsters" were on hand in their gas
masks, heavy bags of hand grenades slung about their necks.

At 7 a.m. a string of empty boxcars was sent rattling down the

Embarcadero behind a locomotive. Strikers shouted at the scab train crew but made no effort to interfere with it.

Shortly before the 8 a.m. deadline a locomotive shunted two refrigerator cars into the Matson docks. A cry went up from 2,000 pickets assembled nearby.

Still no action.

At 8 a.m. promptly the police went into action. Tear gas bombs were hurled into the picket lines and the police charged with their clubs. Gasping and choking, the strikers were driven back to the alleys off the Embarcadero, or retreated up Rincon Hill.

A couple of blocks away from the point of the first attack, two boxcars standing on a siding burst into flames.

Shots rang out as the police opened fire with revolvers. Flying bricks and bullets crashed windows. Tear gas again sent workers in nearby factory and office buildings swarming to the streets. The whole area was swept by a surf of fighting men.

Workers on the San Francisco-Oakland Bay Bridge (then under construction) were forced to abandon the job for the day because of stray bullets whistling around their heads.

One newspaper report read:

Vomiting gas was used in many cases, instead of the comparatively innocuous tear gas, and scores of dreadfully nauseated strikers and civilians were incapacitated. There was no sham about the battles yesterday. Police ran into action with drawn revolvers. Scores of rounds of ammunition were fired, and riot guns were barking throughout the day.

Spectators were amazed by the suddenness with which the conflict began and the high intensity it reached almost instantly. It was like a torch flung into dry straw and flaming to a maximum blaze within a few minutes.

A reporter for the *Chronicle* said:

Don't think of this as a riot. It was a hundred riots, big and little, first here, now there. Don't think of it as one battle, but as a dozen battles.

And again:

At Bryant and Main streets were a couple of hundred strikers in an ugly mood. Police Captain Arthur DeGuire decided to clear them out, and his men went at them with tear gas.

A large number of pickets reassembled on Rincon Hill, down which they charged in a determined mass. Police met them with a fusillade of revolver shots and a barrage of gas shells. It was described:

These boys, a lot of them kids in their teens, came down the hill with a whoop. It sounded bloodcurdling. One policeman stood behind a telephone pole to shelter him from the rocks and started firing with his revolver.

What followed was a hand-to-hand battle that ultimately left the street littered with fallen bodies. A hail of bricks and stones showered the police and laid many of them in the street. Smaller encounters were taking place at a score of points along the front. The streets were filled with running men as pickets, repulsed at one place, quickly moved to another and renewed their efforts to maintain a stand on the Embarcadero.

Seizing upon every object they could find in nearby lots, the pickets threw up a hasty barricade at the foot of Rincon Hill. It did not hold long.

Royce Brier, *Chronicle* reporter, described:

Then DeGuire's men, about twenty of them, unlimbered from Main and Harrison and fired at random up the hill. The down-plunging mob halted, hesitated, and started scrambling up the hill again.

Here the first man fell, a curious bystander. The gunfire fell away.

Up came the tear gas boys, six or eight carloads of them. They hopped out with their masks on, and the gas guns laid down a barrage on the hillside. The hillside spouted blue gas like the valley of the Ten Thousand Smokes.

Up the hill went the moppers-up, phalanxes of policemen with drawn revolvers. The strikers backed sullenly away on Harrison Street, past Fremont Street. Suddenly came half a dozen carloads of men from the Bureau of Inspectors, and right behind them a truckload of shotguns and ammunition.

Firing their revolvers and swinging their long riot sticks, the police charged up the hill, driving the men before them up the steep, grassy slope. The tinkling of glass sounded as bullets crashed through the windows of residences at the top, sending inhabitants screaming to the streets.

Tear gas shells ignited the dry grass of the hillside, producing a roaring inferno. The Fire Department arrived to the scream of sirens and turned high-pressure streams of water on grass and pickets alike, knocking men off their feet and sending them spinning.

Gas and gunfire at last drove the pickets back into the city. Police took command of the hill and surrounded it with guards to prevent recapture.

All morning long the battle raged furiously over a far-flung front. At 12 noon both sides knocked off for lunch. It was the most orderly and systematic chaos imaginable. The grim seriousness of the encounter and the awful casualties which resulted cannot be minimized.

Nevertheless, armies of movie extras on a Hollywood lot could not have observed hours with greater time-clock precision.

Already the possibility of maintaining a picket line on the Embarcadero in the face of gunfire and gas appeared as hopeless. Pickets from all positions drifted back to ILA headquarters on Steuart Street and congregated outside. Most of the morning's fighting had taken place in the south end of the Embarcadero, a more or less out-of-the-way industrial district. ILA headquarters, however, was situated right in the heart of town, a block off Market Street and a stone's throw from the Ferry Building. Strikers felt more or less that they had retired to a "neutral zone" when they assembled here. They were taken completely off their guard when, shortly after 1 o'clock, the police swooped down in full force, staging the most crushing surprise attack of the entire strike.

Tear gas cartridges came hurtling without warning, followed by a loud crackling of pistol fire. Dozens of pickets fell to the pavement where they lay silent, streams of blood pouring from under their coats. Two of them were dead.

Bullets smashed through windows of streetcars. Bystanders fled weeping from clouds of gas amidst sounds of breaking glass and cries of pain.

A newspaper account read:

The hottest battle took place in front of the ILA on Steuart Street, where scores were gassed, clubbed and shot. Police cars literally filled the headquarters with gas from long range guns, and persons entrenched there poured from the doors.

As gas shells crashed into the ILA's windows and strikers were getting out as quickly as possible, the telephone rang. One of the embattled stevedores, holding a handkerchief to his nose, tears flooding his cheeks from inflamed eyes, lifted the receiver.

"Are you willing to arbitrate now?" asked the voice on the other end.

"No!" screamed the stevedore as he slammed down the receiver and fled the hall while gas enveloped the room in a thick cloud.

Police charged into the Seaboard Hotel, where many strikers were quartered, and drove all occupants into the streets, swinging their long riot sticks and cracking skulls right and left. The building was filled with gas and riddled with pistol fire.

Stubbornly holding their ground and fighting every inch of the way, the men were driven back into the city and off the Embarcadero. The battle swept over into the busy downtown district, endangering crowds of pedestrians. One picket entrenched himself in a parking lot, devised a crude slingshot from an old inner tube, and began bombarding Chief Quinn's car with bricks. It took a barrage of tear gas and pistol fire to dislodge him.

A badly wounded man lying on the pavement cursed the police and refused to allow them to remove him. Later he was taken to the hospital in a private car.

Scores of men littered the sidewalk, either lying silently or crawling away painfully on their hands and knees.

A woman alighting from a streetcar at the Ferry Building screamed and collapsed when a bullet struck her in the temple. A man rushed to her assistance, was struck by another bullet, and crumbled to the street beside her.

A *Chronicle* reporter described:

Women who had been shopping in downtown stores arrived at the loop to step into an inferno. With screaming children clinging to them, they disembarked from the cars to find themselves in clouds of smarting tear gas. Guns cracked. Men fell screaming as they went down. Police clubs cracked against skulls.

Smothered and blinded by gas, the women and children staggered about helplessly. Policemen grabbed them as fast as possible and sent them to the hospital where they were horrified by the sight of men dripping with blood, moaning from bullet wounds and injuries.

One lady stepped off a streetcar, took one look at the turmoil, and fainted dead away. She was loaded into an ambulance filled with bleeding pickets and speeded to the hospital. A small dog she carried did not faint, but kept up a constant yipping.

Joe Rosenthal, a cameraman from the *San Francisco News*, slugged and pierced through the ear by a stray bullet, was also hustled off to the tune of screaming sirens.*

People in surrounding buildings were driven out by gas and many were winged by stray shots as they fled.

At the height of the battle a delegation from the strike committee, headed by Harry Bridges, called on Mayor Rossi to protest. The Mayor simply repeated what the Governor had said: "You refused to arbitrate; now take the consequences."

During the entire day an enlarged fleet of ten ramshackle trucks continued hauling freight between the docks and the dummy warehouse.

*This is the same Joe Rosenthal who gained international fame as the photographer who took the classic picture of the flag-raising on bloody Iwo Jima during World War II.

Hospitals were put on a wartime basis to accommodate the wounded. At the morgue, covered over by white sheets, were two cold, quiet bodies. The Harbor Emergency Hospital had a busy day treating hysterical women and children who had suffered the strangling effects of tear and nauseating gas.

The striking unions had men detailed to the hospitals to see that wounded pickets received adequate attention when brought in from the battlefield. These men reported later that injured strikers were threatened and intimidated by police when they stated that their club and gunshot wounds were caused by officers.

A. L. Christopher, one of the observers for the International Seamen's Union at the Harbor Emergency Hospital, stated:

An injured seaman, Joseph Silver of 80 Corn Street, was brought in by Police Officer 1178 to be treated for wounds. While the doctor was dressing his wounds he asked the patient how he came to be hurt. Silver replied that Officer 1178 had struck him. Whereupon the said officer called him a "damned liar" and assaulted the patient while still under the doctor's care. He was forcibly withheld by hospital attendants.

It was later learned that Officer 1178's name was John Honorahan.

At the close of the day Governor Merriam ordered the National Guard onto the waterfront. Two thousand troops marched into the area equipped with rapid-fire guns, machine guns, gas equipment, and bayoneted rifles.

By the time they arrived the fighting had ceased and the pickets had been driven from the Embarcadero. The guardsmen posted themselves at intervals down the whole length of the waterfront and mounted machine guns on the roofs of the piers.

When informed that the National Guard was moving in, Police Chief Quinn remarked, "I do not understand why the National Guard is necessary. The police have the situation well in hand."

Harry Bridges said, "We cannot stand up against police, machine guns, and National Guard bayonets."

Colonel R. E. Mittelstaedt, who commanded the National Guard, said, "In view of the fact that we are equipped with rifles, bayonets, automatic rifles, and machine guns, which are all high-powered weapons, the Embarcadero will not be a safe place for persons whose reasons for being there are not sufficient to run the risk of serious injury."

Troops marched in wearing steel helmets and full service equipment. They set up camp inside the long, covered docks, established field kitchens, and remained there under wartime regulations. Divisions were brought in from Santa Rosa, Napa, Petaluma, Gilroy, and other outlying towns. Rumors were abundant to the effect that certain units had refused service, but strict censorship was maintained and definite confirmations were lacking.

All day long, newspapers uptown had been pouring out extra after extra, delivering veritable hourly reports from the line of battle. Wailing sirens of ambulances careening up and down Market Street aroused speculation and alarm among the public.

Early reports announced 3 dead. Later accounts said 2 dead and 109 injured. Only those casualties which reached the hospital were reported. A far larger number escaped or were carried away by their comrades, since to be taken to the hospital meant automatically to be placed under arrest. Those officially announced as dead were Howard Sperry, member of the ILA, and Nicholas Bordoise, member of the Cooks' Union and the Communist Party. Casualty lists were reminiscent of war days.

In the midst of accounts of unparalleled butchery, Chief Quinn was lauded for a deed of human kindness. A child coming over to San Francisco on a ferryboat poked its finger in an electric light socket and burned its hand. Chief Quinn considerately absented himself from the scene of battle personally to drive the child to a hospital in his own car.

Headlines in largest type read:

"3 KILLED, 106 HURT AS TROOPS MOVE IN!"
"*S. F. Waterfront Rocked By Death, Bloodshed, Riots.*"
"Merriam Calls Out Guard By Proclamation."
"Roaring Guns and Call to Arms!"
"blood floods gutters as police battle strikers!"

The word "blood—blood—blood" recurred every three or four lines in every news story. So much blood had been seen that it obsessed the minds of newswriters, and the word repeated itself again and again, almost involuntarily, as they typed their copy. Reporters had been in the thick of the fighting all day long. Many had bruised limbs and minor injuries to help them remember. These hurts soon healed and passed away. But an experience—a reality—was impressed in their minds that would never wear away, and that would affect their ideas, their decisions, and their loyalties for the rest of their lives.

Typical newspaper lines read:

Blood ran red in the streets of San Francisco yesterday.
San Francisco's broad Embarcadero ran red with blood yesterday.

[116]

Most of us who made that hospital our headquarters yesterday came to hate the sight of red.

There was so much of it.

The color stained clothing, sheets, human flesh.

Drip-drip-drip went the blood on the white tiled floor. Steadily. Drip-drip-drip. Human blood, bright as red begonias in the sun.

Bloody hand-to-hand encounters between mobs of strikers and police.

Badly wounded strikers lie on a San Francisco sidewalk and a thin trickle of crimson crawls toward the curb after desperate fight on the waterfront.

A friend stems the blood of a badly cut hand while he shouts for aid for his wounded companion.

While bloody rioting was shaking the waterfront and creeping toward the lower Market Street business district ...

The strikers named the day "Bloody Thursday," and now every year on this day the workers on ship and dock stop work in honor of their comrades who were slain on July 5, 1934. It is the most impressive and the most reverently observed holiday of the year in San Francisco, even though it is not recognized by the employers or the civic government.

Two years later Gregory Harrison, Esq., on behalf of the Coast Committee for Shipowners, in a booklet issued by the Waterfront Employers' Association, complained bitterly when he said:

On every July 5th there is a complete cessation of work up and down the whole Pacific Coast because of a holiday declared by the unions for the purpose of commemorating a day of violence and bloodshed.

No one authorizes the holiday excepting a 100 per cent accord of the entire maritime profession. Therefore, it is regarded as a completely unauthorized stoppage of work and an illegal act. The maritime unions have nothing by which to defend this annual disregard for "authority" other than an old and almost forgotten phrase in the yellowed documents of the Revolution of 1776, which reads, "... by the consent of the governed. ... "

That night San Francisco vibrated to intense conversation. Every home or gathering place in town hummed with talk. Questions were asked, opinions took shape, and decisions crystallized. A state of alarm prevailed. Doorbells and telephones rang. Neighbors came in from next door. The people upstairs came down. The people downstairs came up. Men had been shot down in cold blood. Authority had taken the shape of force and violence. Bedtime came and went, but still the city talked. Eyewitnesses were besieged by eager listeners.

Young boys from the picket lines described killings and assaults with a ring in their voices. The city was boiling like a vat in ferment.

A General Strike was being forged in the firesides of San Francisco.

In the barroom of the luxurious Union League Club prosperous businessmen were talking in a different vein. Two of them were standing at the illegal, but winked at, gambling machines against one wall, dropping in fifty-cent pieces as fast as the machines would take them, pulling the levers, watching the cherries, bells, and oranges jump around on the celluloid drums behind the little glass windows. Occasionally there would be a metallic gurgitation and one of them would stoop happily to scoop his winnings from the metal hopper.

"If I had my way," said one, "I'd end this strike in thirty minutes. I'd turn machine guns on those bastards and mow them down like wheat."

"What ought to be done," said the other, "is to take that communist bastard Harry Bridges out and string him up to the nearest lamppost."

I was standing just behind them at the bar. The air seemed stuffy —worse than tear gas. I imagined a faint taste of human blood in my drink, and left it unfinished.

Out in the street the air was clearer.

Down on the Embarcadero it was quiet and dark. The lights of an occasional passing car gleamed on bayonets. Frightened boys stood there in the dark holding tightly to army rifles.

They thought they were putting down a Red revolution.

They thought they were defending their country.

Mostly kids in their teens, they were best described by someone who said, "Beardless children tottering under too heavy machine guns...."

The strikers regarded them with mingled disgust and pity, and referred to them as "those goddam sap kids."

I asked the conductor on the streetcar if there was going to be a general strike. He said, "You can bet your damned life there will."

The waiter in the lunch counter said he was ready to go out right away. The proprietor of the place broke in, "Any of my help don't walk out, I'll kick their behinds out the door. That's where I stand."

I bought a newspaper at the corner. It said definitely and positively there would be no general strike. The "responsible" leaders of labor confirmed this.

Joseph P. Ryan had wired from New York:

One thing that prevents settlement is that the Communist Party led by Harry Bridges is in control of the San Francisco situation.

CHAPTER XIII
*Labor Buries Its Dead, The
March of 40,000*

THE MORNING AFTER "Bloody Thursday," strikers chalked a memorial on the sidewalk where their two slain comrades fell, and decorated it with a few bunches of gladioli and two wreaths. The inscription read:

"2 ILA MEN KILLED—SHOT IN THE BACK."

On each side of the inscription, chalked in large letters, were the words "POLICE MURDER."

Soon afterward the police scattered a crowd that gathered to view the spot. They kicked the flowers into the gutter and rubbed out the memorial. They were unable to remove the large and ghastly blood-stain that covered the pavement nearby.

Strikers immediately returned and rewrote the inscription. They picked up the soiled gladioli from the gutter, brushed them off with their sleeves, and relaid them on the spot respectfully.

Mayor Rossi gave them twenty-four hours to remove the writing and flowers from the sidewalk.

When the deadline had passed, the men applied to the Mayor for permission to inscribe a permanent memorial on the spot. The Mayor curtly refused and ordered them to remove it at once.

Thereafter a few men wearing ILA buttons guarded the spot and urged passersby, "Please move on. If we get a crowd here the cops will tear it up again."

An armed peace reigned on the waterfront. Unable to continue picketing, the striking unions threw all their energy toward their last hope, a general strike.

The President's National Longshoremen's Board announced that in compliance with its request that all issues be submitted to arbitration, replies had been received from employers and the strikers. Both sides were willing to arbitrate, provided certain conditions were laid down. But the board found these conditions of such a nature that the situation was not altered in the least.

The longshoremen insisted that the matter of a closed shop and control of the hiring hall be understood before any arbitration began. They also reiterated their position that the grievances of the seamen be considered before any union on strike would return to work.

The employers insisted on the open shop—freedom to hire union or non-union workers at will, and strongly objected to recognition of Harry Bridges as chairman of the strike committee.

The board announced that commencing Monday, July 9, a series of open hearings would be held in a room of the United States District Court to investigate the issues.

That evening a tense meeting was held in the San Francisco Labor Council with representatives present from nearly all the unions in the city. The Joint Marine Strike Committee introduced a strong resolution for a general strike.

Earlier in the day the Steetcarmen's Union, Division 1004, consisting of workers on the Market Street Railway Line, held a meeting and voted to go along with any decision the Labor Council should make.

Under strong pressure from the rank and file, Michael Casey, president of the Teamsters' Union, and a close collaborator with the Industrial Association, had been forced to call a huge membership meeting scheduled for Sunday, July 8, in Dreamland Auditorium to consider general strike action.

The old-time conservative, salaried officials who dominated the Labor Council found themselves in a hot spot at the Friday night meeting. They were determined to block a general strike at all costs. And yet the demand from the membership of the unions for sympathetic action was so overwhelming that they did not dare oppose it too frankly. Such opposition would have resulted in the rank and file's taking the matter out of their hands. Already there was plenty of evidence that the marine strikers were not depending upon the Labor Council officialdom, but were carrying their appeal directly to union memberships throughout the city. The town was literally wading in general strike leaflets circulated by the strikers and sympathetic organizations.

The officials were shrewd enough to realize that if they could not block a general strike, they had better arrange to see that the reins stayed in their hands, so that they could lead it down a blind alley.

In place of the general strike resolution brought in by the marine unions, they substituted another which provided for the appointment of a committee of seven Labor Council officials to be known as the "Strike Strategy Committee," whose duty it would be to work out a common program for all San Francisco labor. The resolution was covertly worded so that it could be interpreted two ways: perhaps it meant a committee to organize a general strike; or perhaps it was only a committee for investigation purposes.

Union men generally took it to mean a general strike would be launched.

In one place the resolution read:

Whereas, the San Francisco Labor Council as the official spokesman for the organized labor movement in San Francisco is deeply and vitally concerned about the vicious and unwarranted attacks now being unleashed upon a substantial portion of its membership by the shipowners and their notorious strikebreaking agency, the "Industrial Association of San Francisco," therefore be it

Resolved, that a committee of seven, etc.

The Industrial Association was sensitive about this paragraph and, when reproducing the document in their official record, deleted the last eight words which named their organization, simply breaking it off after the words "strikebreaking agency."

The Strike Strategy Committee was not "elected," but rather it was appointed by Edward Vandeleur, president of the Labor Council, who named himself chairman. Other appointees were: John A. O'Connell, secretary of the council; Daniel P. Haggerty, past president of the California State Federation of Labor; M. S. Maxwell, president of the California State Federation of Butchers; George Kidwell, secretary-treasurer of the Bakery Wagon Drivers' Union; Frank Brown, business representative of the Molders' Union; and Charles Derry, editor of *Labor Clarion*, official council publication.

Vandeleur afterward explained that the reason why he did not appoint any members of the maritime unions to the committee was because he wanted "a fresh point of view" represented. All appointees were members of the "conservative" wing of labor, which the Industrial Association had always found so congenial to its point of view.

Aside from meetings, proclamations, and intense agitation, Friday passed with few events. The strike was now off the streets and into committees. The National Guard had a quiet day of pacing up and down in the sun.

Next morning when Vandeleur came out of a conference between the Strategy Committee and the marine unions, he said, "We are not considering a general strike at all. What we are trying to do is go in and adjust this thing, to try to get employers to see questions in a different light than they have in the past.

"There is no danger of a general strike at this time, nor is a general strike contemplated."

Other members of the Strategy Committee were equally positive in their assertions that a general strike was completely out of the question.

On the same day fourteen unions voted by overwhelming majorities to support a general strike.

News from Portland and Seattle told of similar "port opening" activities of employers, and corresponding general strike movements in the ranks of labor.

On the afternoon of the 7th, in response to a call from the Joint Marine Strike Committee, delegates from nearly every union in the city assembled in Eagles Hall and voiced unanimous approval of an immediate general strike. The temper of the meeting was indicated when one delegate took the floor and declared, "Any union leader who opposes a general strike at this time is a faker and should be driven out of the ranks of organized labor." The statement drew a tempest of applause that shook the building.

It was originally intended that a definite call for a general strike would be sent out from this meeting. But confusion over the role of the Strategy Committee caused the assemblage to delay action until that body had a chance to "investigate and report."

All day long, scab-driven trucks rumbled on and off the Embarcadero. Scab train crews shunted freight cars in and out of the congested docks. Guardsmen with bayoneted rifles protected all streets leading to the waterfront. Police forces, relieved by troops, moved farther up-town, threw cordons around warehouses, and escorted caravans of "hot cargo" between destinations.

The port was "open." It was open like a festered wound. Commerce was moving again in lame and stumbling fashion. It was moving inefficiently and expensively, like a thin trickle of muddy water down the dry bed of a once mighty river. It was an affectation of "business as usual" designed to weaken the morale of the strikers. How long the employers could have kept up this performance of high cost and low accomplishment is doubtful. And no one was going to wait to find out.

Michael Casey gave emphatic assurance that the teamsters would be content to leave all matters in the hands of the Strategy Committee. But on Sunday night, July 8, the teamsters packed Dreamland Auditorium in one of the most tempestuous meetings since the beginning of the maritime walkout, and voted almost unanimously to go out in general strike on Thursday morning, July 12, regardless of what the Strategy Committee might decide. The vote was taken by secret ballot and carried by a majority of 1,220 to 271.

In vain Casey strove to block action by pointing out that sympathy strikes were in violation of the rules of the international union, as well as contrary to all agreements between the local Teamsters' Union and employers. He confronted them with the possibility of loss of strike benefit funds from the international's treasury, loss of their A. F. of L. charter, loss of agreements, ruination of the union. All his cautions were drowned in a storm of boos.

It was decided that the teamsters would meet again on Wednesday night, July 11, to reaffirm their strike vote. If the grievances of the maritime workers were not settled by that time, they would strike on the morning of the 12th. Such action would completely paralyze all movements of freight or merchandise in the community.

On the same day teamsters across the bay in Alameda County voted identical action by a majority of 369 to 54.

Public sentiment was crystallizing rapidly. People in every walk of life were mobilizing at opposite poles of opinion. Lukewarm or undecided attitudes were becoming fewer. San Francisco was a city divided and moving toward action. In between two camps, representing unqualified support of the strikers and unqualified opposition to the strikers, was a placid lake of neutrals—people who had not the slightest idea what was going on, could not understand it, and did not care about it. They were easy prey for the propagandists who rumored fantastic stories of dynamite plots and bloody revolution. Their brains were pinwheels in publicity breezes, reacting to every wind that blew. Thus, while some people were reacting to the genuine situation, others were merely reacting to propaganda—were, in their own minds, grappling with a situation which was nonexistent.

A good example of this was the state of mind within the ranks of the National Guard. Most of these young men believed, as they were told, that they were going into action to suppress an armed communist uprising.

A few months later I became acquainted with a young guardsman who described his experiences in great detail. He was informed when called to duty in Oakland that a communist revolution was taking place in San Francisco. He did not, he confessed, have any idea what a communist was, aside from the fact that the word had something to do with a "Russian experiment." They were armed with rifles and bayonets, but were not given any cartridges until they landed in San Francisco.

Coming over on the ferryboat they were warned that about 5,000 Reds were mobilized on the waterfront and that they might charge the minute the boat docked. Only a few rounds of ammunition were available, including some belts of bullets for machine guns which were mounted on the bow and held ready for action.

"If they rush us, it means hand-to-hand fighting," said the officer. "A club is as good as a bayonet at close quarters. If they get on this boat before we get off, we'll be sunk."

Most of this division consisted of high school boys or young men of that age. They gripped their rifles in a cold sweat all the way over, expecting within a few minutes to be in the thick of dreadful combat.

"Keep your rifles ready," warned the officers. "If we get ashore without a rush, they're liable to attack the trucks."

Of course their arrival was perfectly peaceful. Nevertheless they were quickly handed ammunition and warned that a surprise attack might be expected momentarily. They spent a nervous, fearful night in front of the docks, holding their guns ready for instant action.

After a week of this they began to sense something ridiculous about the whole proposition. They became restless and irritable. They weren't allowed to leave the piers or talk with anyone.

Some of the guardsmen had taken trips to sea in the fo'c'sle years before. They began telling the conditions they experienced and precipitated widespread discussion about the strike, and whether or not there might be something in the demands of the men. Disillusionment and sympathy for the strikers began to spread.

One afternoon a scab working on one of the docks asked a guardsman for a cigaret. The guardsman told him he had no cigarets for a lousy scab. A fist fight resulted. Other scabs and guardsmen joined in and soon there was a general fracas.

Thereafter the scabs and guardsmen were kept segregated at opposite ends of the pier, with a rope and armed sentries to keep them apart.

Unlike the soldiers in the ranks, officers were allowed to go uptown during the evenings, and frequently came back riotously drunk. This fact was not commonly known, but my young guardsman friend was attached to a battalion telephone section. His duties carried him over the whole front and, while operating the switchboard, he heard numerous interesting conversations which kept him informed.

Near the end of the period the general sentiment among the guardsmen was that they had been duped; that there was no Red revolution, and that they had been called out to break a strike.

When the troops were withdrawn, after the General Strike, this young guardsman asked for a transfer to absence until his enlistment expired. Asked why, he said, "I've had enough of this damned, lousy scabherding."

He is a young artist and has had many exhibitions in local galleries. Before his militia service on the Embarcadero he hadn't even known what a scab was. Organized labor meant nothing to him.

Since that time, whenever there is a strike or labor struggle of any kind, he drops what he is doing and goes down to strike headquarters to offer his services in making signs and placards. Reclining nudes and clusters of fruit have disappeared from his canvases. Instead he paints industrial scenes—men at work and men in struggle.

A neutral became a partisan.

In the midst of the tense situation which prevailed between July 5 (Bloody Thursday) and the General Strike, the Knights Templar arrived in town by the hundreds and were attempting to hold a convention. They strolled the streets in their extraordinary regalia, with white-plumed hats and shining swords, constituting an embarrassment to civic officials. It was much like having company arrive in the midst of a turbulent family altercation. Conservative midwestern businessmen, dressed as nineteenth-century generals, enacted their fraternal pageantry amidst chaos.

On Sunday, July 8, they paraded up Market Street in full regalia. Newspapers described it:

[125]

Their plumes shining and their swords flashing in the sun of a summer's day, hundreds of officers of the commanderies swung up Market Street and into the Auditorium, where they marched with bared heads to the processional "Onward Christian Soldiers."

Reverend David Logan Wilson addressed the assembled Knights:

This world is suffering from a moral slump which is far more important than any material decline. We are cruelly in need of a new sense of religious and moral values.

It is ours to make the cross of Jesus a living reality in our lives, not simply to carry it on our banners, but to feel its weight on our shoulders.

That night a thirty-year-old working woman sat dazed in a cheap apartment house on Fifth Street. Her hands were glazed and worn from the laundry where she worked. Her eyes were red and swollen from tears. She was not crying now. She stared straight ahead of her, apparently unmindful of visiting friends, neighbors, and newspaper reporters.

This was Julia, wife of Nick Bordoise. They had been married six years. Nick was a native of Crete, a culinary worker, a member of the Cooks' Union and the Communist Party.

Ever since their marriage they had lived obscurely in their small apartment. Nick was a hard and steady worker and found employment in some of the biggest restaurants in town. Recently he had undergone an operation for appendicitis, and was convalescing when the maritime strike broke out.

Nick's father had been a working man. His family as far back as he knew had been laborers. Loyalty to the struggles of labor was the familiar philosophy of his home life. It was as natural and binding to him as loyalty to home and family. He heard the call for solidarity and help, and he got up off his sickbed to go down to work, unpaid, in the strikers' relief kitchen. All through the long strike he sweated cheerfully over a hot stove preparing meals for hungry pickets. There was nothing spectacular or grandiose about his contribution. It was a matter of course with him. Unionism was his creed, his belief—the dominating principle that guided him in life. It was his natural duty to his principles and his fellow men, and not a deed performed in expectancy of praise or gratitude.

Three days ago he departed as usual from this small apartment to do his daily bit in the relief kitchen. That was on Bloody Thursday. That night his wife read in the papers that Nick was lying under a sheet in the morgue with a police bullet in his back.

His body was now lying in state in the headquarters of the International Longshoremen's Association on Steuart Street. In another coffin beside him lay Howard Sperry, longshoreman, the second victim of the "opening of the port."

All Sunday long and far into the night crowds swarmed in the street outside the hall, waiting in long, silent lines to pay tribute to the dead. They filed slowly in endless procession past the two coffins. Thousands upon thousands, hour after hour, they passed in silent respect. Young and old, men and women, husky workingmen in dungarees, pale clerks in blue serge, pretty young girls with serious faces, high school boys in corduroys, white-bearded old men—even little children clung tightly to their parents as they gazed at the still white faces in the coffins. Some bent one knee and made the sign of the cross. Others stood erect and raised one fist in workers' salute. Many left small bunches of flowers gathered from home gardens and window boxes. The air was heavy with the scent of flowers from literally hundreds of wreaths from organizations and unions.

Sperry was a World War veteran. Sentries stood guard beside the coffins and outside the door. One of them wore the uniform of the Veterans of Foreign Wars.

A delegation of longshoremen called upon Chief of Police Quinn to obtain permission for a funeral parade on Monday. They demanded that all police be withdrawn from around the ILA hall, where the services were to be held, and from the entire length of Market Street, the line of march.

"You keep the cops away," they said, "and we'll be responsible for maintaining order and directing traffic."

The request was granted. These men, who had been described in newspapers and by public officials as a disorderly mob, asked to take over the entire downtown section for the afternoon of July 9, and their request was granted. No more decisive refutation of the lies and slanders directed against the strikers could have been made. It was also an indication of the enormous public resentment that had been aroused by the attacks of July 3 and 5.

"Okay," said Chief Quinn. "We'll stay away as long as you keep order. But if you don't—"

Early on the morning of July 9 crowds began to gather outside the ILA headquarters. Shortly before noon a living sea of people filled Steuart Street from one end to the other. Latecomers who sought a place in the procession that was forming had to walk a mile and a quarter past one solid mass of men in order to reach the end of the line. Approximately 40,000 men, women, and children of every conceivable trade and profession stood silently with hats off in the hot sun, waiting for the march to begin.

The services began at 12:30 within the ILA hall. They were simple and stark. A spokesman for the ILA began, "We are here to pay the respects of union labor to you, Howard Sperry, and you, Nicholas Bordoise—to bid you farewell."

The harsh clanging of a bell cut in on his words. He paused a moment while everyone listened. It was the ironic clanging of a nearby Belt Line locomotive shunting boxcars with the aid of a scab crew.

The longshoreman continued in a tense voice. He spoke of the supreme sacrifice of the fallen men, the challenge of the Industrial Association, and pledged over the two coffins that the fight would continue until victory.

The coffins were carried down the narrow stairway and placed on trucks. Three additional trucks followed bearing flowers.

A union band struck up the slow cadence of the Beethoven funeral march. The great composer's music was never applied more fittingly to human suffering. Slowly—barely creeping—the trucks moved out into Market Street. With slow, rhythmic steps, the giant procession followed. Faces were hard and serious. Hats were held proudly across chests. Slow-pouring like thick liquid, the great mass flowed out onto Market Street.

Streetcarmen stopped their cars along the line of march and stood silently, holding their uniform caps across their chests, holding their heads high and firm.

Not one smile in the endless blocks of marching men. Crowds on the sidewalk, for the most part, stood with heads erect and hats removed. Others watched the procession with fear and alarm. Here and there well-dressed businessmen from Montgomery Street stood amazed and impressed, but with their hats still on their heads. Sharp voices shot out of the line of march: "Take off your hat!"

The tone of voice was extraordinary. The reaction was immediate. With quick, nervous gestures, the businessmen obeyed.

Hours went by, but still the marchers poured onto Market Street, until the whole length of the street, from the Ferry Building to Valencia, was filled with silent, marching men, women, and children.

Not a policeman was in sight throughout the whole enormous area. Longshoremen wearing blue armbands directed traffic and presided with an air of authority. No police badge or whistle ever received such instant respect and obedience as the calm, authoritative voices of the dock workers.

Labor was burying its own.

Newspapers described it:

A river of men flowing up Market Street like cooling lava ... the solemn strains of dirges and hymns ... unaccountable thousands of spectators lining the streets with uncovered heads ... overhead a brilliant sun in a cloudless sky.

And again:

In life they wouldn't have commanded a second glance on the streets of San Francisco, but in death they were borne the length of Market Street in a stupendous and reverent procession that astounded the city.

Estimates of the length of the procession varied from a mile and a half to two miles. The people marched eight, and sometimes ten abreast.

Even the Industrial Association's official record of the strike bows to the power and dignity of the demonstration. Their record states:

It was one of the strangest and most dramatic spectacles that has ever moved along Market Street. Its passage marked the high tide of united labor action in San Francisco. . . .

As the last marcher broke ranks, the certainty of a general strike, which up to this time had appeared to many to be a visionary dream of a small group of the most radical workers, became for the first time a practical and realizable objective.

The maritime pickets had been driven from the Embarcadero by force. The Industrial Association had assumed the role of government and for three days a slipshod dribble of commerce was carried on with the aid of scabs. For three days the city had been smoldering in anger. Now it was going to act. That was the message everyone read in the silent ranks of marching men.

If a giant strike like that of the maritime workers could be defeated in this manner, then what chance had any smaller strike in the future? A precedent was being established which cast a shadow of doom over all organized labor on the coast. Only one course was left open. Labor must step forward and establish a still greater precedent. Labor was accepting the challenge.

The parade ended at Dugan's funeral parlor on Seventeenth Street just off Valencia.

The body of Howard Sperry remained there until the next day when it was transferred to the Presidio National Cemetery and buried side by side with other veterans of the World War.

Nick Bordoise was placed in a hearse and taken to Cypress Lawn Cemetery. Hundreds piled into every available car or truck and accompanied the body to the burial ground five miles outside the city. There Nick was given a Red funeral with officials of the local Communist Party presiding.

Friends, relatives, union brothers, and party comrades held their fists high and sang the Internationale as the body was lowered into the grave.

As soon as the march was over, the President's mediation board went into secret conference with employers. Later in the day they held a second conference behind closed doors with the members of the Labor Council's Strike Strategy Committee.

The National Guard on the waterfront was strengthened by several new divisions and the area of martial law was extended over wider territory.

That night across the bay at a meeting of the Alameda County Labor Council a brief and businesslike resolution was passed calling on all unions to take an immediate general strike vote. A committee of seven was appointed, not to "investigate," but to proceed with the organization of "an effective General Strike."

CHAPTER XIV
Mediation Hearings, The
General Strike Begins

ON THE SAME DAY that the giant funeral parade took place the National Longshoremen's Board (mediation board) began its series of open hearings on the issues of the strike. They were held in the dignified atmosphere of a federal courtroom and extended over three days, July 9 to 11.

Newspapers described the opening:

Three men fighting to ward off the threat of a general strike, with all its implications of suffering and bloodshed, sat in the Federal Building yesterday and heard labor present its case for settlement of the maritime strike by surrender of the shipowners to union recognition and the closed shop.

Archbishop Edward J. Hanna, Attorney O. K. Cushing, and Edward F. McGrady, Assistant Secretary of Labor, appointed as a board of mediation by President Roosevelt, appealed at the opening of the public hearings for a truce.

They pleaded with the strikers to return to work at once and let the board arbitrate their demands. (*San Francisco Examiner*, July 10.)

On the whole the evidence presented was a repetition of the arguments which had been repeated again and again throughout the whole strike. The principal thing revealed was the unfamiliarity of the three mediators with all matters pertaining to the subject at hand. Their minds had no more practical application to the subject than would a group of bricklayers called in to judge the merits of a medical controversy. They were amazed and puzzled by the most everyday facts of maritime life.

Laughter dispelled the dignity of the court on one occasion when Archbishop Hanna interrupted Harry Bridges to ask him what a "fink" was.

"Just a colorful expression, your Grace," replied Bridges. "The workers know what it means."

Andrew Furuseth, eighty-year-old president of the International Seamen's Union, continually interrupted the proceedings with his opinion that the whole business was foolish.

"This hearing is getting nowhere," he said. "There is an agreement between the banks and the Industrial Association and the shipowners here. This board should get the truth about it, and the only way you can get the truth is to use the full powers granted this board by law, and subpoena their records, by-laws, and constitutions.

"If you don't do that, you are just going to sit here asking questions to which there is no answer."

On another occasion he urged, "Gentlemen, may I suggest that you are merely wasting your time here? You can't get the truth this way. Go to the bottom of this thing. Find out who is who. Use your powers."

Representatives of all the unions on strike took the floor one after another, described conditions in minute detail, and explained the demands.

Harry Bridges said:

There is a lot of talk about independent settlements for each port. Later I will offer proof to show San Francisco is the real headquarters for all the employers on the Coast in their dealings with the unions.

The owners have only one objective—the destruction of labor unions. They haven't made a single concession of any consequence. The men have made three. They have agreed to arbitrate every question except that of control of hiring halls, which involves the fundamental right of labor.

If we can't control the hiring halls, then the right of the longshoremen to organize is just a farce. If we do not control the halls the unions can and will be destroyed by discrimination and blacklisting, and the men who took part in this strike would be driven out of the industry. We can't permit a fink hall....

We don't intend to repeat our former mistake of one group settling without the other. The maritime strikers will go back to work only when all of their controversies are settled.

The employers have had a lot to say about the so-called repudiation of the June 16 agreement. Much has been made of this in the press and by the Industrial Association, the strikebreaking, open shop organization of the employers.

The fact is there never was any June 16 agreement. We never invited Joseph P. Ryan, the international president, to represent us on the West Coast. He spoke only for himself, and he has shown himself to be not in favor of certain conditions which we demand.

Ryan's agreement was never binding on us, no matter how many mayors and representatives of the Industrial Association signed it. It was made without the authorization of the men and therefore there never was any agreement so far as the ILA was concerned, and of course it could not have been repudiated. . . .

From the very beginning the forces of the city and the state have been arrayed on the side of the shipowners. They have instituted a reign of terror under which peaceful pickets have been arrested and beaten without cause. Police Department thugs have committed murder and gone unpunished.

Evidence of this was on the shameful Bloody Thursday, July 5. It was not a battle last Thursday, but an attack by armed men on peaceful pickets —an attack by the shipowners, through the police, on the strikers.

Bridges then read two letters and offered them in evidence. One was the letter written and signed by Thomas G. Plant to Eugene Mills, president of the employers' organization in San Pedro, dated June 21, instructing San Pedro to curtail strike expenses and make use of the Police Department to a greater extent.

The other was a letter signed by numerous San Francisco capitalists in various industries removed from the waterfront, which was sent out to hundreds of local businessmen urging them to contribute money to help break the strike. The specific wording asked that they aid in "retrieving control of the waterfront."

"Contributors were asked to sign pledge cards," said Bridges, "and were given five years to pay. In other words, strikebreaking on the installment plan."

Once again laughter broke the austere dignity of the room. The bailiffs rapped harshly for order.

"We intend to stay on strike," continued Bridges, "until we have reasonable assurance—not merely pledges—that the strikers will have some protection in their jobs. A general strike is impending, and all organized labor is watching this board and the outcome of its negotiations."

The third and final day of the hearings was July 11. That evening the teamsters were scheduled to meet and confirm their decision to walk out in general strike on the following morning. It was a tense afternoon with all concentration centered on producing some kind of result from the mediation hearings that might influence the teamsters and prevent them from going out.

Thomas G. Plant, president of the Waterfront Employers' Union, appeared before the board and read a document outlining the stand of the shipowners. Simultaneously the employers publicly announced their willingness to submit all issues of the "longshoremen's strike" to unconditional arbitration.

Newspapers rushed into print with a wave of extras. Employers were willing to submit to unconditional arbitration. The strikers refused. This, they inferred, was proof positive that the employers were eager for a fair settlement, but that the strike was in control of radicals who sought prolonged strife.

The strikers once more explained that it was not a "longshoremen's strike" but a maritime strike, and that for the longshoremen to sign a separate agreement and return to work, leaving the seamen out on a limb, would be an infamous betrayal. They demanded that the arbitration proposal be extended to include the grievances of the seamen.

This the employers refused to do. They declared it was impossible to arbitrate with the seamen because they did not know what these unions wanted or who represented them.

The unions had already handed in written demands through Mayor Rossi. Furthermore, they had just finished appearing before the mediation board where they had explained their demands in great detail. And if the mediation hearings were not to establish simple fundamentals like these, then what were they for?

Newspapers skipped lightly over these technicalities and laid all emphasis on the accusation that employers were willing to arbitrate, but the strikers were not. A large part of the general public did not comprehend why the longshoremen would not sign a separate agreement. There is evidence, however, that the employers understood the point very well. In the Industrial Association's official record of the strike a very keen understanding of the importance of labor solidarity is shown. There are frequent references to the fact that the strike could have been broken in a few weeks if the teamsters had not supported the longshoremen. Other pages acknowledge that it could have been broken if the seamen had not supported the longshoremen. By the same token, the seamen had very little hope of gaining anything unless they were backed up by the longshoremen.

Members of the general public might reasonably be confused by technicalities concerning labor solidarity. But there is no reason why the conservative officials of the Labor Council should not understand such an issue. Nevertheless they expressed great delight over the separate arbitration offer and professed that it "changed the situation."

John A. O'Connell, secretary of the Labor Council, member of the Teamsters' Union and one of the Strike Strategy Committee, declared, "This should make a big difference in regard to the general strike situation. It is a great deal more than we expected from the employers."

In the ranks of labor, however, there was very little confusion. Teamsters packed Dreamland Auditorium that night in roaring throngs. "We'll hang Michael Casey from a sour apple tree," was a song on hundreds of lips.

Crowds of maritime workers, among them Harry Bridges, thronged the pavement outside, waiting to learn the decision the minute a final vote was taken. Teamsters going in waved assurance to the strikers, shouting, "We're going out with you."

Inside the giant auditorium was a vast rumble of voices and shuffling of feet. It quieted to an intent silence the minute the meeting was called to order. Vandeleur and other members of the Strategy Committee of seven addressed them, urging that all action be postponed. A storm of boos and catcalls split the air. Speeches could not be finished.

Michael Casey came forward and warned that a strike was contrary to union rules and that they would lose benefit funds from the international if they took such action. The hall rocked to rollicking and prolonged laughter.

Voices cried out, "Bridges! We want Bridges!" Cheers, whistles, and stamping of feet swept the hall. A tumult of voices rose on every hand, "Bridges! We want Bridges!"

Michael Casey stood swamped in noise. His voice could not be heard above the uproar.

Several teamsters ran outside to where Bridges was waiting on the sidewalk with the maritime workers. The salaried officials had not even seen fit to invite him to the meeting. He was ushered into the hall to a deafening ovation.

Utter silence fell over the great hall when the rank-and-file leader of the longshoremen began to speak. Firmly and earnestly he reviewed the events leading up to the present deadlock, pointed out the importance of unity, and urged united labor action to defend common interests.

The teamsters decided by unanimous vote to walk out on strike at 7 a.m. the next morning.

Instantly men got up and ran outside to inform the waiting marine workers. "We're out! We're out!" they shouted.

Cheers sounded through the street and echoed for blocks.

A newspaper account said:

Mayor Rossi rode by the auditorium as the meeting was breaking up, shook his head, said "too bad." He went to the Whitcomb Hotel and met Assistant Secretary of Labor Edward F. McGrady. Both were grimly silent when asked for statements. Shortly, Ed Vandeleur, president, and John A. O'Connell, secretary of the Labor Council, arrived from the teamsters' meeting and the four men went into conference.

Events now began occurring with more rapidity, spontaneity, and variety than the eye could follow.

At 7 a.m. the next morning all transportation of freight and merchandise halted as abruptly as if someone had turned off a faucet. East Bay teamsters were already out, their strike having gone into effect at midnight.

Two hundred butchers walked out of the slaughterhouses despite the fact that their union was supposed to await action from the Labor Council Strategy Committee.

Market Street Railway employees voted 700 to 38 to go out on strike.

Cleaners, dyers, and pressers walked out simultaneously with the teamsters.

Employers began hiring scab truck drivers, and teamsters began tipping over scab trucks in the streets.

Scores of other unions voted to abide by whatever decision the Labor Council arrived at.

Chief of Police Quinn issued an alarming order for all hardware stores, pawnshops, and second-hand stores to remove rifles and firearms from their windows. The order was published in all papers and broadcast over the radio.

Several persons who wandered carelessly into the zone of martial law around the waterfront were fired on by the National Guard.

All deliveries of gasoline, food, vegetables, coal, wood, and other vital articles were halted. Housewives instituted a rush on grocery stores, laying in huge food supplies in expectation of shortages. The strikers issued special permits for delivery of food and fuel to hospitals and fire stations.

Every newspaper that rolled off the press looked like a screaming war extra.

Boilermakers in sixty shops got impatient waiting for the Strategy Committee to act, and walked out along with the teamsters.

Picket lines were thrown across all highways leading into the city, and incoming trucks were turned back or turned over. All movement of food supplies was paralyzed within an area of 100 miles around San Francisco. Dealers announced that food on hand was not sufficient to last the million and a half residents of the Bay Region for a week.

Trucks transporting school supplies were equipped with special flags to indicate approval of the strike committee.

Bartenders and waiters voted by a majority of more than 17 to 1 to go out on strike regardless of what the Strategy Committee decided.

Communist newspapers came out describing the Strategy Committee as the "Tragedy Committee," and urging unions to take action of their own accord and elect their own strike leaders instead of letting the Labor Council appoint them from the top.

By the night of the 12th a general strike was already largely in effect and the city was in a fever of excitement. Wealthy residents were already fleeing in great numbers by every conceivable means of transportation.

The next day was Friday the 13th. Morning papers announced:

The city's supply of fresh vegetables and greens will be exhausted by nightfall.
The supply of fresh and smoked meat on hand in the average butcher shop will last through Monday.

Housewives stormed into groceries and purchased the shelves clean.

News came from Los Angeles that every union in the city had voted full support of the maritime strikers and assessed their members 25 cents each to provide funds to carry on the struggle. Movements toward general strikes were developing rapidly in the cities of the Northwest and rumors of sympathy strikes in the agricultural fields were abroad.

From the very start of the strike a large proportion of the small merchants and shopkeepers evidenced willing support of the men. Many of them were already proudly displaying printed cards in their windows: "ILA SYMPATHIZER."

One small grocer said, "I've got enough canned stuff to last maybe a week—and am I going to get a laugh when some of my rich customers start yelling for avocadoes!"

Gasoline stations were rapidly shutting down as supply tanks were drained by unusual demand.

Underwriting companies did a record business in strike and riot insurance. Over a million dollars worth of policies were written in a week, and premiums were increased threefold.

The Knights Templar convention was breaking up, but the Knights were marooned in their hotels with no available means of getting their luggage to the station. As a gesture of hospitality the strike committee issued a special permit to transport their trunks.

Hotel and apartment dwellers found themselves without hot water, owing to the fuel shortage.

Racketeers, posing as army quartermasters, began ordering huge quantities of groceries and saying, "Charge them to the National Guard." Several shops were bilked out of large orders before the fraud was detected.

All other means of transporting merchandise having been shut off, the Post Office became flooded with packages and did a volume of business that exceeded the Christmas rush period.

Additional pressure was put on the conservatives in the Labor Council when the culinary workers, including practically all employees in hotels, restaurants, and cafeterias, voted overwhelmingly to walk out at midnight, July 15, regardless of what action was taken by the Strategy Committee. Taxi drivers took similar action and set the time for their walkout at 5 a.m., July 15.

By this time it was apparent to the Strategy Committee that they could do as they pleased or do nothing at all, San Francisco would have its General Strike nevertheless. A crucial meeting was set for the afternoon of July 13. Delegates to the Labor Council were to assemble, hear the report of the Strategy Committee, and vote on a general strike. They did not dare vote down a general walkout in the face of the rising tide of sentiment. They had all the audacity of King Canute, but less of his impracticality. Instead of ordering the waters to recede, they postponed action until 10 a.m. the next morning.

Newspapers heaved a sigh of relief in a flood of extras. The *San Francisco Chronicle* carried a headline, "MASS STRIKE VOTE PUT OFF." The story read, in part:

In what was obviously an eleventh-hour effort by conservative labor leaders to shield San Francisco from the disastrous and paralyzing grip of a general strike, the Central Labor Council yesterday voted unanimously to postpone the general strike decision. . . .

At 10 a.m. today [NOTE: San Francisco morning papers are on the streets early in the preceding afternoon. Thus, although this story appeared on the afternoon of the 13th, it referred to events scheduled for the 14th as "today," simply because the date on the paper was the 14th.] five accred-

[138]

ited delegates from each of the unions in San Francisco will go into session with the Strike Strategy Committee and the final decision is expected to be made some time before noon. These delegates will comprise a gigantic "strike committee" in the event that the general strike is voted.

Archbishop Hanna immediately broadcast an appeal over the radio urging that a general strike be abandoned and that all issues be submitted to unconditional arbitration. He pointed out the principles of Christian teaching over 2,000 years and that "there should be, in the dispensation of Christ, no conflict between class and class."

Unconditional arbitration, however, had never been offered to date. The only arbitration offer so far applied solely to the longshoremen, who comprised a minority of those on strike.

Another fitful night (and sleepless for many) passed in San Francisco, and the sun of the 14th dawned on a nervous city.

Morning newspaper editorials were headed: "Now Is THE TIME FOR ALL TO KEEP THEIR HEADS."

Simultaneously with such advice the *Chronicle* printed a story that a communist army was marching on San Francisco from the Northwest. How they ever got hold of such a story only God knows. There wasn't a fragment of fact in it. The story read, in part:

The reports stated the communist army planned the destruction of railroad and highway facilities to paralyze transportation and, later, communication, while San Francisco and the Bay Area were made a focal point in a red struggle for revolution and control of government.

First warning communist forces were nearing the Northern California border was relayed from J. R. Given, Southern Pacific superintendent at Dunsmuir, to District State Highway Engineer Fred W. Hazelwood, who immediately reported to State Director of Public Works Earl Lee Kelly.

Mayor Rossi issued another appeal for arbitration. Edward Vandeleur, president of the Labor Council, gave out a warning that general strike action was against the rules of the American Federation of Labor, and that charters of all local unions might be revoked.

All garages and service stations in San Francisco and the Bay Area were now drained of gas and had shut down. Car owners were conserving fuel carefully. Only enough gasoline was allowed through to supply fire stations, hospitals, and doctors.

More than sixty unions, not counting those already out, had voted overwhelmingly for a strike and were waiting impatiently for action by the Labor Council.

Cities and towns hundreds of miles away were already feeling the effects. Millions of eggs were dammed up in Petaluma, the poultry center of the West. Harvesting of crops in the agricultural fields was halted in many places by the cessation of trucking operations.

Railroad ticket offices were swamped by the demands of wealthy persons fleeing the city. The few visitors still arriving at railroad and bus stations found no taxicabs available to take them to hotels.

Governor Merriam, from Sacramento, threatened to place the entire city under martial law.

The Society for the Prevention of Cruelty to Animals was frantic over the predicament of 27,000 live hogs within the city limits who were in danger of starvation if they did not get their swill.

Meanwhile eighty-year-old Andrew Furuseth, president of the International Seamen's Union, broke down from excitement and was carried to a hospital. His was one of the saddest roles in the strike; not because he went to the hospital, for his ailment was not serious and he recovered soon, but because throughout the whole period it was difficult to distinguish him from the general run of reactionary officials with which he surrounded himself. In reality Andy was deeply sincere and had the interests of the union men at heart.

He was unable to grasp the situation around him. At the very moment he was tongue-lashing the Industrial Association for its war against organized labor, the Labor Council officials with whom he leagued himself were cooperating hand in glove with that organization. And he himself was utilized by the employers in their propaganda drive.

"I want to be with the men," he wept as they carried him off to the hospital. But at this very moment "the men" on the waterfront were cursing him for a faker. He was not a faker, although what difference that made is hard to say. The employers wrapped him around their fingers at will and, in practice, he was part and parcel of the reactionary labor element that conspired with the Industrial Association.

Newspapers played him up as a sentimental character, "The Old Man of the Sea," and featured his bewildered utterances as pure gems of labor wisdom. He was still urging the seamen to "accept arbitration" when, as a matter of fact, they had never been offered any arbitration and employers firmly refused to entertain such an idea. With all due respect for his sincerity, he merely cluttered up the scene, created confusion in the public mind, and agitated himself into a nervous breakdown.

The giant committee of five delegates from each union convened in the Labor Temple promptly at 10 a.m. There had been no time to call meetings and elect delegates, so that in nearly all cases the delegates were appointed by the conservative top officials. The meeting dragged out through most of the day as the conservative wing sought to push through a resolution delaying a strike vote until the following Monday. After hours of bickering, time-wasting, and dissension, the resolution was killed.

Earlier in the afternoon, while the meeting was still in progress, the *San Francisco News* came out with an extra that was hysterical in its hopefulness. The headline read: "BRIDGES BEATEN FOR POST IN GENERAL STRIKE MEETING!"

The incident itself was trivial and scarcely merited mention, let alone a headline. Harry Bridges had been nominated for vice-chairmanship of the meeting and had been defeated by another nominee.

Late in the afternoon a definite general strike resolution was put before the meeting:

This convention requests all unions which have voted in favor of a general strike to walk out on Monday at 8 a.m. and also requests all those unions which have not voted, to hold meetings immediately and take action.

Every union present was given one vote, regardless of the size of its membership, and the resolution carried 63 to 3. Forty-nine of the unions did not vote, claiming that their organizations had taken no action yet, and therefore they were not authorized to commit themselves.

Certain delegates, however, saw fit to vote absolutely contrary to the will of their membership. Michael Casey, for example, voted against the resolution in spite of the fact that the teamsters had already approved it by unanimous vote and were now out on strike. During the long afternoon Casey had wearied himself with numerous time-wasting speeches imploring the delegates to vote against a general strike.

The walkout was now a certainty and the deadline was 8 a.m., Monday, July 16, 1934.

Mayor Rossi went on the air that night with an alarming radio speech that concluded:

I am determined that as to those in this city who wilfully seek to prolong strife, either for their own selfish ends or for the disturbance or overthrow of this government, and of the Government of the United States—all of the forces at my command, all others that may be required will be brought to bear to prevent their carrying out their plans.

There was no evidence anywhere of any plot to overthrow the government. The strike was based on clear-cut union demands and was aimed squarely against the Industrial Association and its performance in assuming the role of government.

Roger Lapham, president of the American Hawaiian Steamship Company, telephoned to Secretary of Labor Frances Perkins in Washington, informing her that a communist revolution was taking place, and asking her to intervene for the government. Madame Perkins ridiculed such an idea and told him the employers and workers were acting like two small boys. "How dare you say such a thing," she said over the wire. "If you talk that way you are likely to put false ideas in the heads of the strikers."

Lapham fumed for a while, and then got her on the phone again. This time he poured such impassioned pleas over the wire that she asked him to send her specific suggestions of how he thought she might be helpful.

Lapham sat down and composed a lengthy telegram in which he advised:

As I have previously told you, and as can be verified from the Commanding General of the Ninth Corps Area, or any person familiar with the situation, the present movement is largely led and directed by the Communist Party and its members, most of whom are aliens. The names of such persons are known to the local Police Department and I suggest you exercise the power conferred upon you by the Section above mentioned to cause the arrest of such persons and their deportation. This prompt action will do more than any other thing to clear up this present situation and purge the ranks of the strikers of undesirable elements who are largely responsible for this situation. . . .

The General Strike which includes longshoremen, maritime workers, teamsters, taxicab drivers, and others engaged directly in trade and commerce between states and foreign countries, have openly conspired to restrain such trade and commerce. Not only does this constitute a crime under Federal law punishable by fine and imprisonment, but it is the statutory duty of the United States attorneys and under the direction of the Attorney General to cause proceedings in equity to be instituted to prevent and restrain such violations. . . .

I suggest that a shipping code incorporating the labor provisions of the shipping code which was recently presented to the President for approval be at once announced. Such a code provides methods for collective bargaining and for settlement of disputes and also contains minimum wage provisions which I believe would immediately furnish the basis for the maritime unions' returning to work. . . .

I suggest that the National Longshoremen's Board proceed to hold elections to be participated in by the legitimate longshoremen in which a vote would be taken on the question of arbitrating the longshoremen's dispute and that the board thereupon proceed at once with the arbitration of such dispute. At the same time the board should proceed to determine who the employees of the shipping companies desire to represent them for the purpose of collective bargaining. If the striking longshoremen refuse to put the question of arbitration to a vote, then I suggest that the National Longshoremen's Board proceed immediately to make findings of fact with respect to the merits of the controversy and particularly as to whether the agreement dated June 16, entered into by Joseph Ryan, International President of the Longshoremen's Union, and guaranteed by the Mayor of San Francisco and prominent Labor Leaders, does not constitute a just and fair settlement of the strike.

Meanwhile Chief of Police Quinn applied to Mayor Rossi for permission to swear in 500 additional policemen and make other expenditures totaling an estimated $160,225. The Mayor frugally cut him down to $58,951 but approved the extra policemen.

The department had already purchased $5,000 worth of gas equipment from the Lake Erie Chemical Company, and more recently $14,000 worth from the Federal Laboratories, Inc. This last order amounted to three times the quantity of gas equipment in the hands of the entire National Guard of California. It is still stored in the Hall of Justice and has never been used.

So much surplus gas is on hand that apparently they use the shells for paperweights. Over two years later a public official, prying into an obscure corner of his desk, disturbed a stray gas shell which exploded in his face.

Munitions salesmen were on hand eager to make the most of the opportunity. The Federal Laboratories stored a large quantity of gas in a warehouse within six or eight blocks of the Hall of Justice, in order to make immediate deliveries on demand.

In addition to the huge orders sold to the Police Department, large quantities of gas and equipment were sold to private purchasers, the heaviest buyers being the Waterfront Employers' Union, the Alaska Packers' Association, Bullard Company, the Standard Oil Company, the California Packing Corporation, and the Hearst-owned Examiner Printing Company.

Most important among the many preparations employers were feverishly engaging in as the general strike deadline approached, was the role played by newspaper publishers. This phase is described by Earl Burke in an article in the July 28, 1934, issue of *Editor and Publisher*, a trade journal circulating among publicity executives. The article states:

Just before the zero hour a group of publishers of the Bay region newspapers ... met to devise ways to meet the crisis. John Francis Neylan, general counsel, Hearst newspapers, was chosen for leadership. ... The

Mayor and Governor Merriam welcomed the plans of the publishers. ...

On Sunday, July 15, the *Examiner* and the *Chronicle* published front-page editorials stating that radicals had seized control by intimidation and that the general strike was a revolution against constituted authority. William Randolph Hearst telephoned from London to Clarence Lindner, saying a story was being cabled telling how the general strike in England in 1926 had been crushed when the government took control of the situation. This was published on Monday in the *Examiner, Chronicle, Call-Bulletin, Post-Enquirer,* and all Hearst papers. The *Oakland Tribune* ran a similar story based on other sources. The *News* sounded warnings to unions not to paralyze the vital processes on which the lives of all depended.

By this time the general public, which had generally been sympathetic to the alleged wrongs of the longshoremen, awakened to the menace which caused public hardships and threatened citizens' rights and that the general strike was "revolution."

Under Mr. Neylan's leadership plans were made to crush the revolt. ... Mr. Neylan entered into negotiations with conservative labor leaders. ... Conservative labor leaders welcomed this help as they realized that communists in control of maritime unions had stampeded other unions by saying this was the time for organized labor to take its place in the sun. Newspaper editorials built up the strength and influence of the conservative leaders and aided in splitting the conservative members away from the radicals.

Throughout the entire strike period the Industrial Association maintained a special apparatus for coordinating work between the Police Department and the newspapers. Agents of this intelligence department frequently rode in patrol cars with officers, and it was their duty to keep newspapers and the Industrial Association completely informed. Regular reports were turned in on special forms headed "STRIKE VIOLENCE MEMO." A large part of the newspaper material, particularly referring to violence, was written and supplied through this bureau.

The American Civil Liberties Union, through Chester S. Williams, Ernest Besig, and Austin Lewis, made an investigation of this bureau and their report was published in the *Nation* of October 10, 1934. In an interview with Albert E. Boynton, managing director of the Industrial Association, they were informed:

Early in June a special department was set up to collect information from such places as the police stations and emergency hospitals, from radio reports of the police, and general facts of importance or interest to the Industrial Association.

Mr. James K. Carr, long in the employ of the Association as director of the American Plan Promotion, was put in charge of this special department. ...

Mr. Lewis asked why the Industrial Association should spend time and money helping the newspapers do their job. Mr. Boynton answered that they wanted the papers to get all the strike-violence news possible, and that they wanted a lot of such information direct and quick.

Inquiring into what the American Plan Promotion was which Mr. Carr directed, they learned that:

The task of this official in ordinary times is to promote the hiring of non-union workers wherever possible in order to protect the open-shop policy.

A letter from James K. Carr was quoted describing the setting up of the intelligence bureau:

An office was secured ... telephones and a short-wave radio receiver installed. Three outside employees were engaged ... to visit the various police stations, emergency hospitals, and other locations where news might be obtained. These men, acting in the capacity of reporters, delivered their reports at the office or phoned them in. In addition there were employed two rewrite men and the necessary stenographic service.

Just prior to the General Strike, it was reported in newspapers that since the beginning of the maritime walkout 322 arrested strikers had been tried in the municipal courts, and that 199 cases had been dismissed, 49 had resulted in convictions, 20 were bound over to the Superior Court, and 42 continued. The charges included disturbing the peace, resisting an officer, vagrancy, distribution of handbills, battery, and refusal to move on.

CHAPTER XV
The General Strike

ALTHOUGH THE DEADLINE FOR a general strike was not until 8 a.m. on Monday, July 16, 1934, the walkout was largely in effect Sunday. All but a few streetcars had stopped running. Taxicabs had disappeared from the streets. Countless grocery stores, already stripped of most of their stocks by anxious housewives, had closed their doors and put signs in their windows, "CLOSED TILL THE BOYS WIN," or "CLOSED FOR THE DURATION OF THE GENERAL STRIKE."

Governor Merriam, from Sacramento, had already instructed that food trucks should be sent into the city under armed convoy. He stated, "I am placing at the disposal of each sheriff of his county the State Highway Patrol. I am determined nothing shall interfere with the movement of food supplies."

Mayor Rossi issued a proclamation suspending all provisions of the city charter during the emergency, and taking full reins of dictatorship in his own hands, with freedom to act without recourse to usual formalities and procedure.

In a second proclamation he urged citizens to cooperate with police and civic authorities in breaking the strike. He said, "The present issue being clearly defined, I ask support only from those completely committed in their hearts to the American form of government, it being my intention that those who seek the destruction of this government shall find no comfort in this community."

At the last minute before the deadline two important sections of organized labor decided against a walkout. Electrical and typographical workers remained on the job. Thus light, power, communications, and newspapers continued functioning. Reporters and other editorial employees of the papers were not yet organized in a union. The strike, however, gave great impetus to the formation of new unions, and it was not long afterward that the newspapermen organized themselves into the Northern California Newspaper Guild, which later became affiliated with the A. F. of L., and still later with the CIO.

When the typographical workers met on Sunday afternoon to consider general strike action, sentiment for a walkout was running high and favorable action seemed a foregone conclusion. Charles P. Howard, international president of the typographers, was on hand from the East. He took command of the meeting and argued energetically against a strike. Discussion was heated and wore on far into the afternoon. A strong minority fought vigorously in favor of a walkout. The deciding majority wavered. Howard clinched the deal at the last moment by announcing that employers had just agreed to a 10 per cent increase in wages. The strike was defeated by a vote of three to one.

Despite these gaps in labor's front, the paralysis on the morning of July 16 was effective beyond all expectation. To all intents and purposes, industry was at a complete standstill. The great factories were empty and deserted. No streetcars were running. Virtually all stores were closed. The giant apparatus of commerce was a lifeless, helpless hulk.

Labor had withdrawn its hand. The workers had drained out of the plants and shops like life-blood, leaving only a silent framework embodying millions of dollars worth of invested capital. In the absence of labor, giant machinery loomed as so much idle junk.

Everything was there, all intact as the workers had left it—instruments, equipment, tools, machinery, raw materials, and the buildings themselves. When the men walked out they took only what belonged to them—their labor. And when they took that they might as well have taken everything, because all the elaborate apparatus they left behind was worthless and meaningless without their hand. The machinery was a mere extension of labor, created by and dependent upon labor.

Labor held the life-blood and energy. The owners remained in possession of the corpse.

Highways leading into the city bristled with picket lines. Nothing moved except "By permission of the strike committee." Labor was in control. Employers, however, controlled an important factor. Through the "conservative wing" they held the balance of power within the General Strike Committee. But this "conservative wing" had to buck a strong progressive minority, and dared not move too obviously contrary to the will of the mass.

Three thousand additional troops were brought in from outlying communities—some of them all the way from Los Angeles, 430 miles away. The area of martial law was extended to include the fruit and vegetable wholesale districts adjacent to the waterfront. Barricades were erected in all streets and a cordon of troops flung around the area. Guards with bayoneted rifles stood outside the National Guard Armory on Mission Street. Truckloads of steel-helmeted troops carrying formidable automatic rifles lent a wartime atmosphere as they passed through the streets.

Chief Quinn, in the Hall of Justice on Kearny Street, was busy swearing in his 500 additional policemen.

An atmosphere of panic prevailed in the business districts. But an almost carnival spirit was apparent in working-class neighborhoods. Laboring men appeared on the streets in their Sunday clothes, shiny celluloid union buttons glistening on every coat lapel. Common social barriers were swept away in the spirit of the occasion. Strangers addressed each other warmly as old friends. Labor wore its new-found power with calm dignity.

After all, this great intricate mass of steel, stone, and machinery was their baby. They built it and they ran it. They knew every bolt and cog and screw in the apparatus of civilization. They were as familiar and at ease with its mechanical complexities as they were with the insides of their pockets. They could turn the whole thing off at will, or start it up again in a minute if they pleased. They were organized.

Furthermore, their minds were not inflamed with hysteria about bloody revolution, anarchy and chaos, as was the case with the businessmen and large numbers of white-collar workers. To them the strikers were Joe, Bill, Mike, and Jerry, their pals, their neighbors, their benchmates. To them the hysterical pronouncements of the employers and civic officials, proclaiming that Moscow was trying to seize San Francisco as a colonial possession, were an amusing form of political delirium tremens which had seized upon the upper classes.

It is probable also that employers in the higher brackets were sufficiently aware that this was no revolution. They realized that it was nothing more nor less than a showdown between capital and labor on the issue of the open shop, and they seized upon the strategy of decrying it as a revolution against the government in order to swing the less informed sections of public opinion to their side.

But to thousands of well-dressed businessmen and their slightly less well-dressed white-collar workers, the picture was fogged and incomprehensible, and their imaginations went rioting. I even had one prominent businessman argue with me for hours that an ancient stone had been dug up in Egypt which, when deciphered, predicted that in 1934 the world would revert to savagery, and that this was the beginning.

The Industrial Association issued thousands of "red scare" bulletins which circulated through office buildings warning of armed uprisings and bloody revolution. These devices fed the flames of middle-class hysteria until many persons were afraid to go out in the street for fear they would be shot.

This is easily understandable. For years back these white-collared workers had been infused with the psychology that laboring men who worked in overalls and came home with grimy hands were the "lower classes"—an almost semi-underworld element. Brains, competence, and culture were associated in their minds only with wealth and financial astuteness.

To them the strikers were not Bill, Tom, and Jerry, friend and neighbor, but a vast, unknown quantity—the "lower classes." The strikers were as strange to their way of thinking as a foreign army.

Most people who had witnessed the giant parades of preceding weeks were impressed by the power, dignity, and unity of labor. But to many people in the white-collar class these marches were terrifying spectacles. They saw only a vast, flowing river of big, husky men in soiled clothing. The gnarled fists and weatherbeaten faces of these men did not suggest to their minds a lifetime of toil in the services of humanity. They saw only a mass of faces conforming to their conception of the "underworld." They saw these men as toughs and bullies—men whom they would not want to encounter on a dark night.

One young man, after witnessing one of the parades, told me that it made him "sick to his stomach," and he was glad that we had a strong army, navy, and police force to keep these "morons" in order. This same young man was working ten hours a day for a drapery firm —for $15 a week, and depended on money from "home" to keep his pants pressed. Not many months before, discouraged by long unemployment and poverty, he had tried to commit suicide but the landlady smelled the gas, crashed into the room, and called an ambulance.

Another well-educated young man told me the whole thing was ridiculous and futile—that the thing to do was look after "number one" and go out and make a pile no matter how you made it, because if you didn't do it the next guy would. He was ragged and thin as a sucker stick. He hadn't eaten all day and was sitting on a park bench killing time. I knew him from a long way back and he hadn't worked for years. He had no trade and was sort of "out of things." His mother and small sister were stringing along on relief in a distant country town. He was a capable scholar and had outstripped his fellows in school. Now he spent his time reading in the public library just to distract his mind. He believed America was in trouble because it had no educated aristocracy to rule over the lower classes and keep them in line.

Moving pictures and slick-paper magazines had given this class of people a peculiar conception of humanity. The good man—the intelligent man—as they had been led to believe, was handsome or at least well groomed and polite. The ruffian or underworld character was almost invariably rough-featured and ungainly. Soiled clothes meant the lower classes. Clean collars meant the "better kind of people"— the people to cultivate.

They did not realize that the man who sits all day in the office and the man who stands all day in front of a blast furnace are apt to come out looking like very different creatures. It never occurred to them that the man who worked with his hands, with steel and wood and machinery, was apt to lose fingers, eyes, arms, legs, and gain countless scars.

Consequently they witnessed these parades with terror and came home expecting anything to happen. They did not think with facts and understanding—they simply felt one way or another and arrived at opinions through a series of impressions.

Thus fright and uncertainty swept the business areas, while an easy-going confidence paraded the working-class districts.

The *San Francisco News* ran an advertisement in the lower right-hand corner of its front page:

If you can't get downtown—the *News* can certainly come uptown. You may be accustomed to buying your *News* on the streets. You certainly want accurate, up-to-the-minute information. *News*boys will be in your neighborhood, but you may miss them. So—telephone your subscription. Then you can be sure to get the *News*.

About your food problem—turn to the woman's page today for suggestions on "strike menus."

Office employees pooled what gasoline they had left and rode to work in crowded autos. Others patiently walked miles to report. There was nothing much for them to do when they got there, but employers were keeping offices open as a matter of morale.

Ferryboats were still running, professedly because the union had an agreement with employers whereby a thirty-day notice must be given before a strike. Thousands of office workers lived on the other side of the bay and commuted. They came to work on the morning of the 16th with overnight bags, fearful that the boatmen, agreement or no agreement, might walk out during the day.

Many firms arranged to quarter their office staffs in downtown hotels for the duration of the strike.

Nineteen restaurants at scattered points in the downtown area were left open "By permission of the strike committee." Block-long queues of waiting customers filled the streets outside.

No fresh meat was available in the entire Bay Area.

The strike committee began extending the permit system to assure adequate provisions for the populace. Jack Shelley, secretary of the executive committee, stated, "A definite program is under way for the continuance of all food supplies. Permits will be issued for the transportation of groceries, fruit, vegetables, and meat by the permit committee in cooperation with the local unions affected."

Harry Bridges announced he was recommending establishment of union-controlled food depots throughout the city and committees to prevent profiteering.

Mounted police were handed special equipment in the form of gas masks for their horses.

All theaters, night clubs, and barrooms were shut down. The sale of intoxicating liquors was prohibited by the strike committee as a precaution for preserving order.

The *Examiner* came out with its London General Strike story as wired from Europe by William Randolph Hearst. It appeared on page 1 and was headed: "MEASURES TAKEN BY BRITAIN TO END ITS GENERAL STRIKE BARED." A subhead read: *"Special Citizen Corps*

Helped Police to Keep Order." It combined a strong plea for armed government intervention with the recommendation of direct action by groups of citizens organized along vigilante lines.

The *Chronicle* published the same story under the head: "Citizen Army Broke Mass British Strike; enlisted men, volunteers took over control of isle during big walkout."

The same papers carried a proclamation from Mayor Rossi, declaring he was organizing "citizen committees" to deal with the situation.

Alarming editorials warned that communists had seized control. The *Chronicle's* broadside read, in part:

The radicals have seized control by intimidation.

It has long been evident that radicals were in control of the dock strike. The evidence is that they have shouted down every attempt at peaceful settlement by agreement and at last have ignored the employers' surrender and agreement to submit every point without reserve to the arbitration of the President's mediation board.

The radicals have wanted no settlement.

What they want is revolution.

Organized labor and communism have nothing in common. There are no unions in Russia, where these radicals get their orders.

Are the sane, sober workingmen of San Francisco to permit these communists to use them for their purpose of wreckage, a wreckage bound to carry the unions down with it?

Many inaccuracies can be noted here. For one thing, it is absurd to propose that a small handful of radicals could have intimidated the 40,000 husky men who were on strike, much less the vast numbers now out in the General Strike. For another, the accused "radicals" were the democratically elected representatives of the men. For another, the employers had not "surrendered" and the arbitration offer referred to here applied only to the longshoremen who were a minority among the maritime strikers. For another, no one had even suggested a revolution against the government or a change in the social system. For another, labor in Russia is unionized almost 100 per cent.

Large downtown department stores, after a conference of owners, decided to remain open. There were practically no customers to be waited on, but it was a gesture of defiance. Employees later described how a system of alarm bell signals was worked out and clerks were instructed to mass at entrances to repel an attack by Reds, if one took place. Sentiment among the clerks was divided. Some took it as an amusing joke and related the story with peals of laughter. Others seriously believed that mobs of the "lower classes," armed with pitchforks and brickbats, might storm the revolving doors any minute.

Hotels continued serving meals to guests as well as they could, but they closed their dining rooms to the public. For the most part guests had to shift for themselves, prepare meals, make beds, run the elevators, and wash their own socks.

Hundreds of persons put on roller skates and solved their transportation problem by turning the streets into giant rinks.

Across the bay in Piedmont, an exclusive residential city devoted to wealthy homes, businessmen armed themselves and placed the locality in a state of siege. Two hundred and fifty of them were sworn in as special deputies. Clad in golf knickers and hunting jackets, and flourishing revolvers, shotguns, and rifles, they blocked the entrances to all streets, stopping automobiles and persons for examination.

A partial walkout was already in effect in Oakland, Alameda, and Berkeley, where complete general strikes were scheduled for Tuesday, July 17.

The mediation board now began appealing to employers to include the seamen in their arbitration offer. This was the first time that any realistic attitude had been taken toward the workers' demands that all crafts be considered before anyone settled.

Mayor Rossi, on the afternoon of the 16th, announced the appointment of a "citizens' committee" of 500 men to deal with the situation. The committee was composed entirely of prominent businessmen, members of the Industrial Association and the Chamber of Commerce. They immediately composed an "Americanism pledge" in which the signer vowed to devote his whole energy toward putting down a revolution. These printed pledge cards were distributed by the thousands to business leaders who took them around the offices and handed them to their white-collar workers to sign.

Meanwhile an unexpected embarrassment occurred with the arrival in town of General Hugh S. Johnson, head of the National Recovery Administration. Newspapers and employers viewed his coming with great nervousness. One of the most awkward features of the plan to decry the strike as a Red revolution and suppress it on those grounds was that the federal government consistently ridiculed such an idea. If General Johnson took a similar stand it would put a pretty sharp pin in their red balloon.

A year later General Johnson wrote a book called *The Blue Eagle From Egg To Earth* in which he explained his presence in San Francisco:

... the Secretary of Labor sent my Assistant for Labor, Eddie McGrady (who was also Assistant Secretary of Labor) out there. I am not criticizing that, although as events turned out it was bad judgment.... He ran into a mare's nest, seeming almost to reach agreement on one day only to find himself frustrated the next. I knew what he was doing in a casual way because if there was one thing I had promised myself it was that I would not stick my neck out on that one and he also urged me very strongly to the same effect.

The main point I want to make here is that my arrival in San Francisco on the 15th had nothing whatever to do with that strike. That itinerary was a swing clear around the country in an airplane. It included ten cities and the San Francisco date was fixed by the award to me of a Phi Beta Kappa key from that chapter at my alma mater, the University of California.

When I got to Portland I saw the first results of a general strike. In my speech there I declared I would have nothing to do with it....

Earl Burke, in the July 28, 1934, issue of *Editor and Publisher*, in describing the adventures of the Newspaper Publishers' Council under the leadership of Hearst attorney John Francis Neylan, described General Johnson's arrival thus:

It was evident to the publishers that he might undo all the publishers' council was trying to accomplish. He proposed to grant the request of the general strike committee that the longshoremen's demands for complete control of hiring halls [be accepted] as a condition before any discussion of arbitration should occur. But he was informed this would be a compromise with revolution. Mr. Neylan and the publishers' council sat up with General Johnson until 3 o'clock Tuesday morning giving him a picture of the crisis....

From what follows it would appear that the General was greatly desirous of inserting himself into the situation. Burke continues:

The General quieted down when specifically informed that his tactics had been such that the people of California might have to decide to get along without him. In fact, had decided to get along without him and inasmuch as he had no credentials authorizing him to act for the President in this matter they might even have to ask him to leave San Francisco.... He [later] remarked this was the first time he had "ever been up against a newspaper oligarchy."

General Johnson's good nature is apparent by the fact that even though Neylan had to threaten to run him out of town if he did not bend to the will of the publishers' council, Johnson bore him no ill will. In his book Johnson said:

In my opinion, Jack Nyland [sic] was the man who held that situation in hand during twenty-four hours of the most tense period I have ever lived through. He and I had a beautiful fight at our first conference but I left that place with a great respect for that man and we were in perfect agreement.

The Blue Eagle From Egg To Earth, which Johnson prefaced with the legend: "Everybody in the world's a Rink-Stink but Hughie Johnson and he's all right," also contained the General's personal impressions of the General Strike:

I did not know what a general strike looked like and I hope that you may never know. I soon learned and it gave me cold shivers. We were flying a big army plane which could not land at Presidio on the San Francisco side so we landed on the Oakland side of the Bay expecting to take an automobile to San Francisco. There just weren't any automobiles. The general strike had closed the filling stations and paralyzed the transportation of the city. I took a small plane to the Presidio where General Craig —my captain for many years in the old army—let me use his car to get to town. I had lived several years in San Francisco and what I saw shocked me—physically. The food supply of the population was practically shut off, except by the individual grace and permit of a general strike committee run by an alien communist. Even hotel dining rooms were closed and street cars were held up. A barber at the Palace Hotel sneaked in and offered to "bootleg" me a haircut! The economic life of the city was being strangled. There was fear that the power, light and water supply would be shut off. A foreign enemy could scarcely threaten more than that. Eddie McGrady met me and told that he saw no hope for a settlement. On their own notion, several responsible union labor leaders came to see me. Though they were reticent, it was perfectly apparent, in talking to them, that they had no sympathy with the general strike and that they were being controlled by the influence on some of the men of one Bridges, an avowed communist and a citizen of Australia, and that what they most wanted was to break that influence.

About this time I learned that the University of California had canceled my speech in the Greek Theater for fear I might be injured by communists and there was no police protection because the whole force was needed to watch the situation in Berkeley.

Of course, I could not stand for that. It would have been an acknowledgment that there actually was a communist domination and that an officer of the government was afraid of it. It would have had a serious effect along the Coast and perhaps throughout the country. I insisted on making the speech and while that did not move the Dean, Jack Nyland [sic], whom I shall later introduce, got on the telephone and finally persuaded him.

Not only did Johnson make his Phi Beta Kappa acceptance speech in the Greek Theater. In addition it was broadcast over a radio hookup. The speech was devoted entirely to the General Strike, about which he said, "It is a threat to the community. It is a menace to the government. It is civil war."

The government did not agree with him at all, and when he got back to Washington he got his ears scorched good and plenty by

Madame Perkins and others. In fact, this speech started Johnson on his long downward slide which ended in his resignation.

In seeking to explain his reasons for inserting himself into the situation, Johnson casts some interesting reflections upon the employers, Governor Merriam, and the National Guard:

> As a matter of fact the contestants in the general strike did not want to deal with the President's Board, and the employers would not have dealt with it at all. I called the governor and he told me that he was going to declare martial law next day (the day the general strike was broken). I pleaded with him not to do that. In the tension that existed it would have resulted inevitably in bloodshed on a very broad scale. When you put a loaded rifle into the hands of an amateur soldier he is naturally pretty apt to think that it is for some purpose and when you suspend civil law in a region where a whole community—not just some employer and his employees—are in a state of electrical high tension, something explosive is almost certain to happen. Why, we did not even declare martial law during the Fire in San Francisco, although troops were freely used. After regular troops came in nobody was hurt but in some National Guard zones several people were shot.

Newspapers picked up Johnson's statement that the General Strike was "civil war" and made abundant use of it in their campaign. About the same time William Green, president of the American Federation of Labor, issued a statement from Washington declaring the General Strike as "unauthorized." In still another statement he inferred that the whole thing was being engineered from Moscow. All these utterances were given tremendous emphasis and were used as a battering ram against public opinion.

Meanwhile the General Strike Committee, consisting of about 900 delegates, was in almost continual session in the Labor Temple on Sixteenth Street. From the very start a verbal battle raged hotly between the conservatives and the progressives.

The conservatives were alarmed by the strike and wanted to shave it down by the gradual restoration of business. The progressives wanted to organize all essential services within control of the strike committee in order that the strike hold out until victory.

The progressives, though a minority, had one advantage: they could speak their minds freely. The conservatives, in a constant state of anxiety, had to keep up a pretense of militance and advance their purpose by a series of stratagems and devices. It was the extraordinary situation of a majority, scared to death of a minority, and having to maneuver with kid gloves. For this particular minority had the vast majority of outside mass sentiment on its side.

Many of the conservatives were exactly what the word implies: conservative. But the top salaried officials of the Labor Council who headed the conservative faction were in constant touch with Mayor Rossi, the mediation board, the Industrial Association, the Newspaper Publishers' Council, and the Waterfront Employers' Union. They held continual secret conferences with these interests and acted within the strike committee as virtual agents of the employers.

Conduct of the strike had been placed in the hands of a committee of twenty-five who were hand-picked and appointed by the top officials. They could depend upon this committee to carry out their wishes. As a consequence, although the progressives succeeded many times in putting through resolutions that would have organized the distribution of food, the regulation of housing, and the prevention of profiteering within the hands of the strikers, these resolutions were either ignored or only partially carried out by the committee of twenty-five.

The first step in loosening the strike was the partial restoration of municipal streetcar service. Like the employees of the Belt Line Railroad, these carmen were under civil service status and stood to lose jobs and pension privileges if they went out on strike. As a matter of fact, they never did go out on strike officially. They never took any strike vote. Simply, by a mutual understanding, they all decided not to show up for work on Monday morning, and as a result the tie-up was complete and effective.

The Public Utilities Commission met early in the morning and issued a statement that if the carmen did not come to work immediately they would be fired and lose all privileges automatically. The strike committee, with its gigantic power, could easily have ignored this threat. They could have made full restoration of jobs and status of the municipal carmen a provision of the ending of the strike. Instead, after a long and bitter dispute, the conservatives pushed through a resolution instructing the carmen to go back to work. Even so the municipal lines were only a small part of the city's street railway service. The main line, the Market Street Railway, was still out. But appearance of the big gray cars back in service gave a definite feeling that the strike was on the wane.

On the night of July 16 Governor Merriam broadcast a radio speech over a coast-wise network that conformed precisely to the plan of the newspaper council under Neylan's leadership. The Governor said:

Fully as much as the employers in this state, the workers have been handicapped and exploited by known communists and professional agitators—

men and women who cloak their sinister purposes under hypocritical appeals for human rights, but whose actual purpose is revolution, violent, bloody and destructive.

It is the plotting of such aliens and vicious schemers—not the legitimate and recognized objects of bona fide American workers—that has intensified, magnified and aggravated our labor problems. . . .

Let us be temperate in speech and in action; but above all let us be true to the standards and traditions of an Americanism that counts no cost too great for the protection of the principles and ideals which have governed our people for more than a century and a half.

Next day the strike committee authorized the opening of some thirty-two additional restaurants, which gave increased weight to the feeling that the strike was on the decline.

On the same afternoon the Joint Marine Strike Committee informed the mediation board that they would submit to arbitration on two conditions only: that a union hiring hall be granted to the longshoremen, and that the demands of the seamen be arbitrated also.

Daily papers now published prominent stories designed to discourage the idea of a general strike. "ALL U. S. MASS STRIKES HAVE ENDED IN FAILURE," one was headed. "CANADA'S ONE GENERAL STRIKE WAS FAILURE," said another on the same page. Turn the page and another confronted the reader: "MAJOR STRIKES RECORDED AS FAILURES."

During all this period President Roosevelt was cruising and fishing in the Hawaiian Islands on the warship "Houston." He discarded as nonsense all assertions that the strike in San Francisco was revolution, merely stated that good sense would prevail, and he was confident the mediation board would find some solution to the matter.

Late in the afternoon of the 17th, after a long and turbulent session, the strike committee put through a resolution by a vote of 207 to 180, advising employers and maritime unions to submit all issues in dispute to unconditional arbitration by the President's board. The resolution was passed against strong objections from every maritime delegate present. Later there were complaints that it had been railroaded through by a standing vote in which the count was highly dubious. Although effective as a propaganda instrument for loosening the strike, this resolution did not effect anything, since it was merely advice and imposed no compulsion on either side.

CHAPTER XVI
The Anti-Red Raids,
500 Jailed

WITH ALL THE EXCITED proclamations of public officials and the press urging calmness in the most inflammatory language possible, San Francisco was exceptionally peaceful during the first day and a half of the General Strike. This was not a little embarrassing to those who had proclaimed insurrection. A bloody revolution had been advertised and was not forthcoming. A communist army was declared marching on San Francisco, and it never arrived. The National Guard was out on the waterfront in full force with machine guns, gas equipment, automatic rifles, barbed wire, hand grenades, tanks, and light artillery. But their only encounters had been swatting flies. Some of them had been caught fishing off the end of the docks with lines attached to their bayoneted rifles. Once in a while a curious pedestrian would stray into the zone of martial law and sentries would open fire. But this was hardly fair game for such an array of military power. Something had to be done to justify the militant "patriotism" of officials and employers.

On the afternoon of the 17th the National Guard blocked off both ends of Jackson Street from Drumm to Front with machine guns mounted on trucks. The headquarters of the Marine Workers' Industrial Union was located halfway down the block. When the two ends of the street were sealed, police moved in with clubs swinging. They arrested seventy-five persons who were in the hall, then smashed everything in the place. Furniture was chopped up, windows knocked out, fixtures ripped up, and typewriters smashed. When they were finished nothing remained but a heap of kindling and a vast litter of papers.

From here they moved to the ILA soup kitchen at 84 Embarcadero. Uniformed and plainclothes police combed the line of men, weeding out those resembling, in their opinion, foreigners or Reds and loading them into the patrol wagon. At the station they were booked for vagrancy and thrown in jail.

The Workers' Ex-Servicemen's League, with a majority of unemployed veterans, had its headquarters in a vacant lot on Howard Street between Third and Fourth. An open-air meeting was in progress when the police arrived. The raiding contingent lit into the men with clubs and placed 150 under arrest. Then they systematically wrecked everything on the premises.

From here the flying squadron moved uptown and carried out a series of raids that lasted throughout the day. Scores of buildings and homes were entered and wrecked in a manner so methodical and consistent that it smacked of modern business efficiency. Even in their most vehement rage they moved with the smooth-clicking precision of an Elliott-Fisher billing machine.

Agents of the Industrial Association's intelligence bureau rode with the police, filling out numbered forms recording exact time of each raid, names of men arrested, and other data.

The plan of attack was identical in every instance. A caravan of automobiles containing a gang of men in leather jackets, whom newspapers referred to as "citizen vigilantes," would draw up to the curb in front of a building. They would let fly a hail of bricks, smashing all windows, and then crash into the place, beating up anyone they found, wrecking all furniture, hacking pianos to pieces with axes, throwing typewriters out of windows, and leaving the place a shambles.

Then they would get back into their cars and drive off. The police would arrive immediately, arrest the men who had been beaten up, and take command of the situation.

[160]

Earlier in the day someone had tipped off the Communist Party as to what was coming, so that not many persons were found in their halls and headquarters. Three men found in the Workers' Open Forum at 1223 Fillmore Street were slugged so unmercifully the police had to send them to the Central Emergency Hospital after placing them under arrest.

Offices of the *Western Worker* were deserted when the vigilantes arrived. The building faced on Civic Center, a stone's throw from the City Hall, and contained a bookstore and the main offices of the local Communist Party. The raiders spent their rage on furniture and fixtures, throwing articles through windows and smashing everything they could lay hands on. Large quantities of communist pamphlets were thrown out in the street where winds picked them up and distributed them far and wide in true comradely spirit.

At 121 Haight Street, a large three-story building that once had been the Young Men's Hebrew Association was now a Workers' School where classes in Marxism and trade unionism were conducted. Here the vigilantes wrought havoc on the first floor, but when they attempted to mount the narrow staircase leading to the upper stories they were confronted by the huge bulk of David Merihew, an ex-serviceman who worked as a caretaker in the building. Merihew brandished an old cavalry saber in one hand and a bayonet in the other. Flourishing his weapons he beckoned to them to come ahead. They took a few steps forward and he slashed out with his saber, taking a huge chip out of the banister. The raiders discreetly retired and left the field to the police, to whom Merihew surrendered after striking a bargain with them not to turn him over to the vigilantes if he yielded his weapons.

Across the street and down about a block was the headquarters of Upton Sinclair's "Epic Plan." Apparently the "finger" had been put on this location also, because the records of the Industrial Association state: ". . . and also an attack on Upton Sinclair's Headquarters on Haight Street near 121." (Report No. 300.) Still another entry read: "There were no police in the crowd storming Communist Headquarters at 37 Grove Street, 121 Haight Street, and the Upton Sinclair Headquarters." (Report No. 296.)

These reports were evidently written out ahead of time in anticipation because, as it happened, there was no raid at all on the Sinclair headquarters. The vigilantes either slipped up on their schedule in the excitement or else shied off at the last minute. For another thing, they had to clear out to make way for the police, and it would not have looked right, while the police were taking over 121 Haight Street, for the supposedly unknown and elusive vigilantes to be smashing up a building right across the street.

But if they missed out on one job, they were thorough enough elsewhere. When they had finished with it the Mission Workers' Neighborhood House at 741 Valencia Street looked as if it had been battered by artillery fire. The cavalcade moved from building to building all over town, and when the list of organizational headquarters was exhausted, they started in on private residences. Homes were looted, wrecked, and left in shambles as thoroughly and methodically as halls. By nightfall the jail was packed with some 300 suspected communists, all charged with vagrancy.

Raids of this kind continued for many days and eventually spread through all the towns and cities up and down the Pacific Coast.

Across the bay in Oakland the raids had begun a day earlier. Police announced they had information that the communists were arming. Every communist hall or headquarters in the East Bay was raided and wrecked. No weapons of any sort were found, but scores of men and women were crammed into the jails.

San Francisco papers carried a warning:

"Keep the streets clear of loafers and vagrants."
That order, issued by Police Chief William J. Quinn, early today had resulted in the arrest of 200 men. All were booked at city prison as vagrants or "drunks."
The police are under orders to pick up every man found on the streets who cannot give a good account of himself. The order is effective from sundown to dawn.
Bond for those charged with vagrancy was set at $1,000 each. Police cruising about the city last night arrested every man who was unable to give a good reason for being on the streets.

This was the famous "$1,000 vag law" which the Atherton report revealed as a device for "rousting" underworld characters to make them come through with a "shake-down."

In reporting the raids some newspapers declared the vigilantes were members of the Teamsters' Union. These accusations were vigorously denied by the union. Police said they didn't know who the men were but believed they were "aroused citizens."

It was not until months later that information gradually leaked out as to their identity. Raiders began describing their exploits "in confidence" to friends and acquaintances. Many of them were strikebreakers brought in from Los Angeles by the Industrial Association to run the scab trucks on the waterfront. A lesser number were businessmen, bank managers, and adventurous members of the industrialists' white-collar staffs.

Police announced that they acted absolutely independently in the raids. The simultaneous attacks by vigilantes, and the action of the National Guard in barricading both ends of Jackson Street, were reported as unexplainable coincidences.

Newspapers exulted in the vandalism and praised the vigilantes for their day's work. Side by side with accounts of the smashing of halls and headquarters, anti-communist statements of the most bloodthirsty variety were featured. Typical of these was the pronouncement of Michael F. Shannon, newly installed Grand Exalted Ruler of the Benevolent and Protective Order of Elks, who declared it his intention to mobilize the full strength of his fraternal order into "shock troops to combat and exterminate those who would destroy the business of this country, disrupt forever family relations, abolish religion, liquidate American institutions and tear down the flag."

Mayor Rossi issued a statement:

I pledge to you that as Chief Executive in San Francisco I will, to the full extent of my authority, run out of San Francisco every Communist agitator, and this is going to be a continuing policy in San Francisco.

It may appear that the situation threw an excessive strain on the Mayor's creative powers, so many statements, proclamations, and declarations issued over his signature. But the Mayor maintained a battery of secretaries, expert in the composition of these utterances. Maurice Rapheld, sercetary number one, generally handled the more important pronouncements. Eneas Kane, secretary number two, usually took care of breakfast club, luncheon, and banquet speeches. Malcolm Fraser, secretary number three, specialized in telegrams and letters to women's clubs.

Heaviest emphasis in the press was laid on the phrase "alien agitators," and the central theme was a clamor for their immediate deportation. Communists and aliens were practically synonyms in the language of public officials and the newspapers.

Before the raiding was over, more than 450 persons were packed into the city jail which had been built to accommodate 150. Out of these no more than a dozen turned out to be deportable aliens, and of these no more than three were connected in any way with communist activities. Considering the fact that over a third of the population of San Francisco is foreign-born, this was really remarkable.

Only a small percentage of those arrested were communists at all. Most of them were just people who happened to get in the way of the stampeding anti-radical squad.

One man, when asked at the police station if he was a communist, said, "Hell no. I'm a Baptist."

A morbid comedy took place in the civic courts on the morning of July 18. Attorney George Anderson of the International Labor Defense appeared as representative for the 350 prisoners then behind bars, and declared that each and every one was entitled to a separate jury trial. The cost of such a procedure would literally have drained the public treasury.

Judge Lazarus almost exploded in his chair when confronted with the proposition. He wanted to try them all in a mob. "It's ridiculous," he fumed. "I believe all these men should be tried at once by the trial judge. If they don't like the verdicts, they can appeal."

Anderson pointed out that all these men and women had been arrested while following peaceful pursuits and that a mass trial would be illegal.

"Stepping out of my judicial role," said Lazarus, "I say these men are probably acting to further disturb the industry of the city. They are undesirable citizens, ready to pounce down in time of storm. I recognize we are existing in a time of public peril and I am going to keep that in mind. These men are enemies of the state and government." Then turning to Attorney Anderson, "And if you talk too much, you will be in contempt of court."

This adequately convinced the prisoners that in the mind of the trial judge they were convicted already, and their only hope lay in jury trials. Despite his wrath Judge Lazarus had to continue their cases. The only other alternative would have been to dismiss them, and in his prevailing mood, such a course did not appeal to him.

The Police Department denied that police participated in any of the wrecking. Many times they stated that communists had returned later and smashed their own properties in order to discredit the police. Such denials and countercharges, however, were made with tongue in cheek. Newspapers contained full-page spreads of photographs showing police industriously destroying property in the places they raided.

"The Communist Party is through in San Francisco," said Captain J. J. O'Meara, head of the police anti-radical and crime prevention bureau. "The organization can't face such adverse public sentiment."

That night communist leaflets were distributed thickly throughout the city. Although its surface apparatus had been smashed, the party itself was not seriously affected. All halls and public headquarters had been wrecked and known communists could not show their faces without being arrested. In the preceding weeks usual rallying places and the homes of party leaders had been spotted and reported to the police by stoolpigeons. Police crouched in doorways and around corners ready to pounce on anyone attempting to enter such places.

The Communist Party numbered in its ranks mechanics, longshoremen, seamen, streetcar conductors, printers, laborers, store clerks, delivery boys, college students, stenographers, doctors, lawyers, school teachers, musicians, salesmen, housewives, members of the unemployed, newspaper reporters, bookkeepers, and persons of every conceivable calling. Their influence reached almost everywhere. On the whole, it could be compared with a small plant having tremendous roots. When this vast apparatus swung into action behind the maritime workers it was able to rally enormous support not only in seaports but hundreds of miles inland. The members were not mere dues-paying adherents but active participants in the party work, each one having his own duties and responsibilities.

The popular police conception of a communist was a shaggy man with a stubble beard and a foreign accent. As a consequence their dragnet picked up every man they could lay their hands on whose suit needed pressing. The only real communists arrested were those seized in private homes or who had been spotted in advance. Within the city jail they organized a veritable college of Marxism among the countless unfortunates who were brought in, and carried on active recruiting in the cell blocks. They organized mass singing and other forms of demonstration that nearly drove the turnkeys out of their minds. Crowded to three times its normal capacity, the jail became almost a nightmare—a sort of man-made purgatory into which life's less fortunate were packed like sardines.

The most serious handicap the communists experienced was the crippling of their newspaper, the *Western Worker*. On the eve of the raids they had announced they were increasing publication to twice weekly instead of once weekly. Shortly thereafter the editorial offices were wrecked, the composition shop where the paper was made up was set on fire, and the commercial printer who usually ran it off on his presses was warned that if he did so again his plant would be demolished. The editors and writers were being hunted by the police and did not dare show their faces too prominently.

While party representatives were scouring the city to find a printer who would run off the paper, a mimeographed edition was prepared and distributed. Every printer in town had been warned against accepting the job, and they were unable to find one who would take a chance on it.

Finally they located an old flat-bed printing press and a linotype in a remote part of town. The machinery was antiquated and had been out of commission for a long time. It was doubtful whether it could be put in shape again. Party mechanics set to work on it and after twenty-four hours of continuous work had it running at a low degree of efficiency.

Editors and writers set up makeshift offices in private homes and were pouring out the necessary copy. A score or more of men were ransacking the town for odds and ends of needed parts and type lead to feed the linotype. The old flat-bed press had no modern devices. They had to feed it by hand and peel it by hand and could print only one side of one sheet at a time. An enormous amount of hand labor was required. Nevertheless they succeeded in getting out the first twice-weekly edition on schedule, and continued thereafter without interruption. Only one issue ever appeared in mimeograph form.

Once the paper was printed they faced another serious problem. The paper was legal in every respect, had second-class mailing privileges, and once they could get it into the hands of the U. S. Post Office delivery would be assured. The difficulty was to keep it from falling into the hands of local authorities. The Post Office where they had to deliver it was located right on the Embarcadero, which made the task still more hazardous. A careful study of the most favorable hour was made, and a few men ran the gantlet successfully in an old car.

While all this was going on a group of unidentified men were busy with hammers and nails in Hayward, one of the towns across the bay, erecting a scaffold in the public park opposite the City Hall. It had the customary thirteen steps leading up to it, a large knotted noose, and a sign: "REDS BEWARE!" It was put up, the police said, during the night wthout their knowledge.

Since such a structure could be raised in the dark of night without attracting the police, it would be equally logical to suppose that thieves could dismantle the City Hall itself and make off with it without fear of detection.

Mayor McCracken of Oakland announced he had sworn in 3,000 citizen vigilantes. An additional 500 were mobilized in Berkeley and 500 more in Alameda.

Raids and arrests were continuing in full swing despite the fact that jails in most towns were already packed far beyond capacity. In

Berkeley flying squadrons of vigilantes toured the city in cars, throwing bricks through windows of residences where suspected communists were supposed to live. A note was attached to each brick:

Leave this community immediately or drastic action will be taken.

Members of a committee of Berkeley citizens organized for the purpose of purging the city of communists, bolsheviks, radicals, agitators and other anti-government groups, hereby notify you that you are known to be directly linked with this group that is trying to destroy our government.

We further warn you to leave this community immediately or drastic means will be taken.

A typical newspaper report read:

In San Jose, a crowd of 300 vigilantes, cruising around Santa Clara County in automobiles, captured ten known communist leaders, beat them severely and threatened:

"This is just a sample of what you'll get—if you're not out of here by dawn."

The "vigilantes" met secretly, the roll was called, and pick handles were passed out with instructions to use them.

Moving swiftly, the raiders surrounded three residences just before dawn and forced their way in. They picked up John O'Rourke, alleged communist leader, and nine of his followers and also seized a quantity of communist literature.

After two hours of rigid questioning at a "vigilante" headquarters four of the ten captives were whisked out of town and told to "beat it—and beat it fast!" The other six, admitted aliens, were turned over to authorities in San Francisco for deportation.

Berkeley police reported finding two communist halls literally torn to pieces.

Led by a "Citizens Committee of Twenty-Five," a crowd of 300 men first stormed the Finnish "Tovari Tupa" hall, 1819 Tenth Street, Berkeley.

Swinging clubs, the raiders sent the occupants fleeing and then wrecked the two-story building—smashing four pianos, tearing down the railings, splintering the furniture and ripping out the upstairs plumbing. When police arrived water was flooding down the stairs.

From there the crowd hurried to a communist hall at 2600 San Pablo Avenue, tore IWW posters from the walls, smashed every window and left the place a wreck.

In San Francisco, when the raiders crashed into a hall at 1213 Fillmore Street where the strike benefit dances and entertainments had been held, they found an entertainment device similar to those seen at amusement beaches, where rows of stuffed figures are ranged along shelves for patrons to aim baseballs. In this instance the figures were hairy goblins marked: "Michael Casey—Rossi—Joe Ryan—Vandeleur—Bill Green—Hearst," and others.

A photograph of this array was printed in the *Chronicle* as an example of the hideous entertainments of the Reds.

Even as late as July 21 the *Examiner* came out with headlines: "ENTIRE STATE FIGHTS RED PERIL."

For many days men were simply hauled in off the streets, thrown in jail and left to sleep on the hard floor while newspapers proclaimed that the "Red Menace" was locked in a cage. Later on authorities began to examine their catch.

After scrutinizing the prisoners more closely, Judge Sylvain Lazarus, who had previously denounced them as "enemies of the state and government," underwent a complete reversal of sentiment. He discovered that these men had been arrested, not because they had committed any wrong, but because the police did not like their faces.

"I am disgusted to think that this good old town should have acted like a pack of mad wolves," he said as he apologized to the prisoners and set them free. "I do not know who is responsible, but it should be traced back to its source. Boys never before arrested were thrown in jail for a week. Aging men were also subjected to that humiliation. My heart bleeds for them." He dug down in his pocket and handed fifty-cent pieces to the most destitute as he turned them loose.

"I will stay here all night," he said, "rather than see these unfortunate human beings spend another hour in jail. They have been incarcerated a week already.

"If it had been the son of a leading financier caught in that Howard Street lot there would have been such a stir it would have turned the town upside down."

Out of 101 cases which he had heard on the evening of July 23, Judge Lazarus dismissed 84, continued 11, and set trials for 6 who demanded a jury.

These men had been arrested for no reason at all, except to fill the jail with rumpled-looking men in order to give credence to the theory that a Red revolution had been put down. Nevertheless they were all charged with being vagrants. And it was here that Judge Lazarus combined a personal political prejudice with humanitarian decency. The men whom he released, who had been arrested for vagrancy, were definitely vagrants in every sense of the word. They were penniless, homeless, and without visible means of support. They were vagrants arrested for vagrancy, and he apologized to them and sent them back to their vagrancy.

But the seventeen men and women whom he sent back to the cells, who had been arrested on the same charge, were not vagrants by any stretch of the imagination. They were people of established residence in the community. One was an honor student from the University of California and another was a young writer for whom publishers' representatives from New York were searching at the very moment she was languishing in the city jail. But these people were suspected of being communists. Communists were equally as legal as Democrats or Republicans, but Judge Lazarus did not like them. He was of an opposite political viewpoint so he sent them back to their cells.

J. W. Mailliard, Jr. president of the Chamber of Commerce, was greatly indignant at Judge Lazarus' actions. He composed a form letter which was printed in all newspapers and sent out to local businessmen, together with an "Americanism Pledge Card." It read:

Wholesale release of Communists with apologies to them for their arrest supply whatever fresh proof may be needed to convince the public of its duty to suppress radicalism. If it is "mob hysteria" to prosecute the forces that have been responsible for our troubles, then it is "mob hysteria" to uphold the constituted authority of our government.

Lazarus replied with a flat statement that the men arrested were not agitators, but merely hungry men. In explaining his handing out of fifty-cent pieces, he said, "They wanted to return to jail because they didn't have a place to sleep. The money would at least enable them to get a night's lodging."

Judge George J. Steiger, who also heard the cases of men arrested in the raids, did not share Judge Lazarus' humanitarian views. He said, "Law and order must prevail. This is a conflict between law and order on one side, the government of our city, the state, and nation on one side, and a few irresponsible destroyers on the other side, who would tear down all that is sacred."

In the later vice-graft investigation it was revealed that Judge Steiger pocketed rent from a house of prostitution which he owned at 362 Kearny Street. The investigation disclosed also that rents collected from such establishments were so excessively high that no man could own one and not know the purposes for which it was being used.

Permanent vigilante organizations were being formed in all towns and cities. Vehement demands were made that public libraries be "purged" of all allegedly Red books. Other patriots wanted to reorganize the public school system on a basis of rigid censorship to make certain that no Red ideas were lurking in the primers. Some urged the institution of concentration camps, either in Alaska or on the peninsula of Lower California, to which all communists would be exiled.

Practically all literature pertaining to strikes, Russia, social reforms, economics, or the depression, was regarded as communistic propaganda.

Printers were warned against turning out anything for the Communist Party, and all landlords were cautioned against renting their premises for communist meetings.

Ruth McCord, director of relief work in Contra Costa County, began patriotically striking all persons from relief rolls who were suspected of "communistic leanings." Among the unemployed she was known as "Buzzard McCord." Not long afterwards it was discovered that she was not only embezzling funds, but made a racket of forcing unemployed women to undergo sterilization operations and enter houses of prostitution. She fled the county and became a fugitive from justice.

Dr. Claude Church, a retired lieutenant colonel of marines, and president of the Oakland Chapter of the National Sojourners, demanded of the San Francisco Board of Supervisors that they ban all communist books from the public libraries. He received the terse reply that as soon as the board could get around to it they would read all the books in the county libraries.

John Boynton, librarian of Oakland, declared, "It would be impossible to ban all so-called communistic literature. There is not a modern book on government, economics, or sociology that does not deal with Soviet theories."

Dr. Church decided to choose an example. He picked *Red Virtue,* a book about the Soviet Union written by Ella Winter, wife of Lincoln Steffens, and proclaimed it a volume likely to undermine the patriotic principles of Oakland citizens. He demanded its immediate removal from library shelves.

To this, Librarian Boynton replied, "It is odd that *Red Virtue* should draw such fire at this time when only recently the ultra-conservative Commonwealth Club of San Francisco pronounced the widely read volume as excellent literature.

"True, the book treats Russia and her people from a sympathetic viewpoint, but when the President of the United States sees fit to recognize the present Russian government, certainly a book about the country and its people should not be regarded with distrust."

In some localities the vigilante forces felt the need of more evidence to convince the public at large that a Red revolution was in progress and that raids and sluggings were necessary. An extraordinarily absurd leaflet was turned out on a mimeograph in San Diego and scattered through the streets. It was liberally decorated with hammers and sickles and read:

Join The - Communist
Down With Capitol
Mexican—Negro—Foreing Born—And All Workers—Teachers And Students
Combat the rich, and all FASCIST movements. By arming—Fighting—Rape—Loot—Burn—Over throw all forms of GOVERNMENTS— — — — —
Talk is cheap and does not help the working class. ACTION is needed in the form of World Revolution and overthrow to gain the working class their rights
DEMAND your rights thru ACTION—Organize and ARM in your vicinity, Regardless of RACE—and Creed. Set up the Hammer and Cycle. The emblem of the working class.
What RUSSIA did, WE can do here in America. But do it now. Destroy the christian churches, down with Christienity—Down with the POLICE department—SHERRIFFS office—FASCIST movements, and all groups that oppose the COMMUNIST party—TIME FOR ACTION IS HERE. Wake up??."

Spelling and eccentric typing are reproduced here exactly as on the leaflet. It needs no expert to detect the forgery. Literally thousands of these were printed and handed out by the "League Against Communism" as samples of Red propaganda.

Meanwhile the Communist Party in all cities calmly moved back into their headquarters, swept out the broken glass, restocked their shelves with literature, and resumed "business as usual." While the anti-communist campaign was blazing at its highest, with newspapers printing such headlines as "LEGION ASKS DEATH PENALTY FOR REDS," the Communists launched their state election campaign.

A formal notice appeared in their newspaper advising vigilantes that shotgun squads now occupied all headquarters twenty-four hours a day. A few experimental forays soon established that this was true.

CHAPTER XVII
*General Johnson Takes
A Hand,
The General Strike Ends*

O N THE MORNING OF JULY 18, the third day of the General Strike, it was apparent that the walkout was loosening, and its collapse was a matter of time. Labor had risen to the occasion in a mighty upsurge that had reached its height and now, under the impact of blows from within, was about to recede. It was hoped in some quarters that once the tide turned, the maritime strike and all its demands would be washed down the hopper with the general return to work that would result at the conclusion of the giant walkout.

Businessmen who a few days earlier had been glad enough to obtain permits to transact a minimum amount of trade, now felt the turning tide and began to defy the strike committee. Oil companies asserted, "We are moving our products under the protection of constituted authorities and certainly have no intention of accepting so-called permits from anybody."

Scab drivers piloted trucks through the streets under heavy police guard. The amount of oil moved in this manner was not great; nevertheless it served as a means of weakening the morale of the strike.

The feverish activity of the city's employers during this stage is best described by Mr. Paul Eliel in the Industrial Association's official history.

It is absolutely impossible to attempt to describe here or outline in detail the innumerable conferences which took place between public officials, representatives of the press, publishers, shipowners, the Citizens' Committee, General Johnson and others. During the latter part of July 17 and during the entire day of July 18, running well into the night in each instance, conferences participated in by one or all of these groups were going on simultaneously in a half dozen places.

Some of these conferences were taking place in the offices of the Waterfront Employers' Union, some at the City Hall, some at the offices of the National Longshoremen's Board, and many at the Palace Hotel where a number of business groups had established temporary headquarters, and where General Johnson also made his headquarters during his stay in San Francisco.

All of these meetings, however, were directed toward two principal objectives. One of these was the continued mobilization and direction of public opinion in order to bring it to bear upon the organized labor movement of the city and force it to accept the loss of the general strike which was already indicated by its increasingly accelerated collapse. The other movement was designed to secure an extension of the military lines throughout the entire community and to prevail on Governor Merriam to declare martial law for the entire city and county of San Francisco.

Obvious weakening of the General Strike in San Francisco, manifested by the partial restoration of streetcar service and the opening of restaurants, had its effect in curtailing the East Bay General Strike which, by this time, was just on the upsurge. Plainly there was not much use in promoting general strikes elsewhere if the bans were to be let down in San Francisco. At least this was the attitude taken by labor in other sections. Likewise in Portland, where a general strike was just being organized, it was nipped in the bud by the relaxing of restrictions in San Francisco.

Senator Robert F. Wagner, from Washington, was in Portland at the time, making every effort to prevail upon members of the already elected Labor Strategy Committee to abandon plans for a general strike. It is doubtful if his persuasions would have been effective had it not been for the San Francisco letdown. This letdown, incidentally, was extremely trivial. Only a minute fraction of the city's business was restored. Nevertheless people were not viewing things soberly or precisely; therefore, the psychological effect was tremendous and all out of proportion to the facts. A pinhole in the dikes was regarded as a collapse of the dikes.

Meanwhile raids and arrests of suspected communists were proceeding in full fury and the press was blazing and crackling with the suppression of a communist revolt. Public attention was distracted from the business at hand and fascinated by the theatrics of the anti-radical sideshow.

Newspapers of the 19th carried front-page editorials declaring that both sides had agreed to arbitration and now was the time to go back to work. The *San Francisco News* editorial was typical:

WIND IT UP NOW!

For the first time since the issue between them was joined, no insuperable obstacle today stands between organized labor and the employers of San Francisco to interfere with a prompt and peaceful settlement of their differences.

Both sides have agreed to arbitration by the President's Board—the employers in a communication sent to the board on July 11, and the General Strike Committee by the resolutions adopted yesterday.

The rest of the editorial threatened the direst calamity to anyone opposing an immediate and unanimous return to work.

As a matter of fact, neither side had agreed to arbitration, as every informed person was aware. The employers had agreed to arbitrate the grievances of the longshoremen, but persistently refused to arbitrate with the seamen, who comprised a majority of the strikers. The resolution passed in the General Strike Committee was not an agreement to arbitrate, but merely an expression of sentiment. The General Strike Committee had no authority in the matter. Even the Joint Marine Strike Committee had no authority until the matter was put to a vote of the men; and they refused to put the matter to a vote until the arbitration proposition included the seamen.

At the very moment these editorials were appearing, representatives of the employers were informing the President's mediation board that they had no intention of arbitrating with the seamen. Thomas G. Plant, president of the Waterfront Employers' Union, said that he did not see how the shipowners could arbitrate unless elections were held to determine who was the bona fide spokesman for the seamen.

A. E. Boynton, managing director of the Industrial Association, said that the strikers should go back to work first, then it would be time to talk about arbitration.

Roger D. Lapham, president of the American Hawaiian Steamship Company, said he could see no reason why employers should arbitrate with the seamen at all.

Employers still held to their argument that a blanket agreement was impossible, and that the seamen and longshoremen would have to settle separately, and that separate agreements would have to be worked out between the different ports and different companies.

The strikers argued that if the employers were able to get together and cooperate so closely in order to break the strike, surely this same organization of interests could get together in coming to an agreement.

General Johnson was now established in the Palace Hotel in San Francisco, and had taken over the reins of the mediation board. Early on the afternoon of the 18th, while the conservatives in the General Strike Committee were busy loosening things by authorizing the opening of more stores and restaurants, Johnson issued an ultimatum that there would be no talk of settlement of any kind—arbitration or anything else—until the General Strike was called off.

"I am here," he said, "to do what the federal government can do to aid these coast committees to settle this trouble. It is their job in the first instance. But the federal government cannot act under the continuing coercion of a general strike. The first step to peace and agreement is to lift that strike. Until that is done, I have nothing to offer."

Afternoon papers picked up the statement and spread it over their front pages. The *Examiner* printed it under huge headlines: "BIG STRIKE BROKEN! FOOD AND GAS EMBARGO LIFTED!"

This does not jibe exactly with General Johnson's account in his *The Blue Eagle From Egg To Earth* which says:

Before I got back to San Francisco [from his speech in Berkeley—Q.] responsible union men had ousted several Communist leaders and within a few hours the general strike was broken.

This statement is difficult to understand because no one during this period had ousted anyone, communist or otherwise. He said also:

In all these negotiations John P. Nyland [sic], one of the ablest lawyers on the Coast, gave the responsible union leaders to understand that (while neither he nor I would talk composition of the Longshoremen's strike till the general strike was called off) when it should be called off, he would not only urge submission by employers to the President's Board, *but would represent the interests of the labor unions* before it. He is one of the most powerful advocates on the Coast, and these men trusted him.

This statement is even more difficult to understand. The maritime unions not only distrusted Neylan, but would sooner have had the Devil out of hell represent them than such a character. Neylan was the chief counsel for the Hearst press, and all of the maritime unions had ironclad rules that any of their members caught reading or possessing a Hearst paper would be subject to heavy fine, if not trial and expulsion.

A new angle of propaganda was inserted when newspapers began to publish statements and quotations from foreign papers to the effect that the General Strike and labor troubles nationally were the disastrous result of the NRA. This was the first spark of anti-New Deal propaganda on the Pacific Coast which, under the constant nursing of William Randolph Hearst, was to develop into a blistering fire of invective against President Roosevelt and his policies.

By the morning of July 19, the fourth day of the strike, the mentality of the city was mired in confusion. Conflicting statements and opinions were bandied about to such an extent that the man in the street could not possibly discern between fact and rumor. The newspapers were the only medium that had immediate access to the public brain. And while the majority of people did not place too much faith in the newspapers' reports, they had no other source of knowledge to check with at the moment.

The situation as reported in the press was that both sides had agreed to arbitration, and the Reds, who had been obstructing peace, were now incarcerated in the city jail.

This atmosphere of confusion enabled the conservatives within the General Strike Committee to move without fear that the rank-and-file union men would override or veto their decisions. The strong bloc of progressives within the committee had no means of reaching the public at large with their arguments. This was the weakest point in labor's front; it had no system of communication to keep its members and the public informed—no newspaper, no radio. As a consequence the strikers themselves had to depend on the employers' own publicity apparatus to know what was going on. Mimeographed and printed leaflets were generally depended on, but these could neither reach far enough nor quickly enough to keep pace with developments.

At 1:15 p.m. on July 19, after a turbulent all-day session, a resolution to call off the General Strike was put to a standing vote of the strike committee. It carried by a vote of 191 to 174.

Cries of "Swindle!" and "Faker!" immediately rose in the hall. A standing vote, when so closely divided, is a difficult thing to judge with the eye. The voters simply have to trust and hope in the officials on the platform, who eye the throng and waggle one finger while they supposedly count heads. If they want to be a bit careless or prejudiced in their own favor, there is no way of checking up on them. In this instance the conservatives did the counting.

Edward Vandeleur, Michael Casey, and other top officials had been up until midnight the night before in conference with General Johnson and representatives of the employers. Before going home they promised definitely to throw their full weight toward calling off the strike the next day.

As the delegates poured out of the Labor Temple they shouted to the waiting crowds that the vote had been a "swindle."

Newspapers hit the streets with extras declaring the strike had been "crushed" and "broken." Nothing had been crushed or broken. The strike had been systematically weakened and then called off by the conservative faction in the Labor Temple.

"Mayor Rossi," the *Examiner* reported, "danced around his office for joy when notified by Edward Vandeleur, president of the strike committee, that the strike was over."

Joseph P. Ryan wired from New York congratulating the Mayor "as one good pal to another," and also stated that the top officials of the Labor Council had called the General Strike, not against the employers, but to break the power of Harry Bridges and the Reds on the waterfront.

The Mayor promptly sat down and penned a happy proclamation:

I congratulate the real leaders of organized labor on their decision. San Francisco has stamped out without bargain or compromise an attempt to import into its life the very real danger of revolt.

San Francisco was founded by liberty-loving people. Its traditions are sacred to us. We will tolerate no tyranny, either of Communism or of any other interference with constituted authorities.

Employers, mediators, civic officials, and conservative labor leaders wiped hot necks with handkerchiefs and laughed with the relaxation of a long, nervous tension. Newspapers blossomed with photographs of laughing men shaking hands. And labor poured back into industry like a surf.

Effect of the strike's end was miraculous. Normal traffic returned to the streets, stores and theaters opened, restaurants began serving customers, and thirsty men swarmed into the barrooms. Within a few hours the city was restored to what, on the surface, looked like normalcy. It was hard to believe the thing had ever happened. Labor reached out its hand and instantly the silent corpse was returned to flashing vigor. Trucks rumbled through the streets, smoke appeared from chimneys, hammers sounded, whistles blew. The city shook off a dream.

But it was a convincing dream, and one not likely to be forgotten.

Labor withdrew its hand and all things ceased as abruptly as when the motor of a movie projector breaks and leaves the characters transfixed on the screen. Labor put back its hand, and the whole thing came to life. Labor began to regard its hand with a new respect. Here was a magic never before realized.

In the rush and excitement that accompanied the general return to work, it was difficult to say where it would stop or what the status would be when the sediment went to the bottom. Employers watched anxiously to see if the seamen, longshoremen, and teamsters would be swept along in the tide and carried back to work with the others. By the morning of the 20th the rumble quieted, the fog cleared away, and the scene could be examined. The strike of the maritime workers was as solid as ever and the teamsters were still boycotting the Embarcadero. In addition to this, the Market Street Railway employees had decided to remain out on strike for their own demands.

Although the municipal lines were restored to full operation, their service was limited and many neighborhoods were without streetcar transportation. A few of the green-and-white Market Street Railway cars were operating with scabs under heavy police guard, but they were not enough to count for much. Furthermore, the striking carmen were soaping the rails on down grades, and passengers did not feel safe to ride the scab cars.

Among the longshoremen there was a general sentiment of willingness to submit to arbitration, but they would not even ballot on the question until the seamen were included in the offer. Whether or not longshoremen would still demand control of the hiring hall as a condition to arbitration was uncertain, and could only be determined when the ballot was taken.

The status of the teamsters was also uncertain. As soon as the General Strike was called off, Michael Casey had telephoned to the Industrial Association assuring them that teamsters would return to hauling freight on the waterfront and would also handle the scab freight which was stored in the dummy warehouse where the artificial commerce carried on by scabs had been dumped. However, at a membership meeting that night Casey received such vehement opposition from the teamsters that he did not dare put the issue to a vote. Instead he substituted a motion calling for a secret ballot on the issue to be taken on the evening of the 20th.

The true facts surrounding the calling off of the General Strike were beginning to filter through to the rank and file of the unions and a far-flung rumble of discontent was manifesting itself. Newspapers continued to exult and "rub it in" with blatant declarations that the strike had been "smashed," "crushed," and "broken." San Francisco labor was proud, and all this did not set very well with it. An issue of the *Chronicle* carried headlines: "MASS STRIKE BROKEN! *Citizens Open Food, Gas Sales In Spite Of Unions.* Bridges Admits Defeat Of Plot To Starve City Into Surrender; Conservative Labor In Saddle."

From the employers' standpoint (if not from their point of view) all this undignified crowing was unwise. It was building up a resentment and contempt within the ranks of labor that would never be dissolved. No one had attempted to "starve" the city into surrender. Bridges was the foremost advocate of careful organization of adequate supplies for the populace, and all union men knew it. There was neither shrewdness nor sense in printing statements so ridiculous. On the whole, employers, through the lack of skill and intelligence on the part of their publicity directors, were destroying their strongest tools. They were discrediting their newspapers, making fools of their public officials, arousing the contempt of their workers, and undermining the very conservative labor leaders upon whom they depended for cooperation. And all this was to cost them very dearly in the near future.

Organized labor had just ended the most overwhelming demonstration of power and solidarity in American history, and was quite aware of it. If press agents had realized this and written their copy accordingly, they might have accomplished something.

Every union man in the city knew that the strike had not been "crushed." Every union man also knew that the arrest and incarceration of 450 unfortunates from Skid Row did not comprise the suppression of a Red Rebellion. And the spectacle of Vandeleur, Casey, and other top salaried officials joining hands with the employers and dancing around the table did not go well with them.

Governor Merriam issued a proclamation from Sacramento:

The sane, intelligent, right-thinking leadership in the labor organizations has prevailed over the rash counsel of communistic and radical agitators. . . .

California has served notice upon the radical disturber that his plotting will not be tolerated and is doomed to failure.

The fight against further meddlesome and subversive attacks on our economic and social institutions should now be pushed with vigor and determination. Every alien agitator and revolutionist in the state and nation should be deported.

After the entire city had been combed with a dragnet reinforced by

500 additional policemen, a dozen forlorn foreign-born workers sat in the city jail wondering what in the hell they had done. They had no more connection with the maritime strike or General Strike than you had. And only a few of them were ever deported.

The marine strikers issued a statement:

The Joint Marine Strike Committee, representing the longshoremen and maritime unions that have been on strike for over two months, desires to take this opportunity to express its sincere appreciation to the entire labor movement for its tremendous show of unity.

It became apparent to all organized labor that as the struggle of workers on the waterfront developed, this struggle was becoming more than a waterfront strike. The Industrial Association of San Francisco, by entering into the strike and by its use of force and brutal tactics, emphasized the realization in the minds of organized labor and its supporters that this Association was a destructive force, which has now been shown up in its true colors to the public.

The mass strike of organized labor in San Francisco and the united sympathy of the public at large with the strikers has proved conclusively that this city will not stand for an organization such as the Industrial Association, whose only aim is to destroy, in whatever manner it can, regardless of the monetary costs and the cost of lives, the rights of American workingmen.

The longshoremen and maritime workers feel more strengthened in their position today than at any time during the entire maritime strike. The tremendous cooperation received from the other organizations and from the public at large proves conclusively the justice of our position and points directly to the fact that the American people will give all so that American working men and women shall have the right to organize to strike for just aims.

The strike of the longshoremen and maritime unions is continuing and is stronger today than ever. Our position is fortified by the show of strength from the rest of organized labor and by the fact that the working men and women in this city refuse to be browbeaten by a group of unjust, misled employers, organized in the form of the Industrial Association of San Francisco, whose definite object is to destroy bona fide American labor organizations.

Michael Casey and John McLaughlin, president and secretary of the Teamsters' Union, conducted the balloting on the issue of the Embarcadero boycott. The ballot was worded:

The General Strike Committee has ordered all men on sympathy strike with the longshoremen to return to work. Are you in favor of returning to work.

Thus the men, when they read the ballots, did not know they were voting on the waterfront boycott. According to the wording they were voting on whether or not to continue the General Strike throughout the city, which was already called off anyhow. They voted yes. The majority when announced was 1,138 to 283.

While this was going on an extraordinary conference was taking place thirty-five miles away. Up to now employers had refused consistently to arbitrate with the seamen. But it was apparent to the more intelligent among them that this was a permanent and insurmountable obstacle to peace. The longshoremen under no circumstances would agree to betray the seamen, and unless the strike was settled quickly, the "victory" now being heralded in the newspapers would wear thin and become ridiculous. Paul Eliel, in the official Industrial Association record, describes the conference:

Early on the morning of July 20 representatives of the Waterfront Employers' Union, of the newspaper publishers, and the Industrial Association left San Francisco and went to Woodside, a community some 35 miles to the south, where John Francis Neylan, the western representative of the Hearst interests, has his home. Later this conference was joined by several representatives of the steamship companies. In a conference that lasted during the better part of the day and a portion of the evening, the question of steps to be taken in connection with the maritime strikes was discussed.

The length of this conference indicates the differences of opinion present. Some believed in a rigid and uncompromising stand that would "put the screws down" on the unions once and for all. Other employers present realized the artificial nature of the "victory." They appreciated that they were not confronted by a demoralized laboring class but that, on the contrary, organized labor in San Francisco had discovered its strength and was stirring restlessly. Continuation of the harsh policy that had been pursued on the waterfront might easily reopen the whole general strike issue; and the next time, the subterfuge of calling it a communist revolution would have little effect.

The enthusiasm of uptown employers in supporting the Industrial Association's fight against the maritime unions had definitely sagged. Their efforts so far had resulted in the General Strike, which had thrown the "fear of God" into them. Unions which had lain dormant for years had reawakened, were raising demands and giving evidence of struggle. Witness the Market Street Railway men who were now out. Workers who had never been organized before were forming unions. Witness the warehousemen and the newspapermen.

Employers generally wanted the waterfront strike settled and out of the headlines. They wanted to banish it from the minds and conversation of the populace. It had revitalized the whole labor movement and awakened public interest in labor conditions. Even their clerks were beginning to talk economics, sociology, and politics. The "reliable" officials of the unions had been vastly discredited by the whole affair and it was doubtful if they could "keep things in line" as they had in the past.

The shrewder employers were not deceived by the vote of the teamsters to resume trucking on the Embarcadero. They knew that it was a highly dubious gauge of sentiment, temporary at best, and that if no settlement was achieved, the boycott would break out all over again.

Arguments continued into the night before the more belligerent employers were swung into line with the rest. In the end they decided to grant the demand for inclusion of the seamen's grievances in arbitration.

Paul Eliel said:

There was considerable divergence of opinion as to the best policy to be pursued and it was finally agreed that representations would be made to the various steamship companies, most of whom were not represented at the meeting, urging them to accept a plan of arbitration for the various seagoing crafts providing the Longshoremen's Association voted to submit all differences to the President's Arbitration Board.

The employers promptly issued a statement:

The employers have not heretofore agreed to arbitrate with maritime unions.

In view of the stand of the Teamsters' Union in returning to work and other developments to bring about industrial peace and harmony, the members of this conference believe that in event the Longshoremen's Union should vote to submit all differences to arbitration by the President's Board, the steamship owners should agree to add to their offer already made and should agree to arbitrate hours, wages and working conditions with the maritime unions.

Following the conference steamship representatives consulted the numerous companies involved and have obtained their adherence to a plan of arbitration, if the Longshoremen's Union will make such a course possible.

Thus, once the principal employers made up their minds to do it, the assent of all companies up and down the coast to negotiate a uniform collective agreement with the men was obtained within a few hours. And this was the proposition which for three long months the employers had argued was utterly impossible and beyond achievement.

[182]

The longshoremen immediately agreed to submit the proposal to a referendum vote of their membership in all Pacific Coast ports.

Neither the end of the General Strike, the prospect of maritime peace, nor the discovery that 90 per cent of the men picked up in the police dragnet were destitutes who wanted to remain in jail for the sake of shelter, served to abate the fury of the newspaper campaign against communism. The strike was still proclaimed to be a communist revolution which was allegedly "smashed," "crushed," and "put down by the direct action of patriots."

William Randolph Hearst took this occasion to launch in earnest his campaign of invective against the Roosevelt administration. The *Examiner* of July 23 carried a signed editorial cabled from London by Hearst:

As a matter of frank fact, much of the Administration is more Communistic than the Communists themselves.

And it is the firm opinion of many conservative citizens that the revolution in California against stable government and established order would never have occurred except for the sympathy and encouragement which the fomenters of the revolution were receiving or believed they were receiving from those high in the counsel of the Federal Administration.

This pronouncement was featured on the front page under the legend "Americanism Versus Communism." The headline of the edition was: "VIGILANTES DESTROY RED NESTS."

The *Call-Bulletin* editorial said:

During the terrible trying times of the last two months the San Francisco police have earned the respect and gratitude of the city. . . .

The police have grown mightily in public esteem, as individuals and as guardians of public order and safety.

Chief of Police Quinn announced the organization of a permanent anti-communist squad under the leadership of Captain John J. O'Meara, who commanded the recent "extermination raids." Raids would continue, he affirmed, until every communist had been driven from the city.

"We find there is a general retreat of this element from San Francisco," said the chief. "We cannot have in this city propagandists who continually foment trouble."

In explaining the battles of July 3 and 5 he said, "If that mob had broken through police lines on Bloody Thursday, it planned to move straight up Market Street and start sabotage and pillage."

As a matter of fact, the police lines had their backs to the waterfront and if the pickets had "broken through" they would have tumbled into the waters of the bay. The police drove them "straight up Market Street" and back into the city where scarcely any police were on duty, owing to the concentration on the piers.

At the same time that Chief Quinn was announcing a "general retreat," the *Examiner* blew the bugles of a "general advance." It published headlines: "Communist Chiefs Swarm to State for New Uprising; S. F. Strike Called Just Rehearsal of Big Show."

In the midst of this situation the Communists moved back into their halls and the *Western Worker* resumed publication. The Knights of the Red Branch Hall was rented for a free speech meeting and was jammed to the rafters with an enthusiastic audience. Across the street from the City Hall the Communist headquarters blossomed with new banners. Glass was replaced in the windows and displays of literature stacked high. Inside was a furious crackling of typewriters. They were busily engaged with their election campaign, with candidates for nearly all public offices. Soon scores of Communist election campaign headquarters opened up all over town with large signboards proclaiming their platform.

A strong protest movement was launched against civic officials for their activities in the strike. Letters even began to appear in the Open Forum sections of the newspapers. One in the *San Francisco News* of July 20 read:

EDITOR: After the recent heroic demonstration by our local Fascists against the "reds," and after the noble defense made by the police of the rights of lawful assembly, free speech and private property guaranteed by the U. S. Constitution, the people of San Francisco will no longer be in a position to criticize the Nazis or any other persecutors of helpless minorities.

The red scare now being fostered by certain newspapers will not blind the decent people of this city to the real issues at stake, nor will union labor be frightened into submission by this cheap trick of attempting to confuse militant unionism with Communism.

The working people of San Francisco are, I believe, 100 per cent behind the striking unions in their effort to obtain decent working conditions for the waterfront and marine employees, and the methods being used by the press and the employers to defeat that purpose are a disgrace to the principles of justice and fair play upon which this country was founded.

G. A. BALDWIN

Another letter read:

EDITOR: The writer is by no means a Communist, just one of those old-fashioned fools who still believes in freedom of press and speech.

The hysteria and mob law, fostered by the police of the past few days makes me wonder whether this is Germany or America.

Another in the "People's Safety Valve" department of the *Chronicle* read:

Editor the *Chronicle*—Sir: Now that the white-winged dove of peace has settled down in San Francisco would it not be in order to suggest to Governor Merriam that he should invite the President's calliope, General Hugh I. I. I. I. Johnson, to use the return part of his ticket to Washington as soon as possible? He might use the old expression so familiar in army orders, "The travel enjoined is necessary for the public service."

T. C. WEST

Annie Laurie, famed sob sister of the Hearst *Examiner,* penned a eulogy to the Mayor:

Why, you can't speak his name this morning without a thrill in your voice, you can't to save your life—no matter who you are, as long as you are an honest lover of human nature and a true son or daughter of the gayest, most generous, freest, most liberty-loving city under the shining sun.

Handsome man, this Angelo Rossi of ours, calm, dignified, self-possessed. Why, they'd be proud of him in Rome itself, the city of proud and loving loyalty....

Unprejudiced, unbiased, as brave as a lion, and as solid as the rock of Gibraltar—until this strange week which has blown the hours through San Francisco as a mighty wind blows the bubbles along the crest of a wild sea.

The Mayor's personal bodyguard clipped it out and had it framed for him to hang up in his office. "We had it framed, Mayor," they said, "so you can preserve it. Usually one has to die to learn what folks think of him. You have the good luck to learn while you are still hale and hearty."

On Thursday, July 26, the results of the longshoremen's ballot were made known. The men approved arbitration by a majority of four to one, provided the seamen were included. On the same day the Market Street Railway strikers agreed to return to work and submit their grievances to arbitration. Governor Merriam ordered evacuation of the troops from the Embarcadero.

All this received secondary attention on the front pages, and was submerged in a riot of headlines:

"READY TO FIGHT: MUSSOLINI."

"CIVIL WAR SWEEPS AUSTRIA."

"Dillinger Face-Lift Aide Ends Life."

"JUMPS 19 FLOORS TO DEATH."

"Nazi Assassins Let Dollfuss Bleed Slowly To Death."

"ARMED NAZIS BATTLE FOR PROVINCES."

"Duce Orders Troops To Mobilize."

"Envoy To Austria Is Dismissed By Hitler."

"Frau Dollfuss Alone At Bier."

"Garbo Has A Cold. Cameras Grind On."

And sandwiched in between it all: "Troops Will Move From Pier Front; Evacuation To Start At Once As Strikers Vote Quick Return To Jobs."

But they weren't back yet, and were not to return for another five days. Quite a few matters remained to be settled.

FINK HALL GRAVE

U

NDER WHAT CONDITIONS
would the men return to work during the prolonged period of arbitration? That was the question now to be settled.

The longshoremen insisted on five main points:

(1) They would not go back on the docks until the seamen had received satisfactory guarantees and were ready to return also.

(2) All men who had been working as strikebreakers must be discharged.

(3) There must be no discrimination in employment against men who had taken a prominent role in the strike.

(4) Pending decision of the arbitration board, temporary hiring halls must be established, jointly controlled by unions and employers.

(5) Any pay increases decided on by the arbitration board must be retroactive to the day men returned to work.

Employers agreed to retroactive pay increases. But on all other points they took an exactly opposite stand. They demanded that longshoremen return to work immediately, regardless of what happened to the seamen; that certain strikebreakers whom the employers did not want to fire, remain at work; that hiring should be conducted from the pierheads in the same manner as before the strike.

Starting at these opposite poles of attitude, they argued it out for five days in the presence of the mediation board.

Meanwhile the board lost no time in taking a ballot of the seamen to establish who should represent them in collective bargaining. Prior to the strike some of them belonged to the Marine Workers' Industrial Union, a larger group belonged to the International Seamen's Union, and a still larger group belonged to no union at all. A vote of 4,305 to 509 favored return to work pending arbitration and established the International Seamen's Union as official bargaining representative. This disposed of the main obstacle.

After long dispute a compromise was worked out on the other issues. Prior to the strike, in some of the smaller ports company-controlled hiring halls had existed. The experience of the men with these halls had been bitter, and this was one of the factors which strengthened the demand for union control. However, it was agreed that wherever hiring halls existed before, they should continue during the period of arbitration, but that the men should place union representatives in these agencies to see to it that there was no discrimination.

In San Francisco, where previously no hiring hall existed, hiring was to continue from the docks until the arbitration award was handed down. It was promised that there would be no discrimination for union activity.

As for the strikebreakers, employers agreed to discharge them all except a few who had worked on the docks prior to the strike and had remained at work instead of going out with the rest.

On the evening before the return to work, hundreds of seamen gathered in a vacant lot at the corner of Clay Street and the Embarcadero and made a bonfire of their "fink books." These were the hated registration cards of the Marine Service Bureau, the company-controlled hiring hall through which seamen had to ship prior to the strike. Andrew Furuseth, eighty-year-old president of the International Seamen's Union, still feeble from his recent breakdown, came to the waterfront and joined the boys in their celebration. A wooden cross stuck up beside the bonfire was marked "FINK HALL GRAVE."

Next morning 40,000 longshoremen and seamen poured back onto the docks and ships, restoring life and vitality to the industry. Deep engine rooms once more rang with the voices of men. Oilcans limbered up long idle machinery. Fires were lit under boilers. Pistons and turbines came to life under the hot pressure of steam. Rags moved swiftly and vigorously over brasswork, removing three months of tarnish and restoring it to flashing brilliance. Pots and pans rattled in the long-vacant galleys. Decks were holy-stoned and bulkheads washed down with soujey. Smoke rose from the stacks and the longshoremen dug their hooks into a mountain of congested cargo.

The long, endless parade of cargo that gave San Francisco its place among the major cities of the earth began moving again.

The mediation board heaved a sigh of relief and settled down to arbitration proceedings.

Meanwhile thirty-one men and women were still sitting in the city jail wondering if they had been forgotten. Out of some five hundred arrests during the anti-communist raids, they were all that civic authorities had left to show for their tremendous expenditure of frenzy and public funds. They were all suspected "Reds." Some of them were and some of them weren't. Whatever the case may be, they had nothing whatsoever to do with the strike. Still less had they made any attempt or voiced any intention to overthrow the government. Most of them were young kids.

Their situation was really desperate. Since they were being held as "$1,000 vags," their friends on the outside could not raise the money for bail. They had only a fragmentary notion of what was going on outside and, considering the hysterical circumstances of their arrest and the lurid anti-Red statements in the papers, they did not know what to expect next. For a long time they were denied visitors or any contact with the outside world.

The raids had swept all through California, and farther north in the state capital twenty-four young men and women were being held in the Sacramento jail.

The plight of the prisoners was ridiculed and made light of in the newspapers. But it was no laughing matter, as later events proved. The San Francisco prisoners were released ultimately. But eight young men and women in Sacramento went to the penitentiary for terms of one to fourteen years.

It was a dramatic scene that was enacted in the San Francisco jail, for all the sarcastic comment in the daily press. In a final, desperate effort the prisoners went on a hunger strike and starved themselves for eight days.

Newspapers, in making comedy of the affair, directed public attention to the situation. The decent-minded people of the city did not approve of locking young people in jail because they sympathized with a labor strike. Furthermore, no one with a grain of sense believed these thirty-one people had anything to do with the General Strike or that a communist revolution had taken place at all. A very substantial public protest developed and authorities felt the cold shadow of scorn creeping over them.

The Police Department was especially alarmed. The Atherton report indicates that they were not at all desirous of attracting public attention to the conduct of their affairs or the conditions within the city jail, which was a veritable hive of graft and a network of "shake-down" rackets. In vain they pleaded with the prisoners to abandon their strike, and tempted them with all sorts of delicacies.

On the eighth day, yielding to the advice of friends on the outside, the prisoners called off their fast. This "giving in" disgusted a young Mexican prisoner. He cursed his partners for lack of resolve and continued his fast for another two days.

The prison menu became sumptuous. A diet hitherto unheard of within the iron confines of the prison was accorded the "political prisoners." Not since the famous "Arbuckle splurge" had the city jail experienced such luxury.

Many years before, Roscoe "Fatty" Arbuckle had been arrested for assertedly raping a woman in the St. Francis Hotel. The wealthy moving picture actor found the bunks in the felony tank far from what he was accustomed to. He wanted to improve his condition but, at the same time, had some respect for the feelings of his fellow unfortunates. He ordered the very finest mattresses, not only for his own bunk, but for everyone else in the tank.

The mattresses are still there, but they have become inhabitated by such armies of bedbugs and cockroaches that the luxury is now questionable.

After a few days of exceptional diet, the alleged Reds were confronted one morning with sticky oatmeal and "blue" milk. Not a word was spoken, but the jailers found a row of untouched bowls stuck outside the cells. A state of alarm resulted. Within half an hour a new breakfast was provided including rich, creamy milk, orange juice, and fresh fruit.

Soon afterwards the prisoners were released and the alleged Red Rebellion dissolved into thin air.

The Sacramento prisoners did not fare so well. Eleven of them were sentenced to maximum terms for vagrancy and eighteen of them were indicted for criminal syndicalism.

Sacramento is the state capital and also the center of the agricultural regions. It is the terminus for river steamers plying to San Francisco harbor. California agriculture is predominantly large scale and harvesting is done by about 20,000 migratory workers who roam from crop to crop, setting up camp during the season and moving on again when it is over. Most of them are families in which men, women, and children work in the fields for wages averaging 15 or 20 cents an hour. Sacramento is also the headquarters for this transient population.

At the outset of the maritime strike this large section of people accustomed to hard work at low wages was regarded as the most probable source of strikebreakers. Arrangements were made to recruit them in Sacramento and bring them down the river on steamboats. This plan was frustrated by the activities of five organizations: the Cannery and Agricultural Workers' Industrial Union, the Workers' School, the Unemployed Council, the International Labor Defense, and the Communist Party. Leaflets were spread thickly all over town and mass meetings were held in the parks urging support of the marine workers. Money was collected to aid the strike and small farmers were contacted for contributions of produce for the strikers' relief kitchen.

When the raids began they concentrated on these organizations and practically all of their leaders were arrested. But there was something more than the maritime strike involved here.

The Cannery and Agricultural Workers' Industrial Union had organized scores of strikes among the migratory field workers and in the canneries which were no less spectacular than the maritime situation. In 1933 they led 15,000 cotton pickers in the largest agricultural strike in American history, with picket lines flung over a hundred-mile front. The strike succeeded in raising wages from 60 cents to 75 cents per hundred pounds for pickers, thus costing the growers an average of a million dollars a year in pay raises. Bitterness of the dispute is indicated by the fact that three strikers were killed and scores wounded when armed vigilantes fired into the ranks of the picket lines. Responsibility for the violence is apparent in the fact that in the whole struggle no grower was injured or harmed.

The huge corporation ranches and banking interests which control California agriculture are organized in the Associated Farmers, a group very similar to and working closely with the San Francisco Industrial Association. The greatest object of this organization at the moment was to do away with the Cannery and Agricultural Workers'

Industrial Union. It was the raids that gave them their opportunity.

Leaders of the union were accused of a plot to overthrow the government of the United States by force and violence. Neil R. McAllister, the prosecutor, announced he had documentary proof they had conspired to kidnap the President out of the White House. Newspapers picked up the statement and printed it in a manner to imply that such a scheme had actually been thwarted. Nicknames and initials in the personal correspondence of the prisoners were scrutinized by the prosecutors who declared that prominent Hollywood movie actors were financing the plot. Once again the headlines blared with sensational nonsense.

The trial was the longest in California court history and lasted until April 1, 1935. The evidence consisted of 190 items of printed literature—newspapers, books, pamphlets, magazines—which were legally printed, legally sold, and passed through the U. S. mail. They were for sale on Sacramento newsstands while the trial was going on, and many of them were on the shelves of the public library a block away from the courthouse. Yet the defendants were on trial for possessing them.

Three professional labor spies, one in the employ of the Associated Farmers, one in the employ of the State Bureau of Criminal Identification, and one in the employ of the prosecuting attorney, testified that they heard the defendants say they were going to overthrow the government.

Two amateur spies in the employ of the National Guard, and a clerk from the Bureau of Identification testified, but said nothing that could be construed as evidence.

To the jury of middle-class, well-to-do people the whole thing was bewildering. All they knew was that before being sworn in they had read in the newspapers that a Red Rebellion had been suppressed in San Francisco and that these people had some kind of connection with it.

The whole parade of evidence dwindled down to an accusation that violence and sabotage had been advocated and used in the agricultural strikes of preceding years. A few growers and police officials took the stand and testified to this effect. But they could cite no specific incident.

As a matter of fact, although strikers were killed and maimed, one of them, a nineteen-year-old boy having had an arm blown off by a shotgun, not a grower had been scratched. The only sabotage that took place was when vigilantes burned the camps of the pickers and drove them out onto the highways.

When the time came for the defense to testify, so many small farmers and laborers came forward to vindicate the defendants that the judge cut them short and refused to allow any more witnesses. The prosecution witnesses had consisted exclusively of police officers, paid labor spies, and three farmers.

The jury acquitted the defendants of plots against the government and found no evidence of any violence or sabotage. But it declared eight of the people guilty of having conspired to commit such acts, and sent them to the penitentiary for terms of one to fourteen years. They were: Pat Chambers, young organizer of the union and leader of the famous cotton strike; Caroline Decker, youthful secretary of the union; Martin Wilson, young organizer of the International Labor Defense; Nora Conklin, leader of the Unemployed Council; Albert Hougardy, organizer of the Communist Party; Jack Crane, a young violinist and radio technician who taught a class in Marxism at the Workers' School; and Lorene Norman, a member of the International Labor Defense.*

In asking for a verdict of guilty Prosecutor McAllister said:

You are here today *making history*. We stand today on a crossroads. One road points toward Americanism. [Goes up to the flag which hangs by the witness stand. Grasps its edge and pulls out the folds.] The other points toward Communism. [Points at the defendants.]

Now let us consider the position of the Associated Farmers. What are the farmers to do in the state of California? Sit idly by while these *conspirators*, these *leaders*, these *propagandists*, these *agitators*, these *agit props*— that's what they call themselves and every last one of them is an *agit prop* —they don't need Mr. Gallagher to appoint an *Agit Prop Department*, because every last one of them is unto himself an *agit prop*. They live for nothing else. It's in their blood. It's all they live for. It's all they sleep for. It's all they eat for. It's all they dream of. It's all they desire. Scheming how they can *agit prop*. What can they *agit prop*.... Well, the farmers certainly have to organize to protect themselves.... But they will be able to disband their organization and save the cost of maintaining it if you do your duty in this case, as I believe you will....

They advocate the overthrow of the government of the United States by force and violence. *By force and violence!*... The prosecution cannot stop it. The court cannot stop it. There is only one way it can be stopped. There is only one body that has the jurisdiction and the power to stop it, and that is *you*, ladies and gentlemen of the jury. If you don't an aroused

*The "Criminal Syndicalism" trial prisoners were later released, after winning an appeal to higher courts.

public will stop it, *and the vigilantes will be the thing that will stop it.* You'll have *bloodshed*, another Pixley and another Harlan, Kentucky. . . .

They attempted to justify this revolution by what? By the *majority*. A majority has no more right to undertake to overthrow this government than has a minority. The judge will so instruct you. . . .

Out of this primitive wilderness, ladies and gentlemen, sprang up the greatest Democracy in the world. . . . Think of the covered wagons. Think of the Donner party coming through the snow and getting frozen to death. . . . They propose to agitate the country and take away from you what you have and overthrow the government. From Moscow! They are paid by Moscow! . . . The eyes of the nation are on you, asking you, begging you, pleading with you to *stamp out this insurrection*, this advocacy of revolution and the overthrow of your government and institutions, which you love, honor and revere, and which you hope to pass down to your children and your children's children.

In closing he walked over to the flag, took a notebook from his pocket, thumbed to a page, lifted his hand to salute, and read:

I now pledge allegiance to the flag of the United States of America. One nation, indivisible, with liberty and justice for all.

Then turning to the jury:

Ladies and gentlemen, I ask you to think of that flag in the jury room, and I ask you to think of what it stands for. I ask you to bring in a vote for that flag—for the good old U.S.A.—for "My Country 'Tis of Thee"—for the Star-Spangled Banner—for the United States of America—and God will bless you.

The convictions effectively smashed the union and left the agricultural workers without any device for protection. Conditions of poverty and disease became so bad that they were a menace to the whole population and the government was forced to step in and investigate. Little children were plagued with rickets and wasted away from malnutrition. People were living in dirt hovels, starving in the heart of the richest food-growing region of America. Wages were so low that despite the meagerness of the dole, families could get more money on the relief roll than by working long hours in the fields. Artistic photographers visited the region and brought back pictures of tired babies fumbling with the wasted breasts of tragic-looking women, while swarms of flies buzzed about. The camps of the laborers literally stank with poverty and degradation.

When union organizers ventured into the region they were tarred and feathered by the vigilantes.

Reports of qualified government investigators read like descriptions of Chinese famine areas.

Pat Chambers, the union organizer, a youth in corduroys and a leather jacket, when asking the jury for a verdict of not guilty, said:

No strike leader will incite violence. Calling a strike is a great responsibility. I want to point out that if any of these strikes had not been conducted correctly by us, not only growers would have condemned the organization, but workers would have been the first to do so. Yet not a single worker came forward to testify against the organization.

You, yourselves, are more or less sheltered. I ask you, irrespective of your decision in this case, to do one thing. Go to the agricultural fields and see for yourselves how miserable the conditions of life are there. You will see children with the terrible imprint of hunger on their faces.

I swore to fight against all organizations that use their power to browbeat the poor. I swore above all that these children would not go hungry. I have seen so much misery, starvation, brutality, I am glad I took part to a small extent in the struggle against them, and against the banks that caused them.

It will seem illogical that no criminal syndicalism charges were brought against communists in San Francisco. This is explainable in two ways.

District Attorney Matthew Brady of San Francisco regards the law as so manifestly unjust and ridiculous that he has repeatedly proclaimed that as long as he occupies office, no one in the city will be prosecuted on a C. S. charge.

The law was enacted during the days of hysteria that followed the World War, and its terms are so vague and sprawling that if rigidly applied, persons could be imprisoned for having in their possession books that may be obtained from any public library. It is an unpopular law, and prosecutions under its terms are equally unpopular.

District Attorney Neil R. McAllister of Sacramento, who tried to campaign on the basis of his prosecution of the C. S. case, was defeated for reelection by such an overwhelming majority that it amounted to a slap in the face.

For another thing, Sacramento, even though it is the state capital, is a comparatively small and provincial city. It took four and a half months of trial to put over such a prosecution even there. In San Francisco such a thing was out of the question. To put over such a trial in the stronghold of organized labor was beyond practicability.

T

HE MEDIATION BOARD
handed down its award to the longshoremen on October 12, 1934.
Throughout the long proceedings, which dragged out over two
months, employers refused to permit any discussion of operating
costs and profits. This was inconvenient to the men because they
came equipped with full data on this subject. But the employers insisted that they were not arguing inability to pay, therefore such
matters had no place in the proceedings.

The award (see full document in Appendix 11) comprised a working agreement between the longshoremen and employers to be effective until September 30, 1935. Thereafter it would be renewed
automatically each year on September 30 unless either party served
written notice not less than forty days prior to the expiration date
that they wanted to cancel it.

The men were granted the six-hour day, a thirty-hour week, and
time and a half for overtime. The wage was set at 95 cents per hour

for straight time and $1.40 for overtime. Higher rates were established for special types of difficult or dangerous cargo.

All hiring was to be done through a dispatching hall controlled jointly by employers and the union. The personnel of the hall was to be appointed by the Labor Relations Committee, with the exception of the dispatcher, who was to be selected by the ILA.

The "Labor Relations Committee" referred to was to consist of three representatives of the employers and three representatives of the International Longshoremen's Association, and they were to handle all disputes which might arise.

There were two clauses in Section 11 of the award that were ultimately to give rise to endless controversy. They could be interpreted any way the reader saw fit. They were:

The employers shall be free to select their men within those eligible under the policies jointly determined, and the men likewise shall be free to select their jobs;

and

The employees must perform all work as ordered by the employer.

The phrase "must perform all work as ordered" was negated by the phrase "the men likewise shall be free to select their jobs."

From the very start the men defended their gains to the letter, and the phrasing of the award helped them to do so. Whenever any grievance arose, whether it was over an infraction of the rules, an increase in slingloads, an unfair discharge, or a hot cargo dispute, the men working on that dock would walk off the job. The employers would get ILA headquarters on the phone and call their attention to the "work as ordered" clause.

The ILA, which was now the hiring hall, would dispatch another gang immediately. They too would refuse to work until the grievance was adjusted. Once more the employers would phone the ILA and receive the reply, "The award says the men are free to select their jobs. We can't order them to violate their own rights. Shall we dispatch you another gang?"

No matter how many gangs were dispatched, the result would be the same. The men stuck together with the accord of a single person.

This job action began the minute the men returned to work, and twenty-nine such stoppages occurred up and down the coast before the award was even handed down.

For the most part, the men found the agreement reasonably satisfactory. The employers were less content.

The hiring hall was established in ILA headquarters and to all intents and purposes was controlled by the union through the dispatcher whom the award permitted the union to select. True, the employer could have his representative there to keep an eye on things, but what was the use? The longshoremen were perfectly capable of managing the hall and they, better than anyone else, could judge the efficiency and qualifications of the men. They were not apt to dispatch an incompetent or lazy man because this would throw an extra burden of work on the other members of the gang and raise democratic complaints.

The hall became a model of efficiency and the ILA issued a permanent invitation for members of the general public to come down and inspect it. Even Roger Lapham, one of the most bitterly anti-union shipowners, upon examining the hall, marveled at its conduct and praised it highly.

Jobs were rotated in a manner to give every man on the front an equal amount of work with adequate periods of rest. There was no longer any waiting around for jobs to turn up—no wild scramble to get ahead of the other fellow—no toadying to straw bosses. Each man had his rights and democratic channels through which to redress any grievance.

Harry Bridges, the rank-and-file leader who was decried in the press as a Red, an alien, and an agitator, was elected to presidency of the San Francisco local of the ILA, and later to presidency of the entire West Coast District. He became, by all odds, the most influential labor leader west of the Rockies, and one of the most distinguished in the country. At all public gatherings he was accorded standing ovations and storms of applause such as the Mayor had never experienced. When marching in Labor Day parades, he stirred up a thunder of acclamation from one end of Market Street to the other.

But all this did not bring peace to the waterfront. Instead there ensued a period of industrial guerrilla warfare which persisted for more than two years, ultimately resulting in the whole Pacific Coast maritime strike's breaking out again in greater force than ever. On the whole, this period was as interesting and eventful as were the more concentrated struggles of the maritime and general strikes. And just as important to understand.

The most bitter and recurrent dispute was that of "hot cargo." The longshoremen knew well enough that they would not be enjoying the advantages they had were it not for the solidarity support that they received from other unions and other sections of the populace. Thus they persistently backed up every struggle of organized labor anywhere in the world and were a strong factor in developing unionism generally.

There was more than sentimentality involved here. They realized that their gains were founded on solidarity, and the stronger organized labor became everywhere the more secure would be their gains.

They refused to lay hands on any cargo which came from a strike area and had previously been handled by scabs.

Another frequent dispute was the matter of speed-up. Speed-up not only increased the labor and danger of the work but cut down on the amount of work available for all. Longshoremen would be loading sacks so many to a sling, a number they regarded as safe and not apt to snap the cable and cause injury. The dock foreman would order them to increase the number of sacks to a sling. They would refuse and be fired off the job. Another gang would be ordered, and they too would refuse and be fired. This would go on until the men won their point.

Two spectacular applications of the "choose your job" clause occurred in 1935. One was when the German cruiser "Karlsruhe" arrived in port flying the Nazi flag. Longshoremen refused to service the vessel and finally German sailors had to be put ashore to fasten their own lines before the vessel could be docked.

The other was when the University of California football team was embarking on the steamer "Yale." Not only longshoremen but seamen also refused to service the ship, which was delayed for several hours. The University of California football team had scabbed on the docks during the 1934 strike. Now they had to carry their own luggage, grope for their own staterooms, and ring the service bells until they wore the ends off their fingers, without getting any response.

On July 5, Bloody Thursday, of 1935 and succeeding years, the maritime workers took unauthorized holidays in honor of the two dead pickets lying under grass. They staged mass parades up Market Street, the length and dignity of which almost equaled the famous funeral parade.

An arbitration award for the seamen was not handed down until April 10, 1935, and it was pretty slim pickings as compared with what the longshoremen gained. They did not even get the eight-hour day for all departments, let alone the six-hour day. Wages in many cases were as low as $45 per month, with licensed navigators frequently receiving far less than ordinary clerks ashore. Overtime was not paid for in cash, but in time off at a later date—and perhaps in some isolated port where the time was not worth anything. Employers could hire from the pierhead or the union hall, just as they pleased. Job strikes or stoppages of work were outlawed for the duration of the award. The seamen felt—and rightly so—that they had been handed the dirty end of the stick. When the mediation board handed down that award they handed down a barrel of trouble. Apparently it was felt that the seamen, away from port most of the time, could not very well do anything about it, and the longshoremen, endowed with reasonable conditions, would not be eager to endanger this state of affairs by backing up the seamen. Whatever was thought or felt, and whoever thought or felt it, they were mistaken.

Another factor which influenced this disparity in awards was that the longshoremen had negotiated under their own democratically elected leaders. The seamen, however, were under the domination of conservative salaried officials of the Ryan-Casey-Vandeleur type, outstanding among whom was Paul Scharrenberg of the International Seamen's Union.

Thus the strike of 1934 ended with a very unhealthy and uneven situation. The longshoremen were the only ones who made substantial gains. This was not their fault. They realized that such unevenness did not make for security of their own improvements. And they had exerted every effort to assure the seamen of similar advantages.

Another disparity bound ultimately to give rise to new struggles was the difference in working conditions between the West Coast, the East Coast, and the Gulf of Mexico. This unnatural situation was bound to seek a level, and if the rest of the maritime industry could not be lifted to accord with the high standards of the West Coast longshoremen, those standards would soon be pulled down again.

The first step taken by West Coast rank-and-file leaders was the organization of a Maritime Federation of the Pacific, which drew all the separate craft unions into a coordinated body capable of handling all matters on an industrial instead of a craft basis. District councils were set up in all Pacific ports with delegates from all unions, and a weekly newspaper, the *Voice of the Federation,* was established with editorial offices in San Francisco.

All informed trade unionists realized the importance of coordinating activities on an industrial basis. The various crafts were so closely related that one could not take action without seriously affecting all. The utmost cooperation was needed, and this cooperation was not forthcoming from the old-line salaried officials. Although the San

Francisco longshoremen were under progressive leadership, the Pacific Coast District, during 1935, was still headed by conservatives. The International Seamen's Union was almost entirely under the domination of such officials. Thus a long internal struggle within the unions themselves began which has not worked itself out even up to this writing.

The first serious result of these differences was a belligerent action taken by Paul Scharrenberg, secretary-treasurer of the Sailors' Union of the Pacific, early in 1935, which almost upset the apple cart of the newly formed federation. Without making any preparations or consulting the other unions he called a strike of all seamen on oil tankers. It was a hopeless and inadvisable strike, and the union men themselves have good reason to believe that he called it for the sole purpose of destroying the Maritime Federation. A small booklet, *Modesto Frame-up,* published under the auspices of the Pacific Coast maritime unions, sets forth their official view of the deed:

In the settlement of the strikes of 1934 the sailors had particularly been left with many grievances that had not been adjusted, and the conditions in the oil-carrying branch of the transportation industry were very bad. The crews of the tankers were becoming impatient for some amelioration of their conditions.

The strategists of Standard Oil saw in this situation their opportunity to strike a blow at the Maritime Federation. They had a willing ally in Paul Scharrenberg, Secretary-Treasury of the Sailors' Union of the Pacific. For thirty years Scharrenberg had successfully served two masters. How successfully he had served the sailors on the ships is open to question. But he had managed to remain in office and waxed fat and prosperous on the per capita tax they paid, while he successfully served the shipowners and their industrial allies, as the leading labor lieutenant of the captains of industry of California.

Somebody saw Scharrenberg, and Scharrenberg saw the way to smash the Maritime Federation. The old trick of calling a premature strike, while the workers were in the midst of preparations for a really effective move at a later date, was resorted to.

The strike was called on March 9, 1935, and called off on June 18 when the Maritime Federation stepped into the picture to pick up the pieces. It never gained anyone anything. But it sent eight union men to the penitentiary.

The arrest and conviction of these men provides a crude and incredible story that would sound like the wildest fiction were it not that every fact has been carefully confirmed by a special investigating committee of the state assembly.

James Scrudder, a labor spy in the employ of the San Francisco

Police Department, and Hal Marchant, a private detective in the employ of the Standard Oil Company, were both working within the ranks of the strikers and submitting reports to their respective chiefs. Scrudder was posing as an ordinary striker, but Marchant was a member of the Joint Tanker Strike Committee, sitting as a delegate from Portland, Oregon. He was also serving on the mediation board appointed by President Roosevelt to arbitrate the tanker strike.

Together these two secret agents either stole or prevailed upon others to steal (this exact fact has not yet been established) a quantity of dynamite from a quarry in Marin County.

About this time it came to the attention of the strike committee that the Standard Oil Company was housing strikebreakers in the Del Puerto Hotel in the small town of Patterson, Stanislaus County. It was decided to send a sufficient number of men down there to throw a picket line in front of the hotel. But first they were instructed to investigate and find out whether or not there was sufficient pro-union sentiment in the town to make such a move effective. Also to determine whether the proprietor was aware of what his hotel was being used for and if the employees in the hotel were unionized.

Meanwhile Scrudder informed the San Francisco police that the dynamite had been stolen and where it was located. Then both Scrudder and Marchant arranged to get themselves included in the party that was to go to Patterson.

Whether they planted the dynamite in the two cars from the start or whether it was turned over to other agents and planted after the arrests has not yet been verified. But one thing has been verified, and that is that none of the union men traveling in those cars knew anything about the dynamite.

Before the two cars left for Stanislaus County Scrudder and Marchant advised the San Francisco police and Standard Oil authorities. On the outskirts of Patterson the cars were stopped by private guards in the employ of the Standard Oil Company and the men ordered out at the point of guns. A short while later the sheriff arrived and placed them under arrest. It was claimed that the dynamite was found in the cars and that these men intended to blow up the Del Puerto Hotel and numerous gas stations.

They were convicted in a Modesto court solely on the testimony of Scrudder and Marchant, neither of whom was ever prosecuted. Eight men were sent to the penitentiary for terms of six months to five years for reckless possession of dynamite. It was later ascertained that the Standard Oil Company spent $15,000 prosecuting the case.

The tongue of James Scrudder was fixed loosely in his jaw and fluttered like a flag in the breeze to every thought that entered his head. A year and a half later, in Hollywood, California, he bragged to a new-found acquaintance of his role in the Modesto case and complained bitterly of his small reward. "And what did I get out of it?" he said. "Nothing but a measly job in a Culver City substation for $5 a day, while Marchant got a roll of bills that would choke a horse."

The man to whom he was talking was William S. Briggs, a union chauffeur, who had heard about the Modesto business. He communicated immediately with Grover Johnson, International Labor Defense attorney. Johnson communicated with Aaron Sapiro, attorney for the Sailors' Union, and others, and arranged to plant a dictograph in Briggs' home and invite Scrudder and his wife in to play rummy. On December 1, 1936, Scrudder played cards and talked freely while eighteen dictograph records were made in an adjoining room.

As a result of this evidence the state assembly appointed a special committee to investigate, which reported that the Standard Oil Company had deliberately "framed" these men on "perjured evidence."

All this, of course, was a much later development, happening after the abortive tanker strike had passed into history. The San Francisco Industrial Association, before the frame-up was exposed, made lavish use of the incident to discredit the unions. In the August 1935 issue of *American Plan*, a journal published by the Association, they stated:

The red leadership of the marine unions with the *Western Worker*, official Communist organ, immediately charged that the arrest of the dynamiters was a "frame-up" to discredit the unions, and the dispatches from Modesto stated that men claiming to be representatives of the marine unions in San Francisco appeared there and attempted to bail them out. Led by the *Western Worker*, Communist organizations and the radical leadership in the seafaring unions, including the longshoremen, began a money-raising, propaganda campaign to free the prisoners.

Paul Scharrenberg himself fared very badly as a result of the tanker strike, but for different reasons. He was placed on trial by the membership of the Sailors' Union and expelled for union betrayal, not only in this instance, but on numerous other occasions which were cited.

The expulsion of Scharrenberg caused great alarm amongst the top officials, not only in the San Francisco Labor Council, but among the international executives. They viewed it as "the handwriting on the wall" and fought it with every power they had. He was one of the most powerful of the old-line conservatives and the fact that he could be ousted so summarily was something of a thunderbolt.

Executives of the International Seamen's Union in the East promptly informed the sailors that they had no authority to expel an officer, and ordered the reinstatement of Scharrenberg. The sailors flatly refused.

Scharrenberg was also secretary of the California State Federation of Labor, and his expulsion left him in the position of a high labor official without a union. His fellow officials protected his status there by "smuggling" him into the Office Workers' Union of San Francisco.

The Office Workers' Union, to date, has been a dummy organization designed to prevent the organization of office workers. Although there are over 100,000 such workers in San Francisco, this union has a membership of less than 50, no more than a handful of whom ever show up at meetings. It is as difficult to get into as an exclusive millionaires' club. As an experiment I asked a friend of mine to try to join. After six months of endeavor he was granted an interview with the officials who told him, "We don't see what you want to join for. We can't do anything for you."

Scharrenberg still holds his high office and the top officials of the International Seamen's Union in the East recently sent him to Geneva as a delegate to the international seamen's convention. But so far as the Pacific Coast maritime workers are concerned, he has been expelled and discredited.

All this is evidence of the long and bitter internal struggle that has been going on within the unions ever since the 1934 strike, and which still persists. One by one the old-line conservatives have been forced out and replaced by new blood elected out of the ranks. Even the San Francisco Labor Council underwent a transition until it came to be regarded by some to have a progressive majority.

The conservatives, however, still command a tremendous amount of formal authority. They entrenched themselves in the State Federation of Labor Executive Committee with Scharrenberg, and a long hard fight lay ahead in order to throw off their influence.

This internal struggle broke out into gangsterism in San Pedro during 1935 when "Boss" Friedel, reactionary head of the local Marine Firemen's Union, organized "Beef Squads" and instituted a reign of terror against his opponents, whom he characterized as communists. For many days he rampaged through the streets of San Pedro at the head of his gangsters, raiding homes, slugging progressive union men, and committing wholesale hoodlumism. Union meetings were presided over by gangsters and anyone who opposed his reactionary dictatorship was taking his life in his hands.

Friedel's career terminated in a hideous manner when the police mistook him for a radical and blew off his head with a sawed-off shotgun. Someone had phoned the Los Angeles police "Red Squad" informing them that "communists" were on the rampage in San Pedro, and directed them to Friedel's address. When they entered to investigate, Friedel mistook them for union men and opened fire. They replied with shotguns at close range.

Next day the police declared it was all an awful mistake, that they had understood he was a communist.

During the slow, steady progression of this internal union struggle, many union officials hitherto regarded as "conservatives" changed their attitude and became "progressives." In some instances this has been due to a sincere change of opinion, and a realization that if organized labor is to advance it must take a hand in politics and organize its struggles on an industrial basis instead of along craft lines. The importance of political action was brought home very definitely during the presidential elections of 1936 when Roosevelt defeated Landon. Both employers and labor on the West Coast watched the balloting with a realization that the whole future of industrial relations was bound up in the opposing philosophies of the two candidates. Labor in vast majority backed Roosevelt with a reason. Capital in vast majority backed Landon with a reason.

But some of the "conservatives" gone "progressive" have been shrewd opportunists who saw which way the wind was blowing and set their sails to suit it. Likewise it can be pointed out that many of the top officials within organized labor are no more than jumping jacks at the ends of Industrial Association buzzer buttons. Employers long ago discovered the effectiveness of sending their own men into the ranks of labor to attain high positions. A good example of this kind of strategy is the case of Hal Marchant, one of the spies in the Modesto frame-up. Although a private detective in the employ of Standard Oil, Marchant acted the role of a militant trade unionist so successfully that he got himself on the Joint Tanker Strike Committee and the President's mediation board. Such men are apt to be skilled in public speaking and intrigue and capable of deceiving inexperienced unionists. The surest defense against them is the institution of complete rank-and-file democracy which prevents such men from creeping in and gaining dictatorial powers.

Numerous detective and strikebreaking agencies throughout America make a business of training these men and supplying them on demand. The famous Bergoff agency in New York issued a printed prospectus for business executives, which sets forth the various classifications of men available:

Strike Prevention Department.—This department is composed of men possessing natural leadership qualifications. Men of intelligence, courage, and great persuasive powers to counteract the evil influence of strike agitators and the radical element.

Undercover Department.—Our undercover department is composed of carefully selected male and female mechanics and workpeople. They furnish accurate information of the movements and contemplated actions of their fellow employees—"Forewarned is forearmed."

Openshop Labor Department.—This department is composed of an organization equipped to supply all classes of competent mechanics and workpeople to keep the wheels of industry moving during a strike.

Protection Department.—This department is composed of big, disciplined men with military or police experience, for the protection of life and property.

Investigation Department.—Our investigation department is international in scope and embraces all branches. The personnel is composed of male and female operatives of the highest caliber.

Edward Levinson, in his history of the Bergoff agency, *I Break Strikes,* gives convincing evidence to show that the Bergoff army consists of such an outlandish gang of hooligans and underworld characters that sensible employers will no longer utilize them. He also describes an amusing sidelight to the San Francisco General Strike. Bergoff, anxious to make the most of the situation, let it leak out to the press that he was sending an army to San Francisco and would soon be in command of the situation. The report was false and, according to Levinson, Bergoff had not received an order for a single man. Relates Levinson:

The day after this story apeared, the Red Demon (as Bergoff styled himself) was sitting in his inner office, speculating on plans to exploit his gratuitous publicity. Suddenly a dentist who had offices on the same floor pushed through the door in great agitation and announced that a menacing crowd had gathered outside the building. The plump Red Demon turned pale. He sent Eddie Klein over to the window to report on the situation. Below him in the Circle [Columbus Circle in New York.—Q.] Klein saw a large crowd of young men and women. They carried banners with signs: "DOWN WITH THE SCABHERDER BERGOFF"; "BERGOFF'S THUGS THREATEN SAN FRANCISCO'S WORKERS."

"Good God, they're after me," the Red Demon shouted. Hastily he called for the police and locked and barricaded his door.

One of the most amazing of all incidents between the close of the 1934 strike and the beginning of the 1936-37 strike occurred in connection with Captain Bakcsy, sometimes known as Captain X, one of the most spectacular spies in American history. Bakcsy was the man who trapped Big Bill Haywood, militant IWW leader, during the days of the World War. He is a short, squat man with a wrestler's build, two cauliflower ears, light blue eyes, grizzled, thinning hair, and a broad nose. He speaks with a strong Hungarian accent and has an insatiable appetite for publicity.

Bakcsy first turned up in California as a spectator at the criminal syndicalism trial in Sacramento, at which time he received a brief flurry of publicity. Months later, in September 1935, he appeared before the Waterfront Employers' Union with an astonishing proposition.

About a hundred miles south of San Francisco on the seacoast is the little town of Carmel, famed art colony and summer haven for wealthy people. Here Lincoln Steffens, America's most outstanding newspaperman, had settled down with his wife Ella Winter and his young son Pete, to spend his last days in reflective peace. Bedridden and nearing the end of his road, Steffens spent his time reading, writing a little, and entertaining visitors from all over the world who came to pay tribute to his international fame. At one time he had been a friend of Nicolai Lenin, the Russian revolutionary leader. People frequently asked him if he was a communist, and he would reply, "I appreciate the compliment, but I am really only a useless liberal."

It was Bakcsy's theory that Carmel was the headquarters of the "Red Network," and that the maritime strikes had been financed by "Moscow Gold" which poured in through Lincoln Steffens, the secret leader. It is hard to judge which is the most amazing, the story itself or the fact that he was able to sell it to the waterfront employers. But sell it he did, and for good hard cash.

Having secured financing, Bakcsy rented a house in Carmel from Mr. Byington Ford, son of a San Francisco corporation attorney, and brother of a member of the Waterfront Employers' Union. He equipped it with dictographs from top to bottom. There were even dictographs in the bathroom and a cluster of them in the Christmas tree. Posing as a master mariner and world traveler under the name of Captain Y. Sharkey, he began giving a long series of parties and invited the pleasure-loving population of Carmel to use his house, where drinks always flowed freely, as a hangout. Meanwhile secretaries sat with earphones on, jotting down the heterogeneous hodgepodge of inconsequential chatter that went on in Bakcsy's "house of a million ears." When the guests departed, fingerprints were taken from their liquor glasses.

By the time Bakcsy's investigation had consumed two months and $7,000, Thomas G. Plant, president of the Waterfront Employers' Union, began to suspect that the whole thing was foolish. The only piece of evidence Bakcsy had uncovered was a plaque with a hammer-and-sickle design on it, which he had hired a young man in Carmel to make for him. In the meantime he was demanding more thousands of dollars to meet his current bills. The whole thing ended in a dismal fiasco, and the waterfront employers realized they had been duped out of $7,000 or $8,000 by a new kind of racket. The Carmel local press blistered the ears of Bakcsy, alias Sharkey, and of Byington Ford, who was implicated. The populace flared with righteous rage at the discovery of the intricately wired "Red trap" in their midst. Ford was bitterly censured by the local American Legion post which disclaimed any connection with the affair, although Ford was its leading member.

Another affair of more serious consequences marked the two-year period of restless hostility between the two strikes, and added three more names to the long list of labor prisoners within the penitentiary.

On the morning of Sunday, March 22, 1936, George W. Alberts, chief engineer of the Swayne and Hoyt freighter "Point Lobos," was found stabbed to death in his cabin while the vessel lay berthed in Alameda. No one knows to this day who killed him or why.

Five months later George Wallace, a member of the Marine Firemen's, Oilers, Watertenders and Wipers Union, was arrested in Brownsville, Texas, and brought back to Alameda. How he could have been traced this distance, since the police were equipped with neither his name nor description, has never been disclosed. However, after being in custody for some time he was said to have confessed that, although he took no part in the slaying, he had accompanied two unidentified men to the "Point Lobos" who committed the murder. These men have never been located, nor is there any certainty that they exist. Wallace did accuse, though, several prominent rank-and-file unionists, who he claimed had instructed the two unidentified and unknown men to kill Alberts.

Wallace was nervous, shifty, and not overbright. He could neither read nor write and was the typical weak character whom police universally intimidate into serving their purposes as informers and stoolpigeons. Certainly his was not the word on which to send three men to the penitentiary. And yet on his word, and his word alone, this very thing was done.

Wallace, according to his own testimony, was never personally instructed to harm Alberts. And he never heard anyone else instruct anyone to harm Alberts. Even his weak and wavering testimony was a sheer matter of implication.

Nevertheless Earl King, leader of the Pacific Coast Marine Firemen's, Oilers, Watertenders and Wipers Association, a man with a record for honest unionism, was arrested and accused of instructing two unknown men to kill Alberts. No one had ever heard him order such a purposeless killing. But a weak and jittery character who had been under police pressure for some time, was alleged to be under the impression that such was the case.

Likewise, E. G. Ramsay, formerly a patrolman of the union and then engaged in organizing the Fish Reduction Workers' Union in San Francisco, was arrested and accused. Neither he nor King had been near the vessel or the town of Alameda on the day of the killing.

A short while later Frank J. Conner, an oiler in the engineroom of the "Point Lobos," and ship's delegate for the union, was arrested in Seattle and accused of complicity. The fact that he was nowhere near Alberts' stateroom on the day of the murder was clearly established by the evidence—so clearly, in fact, that no one questioned it. The only thing existing to link these three men with the murder was the word of Wallace.

Yet all three, including Wallace, were exonerated of the actual murder and sent to the penitentiary for complicity with it. Wallace had been implicated in knife killings before and it is the opinion of union observers at the trial, and also of union attorneys, that Wallace had committed the murder and, under pressure, had implicated the others in order to save his own neck.

The fact remains that three union men of fine record and high character—three men widely esteemed and respected by all maritime labor—were sent to the penitentiary on the sole testimony of a man of dubious character and intellect.

Among the maritime unions the case is known as the King-Ramsay-Conner frame-up. A large section of the public remains unconvinced. They feel that every time a laboring man is arrested in connection with union activities, the unions raise the cry of "frame-up." The fact that employing interests will spend thousands of dollars and engage in intrigue and stoolpigeoning to send union leaders to prison on false charges is beyond the imagination of a large part of the general public.

That was the way they felt about the Modesto Dynamite Case, until the infamy involved was proved beyond any doubt. The King-Ramsay-Conner case remains to be proved in this manner—and such things are difficult to prove. But the waterfront needs no further proof. To · them King, Ramsay, and Conner are honored martyrs to the cause of labor—men who could not be bought and had to be framed. To maritime labor they are akin to Howard Sperry and Nicholas Bordoise, who lie buried in the city's cemeteries. And these things are not easily forgotten.

Newspapers used the case to point to the waterfront as a region of excessive crime and disorder. They had to seize upon the case because murders and crimes are so rare on the waterfront. They are not so rare in the exclusive residential sections of the city where atrocities of sex and greed are almost daily occurrences.

Murder among the mansions is a monotonous everyday fact. But murder on the waterfront was an exceptional novelty, and received much prominence in the press.

It may be pointed out for what it is worth that certain interests were highly desirous of getting King out of the way. Four separate attempts were made on his life in preceding months. He was disliked, not only by employers, but by the international executives of the union. On April 7, 1936, Ivan Hunter, secretary-treasurer of the International Seamen's Union, was arrested in San Francisco on the charge of having attempted to pay a gunman $500 to murder King. The case was only loosely investigated and ultimately Hunter was dismissed for the reason that the word "kill" had never been uttered in the arrangements.

CHAPTER XX
*The "March Inland," A
Lockout Is Planned*

THROUGHOUT THE WHOLE PERIOD
of 1935 and 1936 there was hardly a day in which struggles, large or
small, were not taking place on the waterfront. In the fall of 1935 the
famous Vancouver "hot cargo" incident occurred which resulted in a
lockout when longshoremen refused to handle scab cargo from or to
British Columbia where the dock workers were on strike. There was
also a strike of barge workers and a strike of the seamen on steam
schooners. In all some 561 stoppages of work occurred, ranging from
a few hours to a few months, and involving disputes all the way from
small handfuls of cargo to large fleets of vessels.

These situations required an enormous amount of tact and skillful
maneuvering on the part of rank-and-file leaders. If the maritime
unions failed to extend support to organized labor elsewhere they
would be destroying the very bond of loyalty that had enabled them
to win their present gains. If they allowed these incidents to provoke
major strikes, unprepared for and in violation of the arbitration
award, they would again be endangering their gains. It was perhaps
the most difficult period ever undergone in the history of American

labor struggles—difficult because it required great understanding and diplomacy. The whole East Coast and Gulf sections of maritime labor were still under the thumb of old-line conservative officials, and their working conditions were far below the West Coast. Furthermore, the West Coast seamen still had bitter grievances which were not adjusted in 1934, and the top officialdom of the West Coast unions was still of the conservative variety. A bitter internal struggle was going on simultaneously with the struggle to defend the strike gains.

During this period the longshoremen continued their "march inland" and proceeded to organize warehouse after warehouse into an auxiliary unit of the ILA. There could be some dispute as to whether the warehousemen came under the jurisdiction of the Teamsters' Union or the longshoremen. But for a third of a century the teamsters, under their conservative leadership typified by Michael Casey, had sat back and made no effort to organize the warehousemen, one of the most vital sections of labor in the community.

It was also a period in which the maritime unions, and the longshoremen in particular, grew tremendously in strength and prestige, and became a powerful influence in the community. Resolutions and opinions expressed by the waterfront unions set the tone for the progressive labor movement generally, and also influenced large sections of public opinion outside the labor movement. There developed a general attitude of "If the longshoremen think it's all right, it must be all right."

Whereas in most American cities the Mayor and the Chamber of Commerce are regarded as the civic leadership, in San Francisco this sentiment was split. An enormous proportion of the public now looked to the maritime unions and their leaders. In labor parades, when the longshoremen march in uniform hickory shirts, clean black dungarees, and white caps, they are hailed in the manner that some European cities hail crack regiments of the king's own guard.

The ILA set up an efficient publicity bureau which turned out booklets and literature to keep the public informed on waterfront affairs. All and sundry were invited to come down to the waterfront, inspect the hiring hall, and be conducted around the docks by official ILA guides. Hitherto the relations between the public and industry had been through the Chamber of Commerce. The ILA was now functioning as a veritable "Chamber of Labor." Hitherto the public's attention had been directed to the graceful lines of the ships, the palatial decorations in first-class cabins, and the "romantic" side of the maritime industry. Now their attention was directed to the complex and fascinating particulars of maritime labor—the skill and knowledge required—the importance of human muscles, brains, and hands in the conduct of commerce.

Within two short years the whole psychology of a city was transformed. The longshoremen were no longer regarded as ragamuffins or roustabouts. They were a skilled, important and proud element in the community. An ILA union button commanded respect. A longshoreman's credit was good. His opinion was something to listen to. And his kids clogged to school with good thick leather on their feet.

Meanwhile the seamen were also consolidating their gains. Although they were not granted a union hiring hall in the arbitration award, they soon had one. They had one because seamen refused to hire off the pierheads or in any other way but through a union hall.

Every vessel had its ship's delegate who represented the seamen in their differences with the companies. Any grievance, be it a cockroach in the hash or a dollar too little in the pay envelope, was taken up through the ship's delegate and adjusted in an organized manner. When the ship's delegate talked, he had better be listened to. His word was backed up by every seaman on the vessel, and every vessel on the coast.

However, a situation regarding the seamen arose which, according to the majority of opinion on the subject, gave the shipowners their strongest hope of breaking this great power of labor. The seamen got the "dirty end of the stick" in the 1934 strike. That was not the fault of the longshoremen, but it was a fact. The basis for a certain amount of jealousy existed. And if this jealousy could be fanned into open friction between the seamen and the longshoremen, the power of maritime labor would be gone. The whole strength of the unions rested squarely upon the solidarity of seamen and longshoremen.

September 1935 was the time for renewal of agreements. Seamen looked forward to this time in order to voice their grievances. Cooperation of the longshoremen was important. But the West Coast district of the longshoremen was still headed by William J. Lewis and Paddy Morris, two lieutenants of Joseph P. Ryan. They promptly renewed the longshore agreement without so much as a blink at the difficulties of the seamen. This cut off the possibility of longshore support and, when the seamen presented their demands the employers could afford to ignore them.

Rumors began to spread that the longshoremen were "pork chop conscious" and would not support the seamen because they were afraid of losing their own advantages. It was not true, but it gained ground nevertheless. As a matter of fact, most seamen were more sensible than this, and the ground that the rumor gained was not enough to plant a blade of grass in it, let alone a lily. But on the surface it appeared that there was some possibility of stirring up strife. And certain interests thought the ground was wide enough to yield a bumper crop of open-shop weeds.

Among the seamen there were still remnants of syndicalist sentiment which placed very little value on political action or the practice of winning public support. The attitude of the syndicalist elements, roughly, was, "We've got the men. To hell with everything else." Some were honest trade unionists, but honesty is not enough, as many people learn when they are operated on by humane but unskilled surgeons. There were others, a small group, whose honesty was dubious at best, who played on syndicalist sentiment to advance their own designs.

Since the ousting of Scharrenberg, Harry Lundeberg had risen to the head of the Sailors' Union. He professed the belief that the power of labor rested solely in its hairy arm and "to hell with politics, publicity and strategy." * He resented the power and prestige of the longshoremen and their leaders.

Under Lundeberg's leadership the sailors embarked on a provocative policy of "job action" which threatened to upset the canoe of the Maritime Federation. As has been pointed out, no portion of maritime labor could indulge in any action without seriously affecting all other crafts. Therefore, it was important that all crafts be consulted before such action was taken. This was the fundamental reason for the federation. All unions had consistently engaged in "job strikes" or "quickie strikes" to maintain the gains of the 1934 conflict. But all of the more informed unionists realized that major demands could be won by a major strike only, and that "job strikes" had no value in this regard. (See Appendix 12.)

The Lundeberg "job action" campaign, however, did not follow this

*Subsequent developments demonstrated that Lundeberg's supposed opposition to political action did not stem from a distaste for politics in general, but for the sort of politics in which labor asserted its independent strength. He has since become an adroit politician in his own right, and for the Republican Party is The Old Reliable whenever a "labor" endorsement is needed for a Republican candidate particularly obnoxious to the workers.

As with political program, so with economic action. Despite his blustering show of militancy, Lundeberg has become the shipowners' preferred maritime labor leader. The furtive affection shown for him by both employers and the commercial press in 1936 has since blossomed into unashamed passion, and Lundeberg is the "fair-haired boy" of every employer agency and mouthpiece.

[214]

reasoning. Such strikes were called in demand of major items not included in awards or agreements. Early in 1936 sixty steam schooners struck for the six-hour day and overtime pay, a demand that obviously could not be won by anything but major action. This unwise strike resulted in a virtual lockout of all crafts.

International executives seized upon the opportunity to revoke the Sailors' Union charter issued by the American Federation of Labor. This was really a serious matter because it isolated the Sailors' Union from the rest of organized labor. But the syndicalist element did not see it that way. Their attitude was, "We've got the men, let them have the charter," and they advanced a theory of dual unionism. The majority of the membership of the Sailors' Union perceived the folly of such a course and insisted on a policy of fighting to retain the A. F. of L. charter. In this fight they were backed up by the whole of the progressive labor movement and, although at this writing they have not yet regained their charter, there is every probability that they will in the near future.

The most important objective of all maritime unions was to achieve democracy and rank-and-file control in the East Coast and Gulf unions, and then to form a national maritime federation. If individual unions like the Sailors' Union should break away from the A. F. of L., it would seriously disrupt such a program. Likewise, if the Maritime Federation of the Pacific Coast were to break away and constitute itself an industrial union, this would create a serious split, isolating the West Coast workers from the East Coast workers. Unity among all crafts and between East and West coasts and the Gulf was the first and most important thing to attain.

Almost everyone realized that the existing hostile peace was a very temporary thing and that sooner or later the issues of the 1934 strike would have to be fought out all over again. And it was well known that the shipowners were amassing an enormous war chest in preparation for the coming struggle. By the end of 1936 they were reputed to have collected a fund of $200,000,000 by a tonnage tax. They admitted frankly that the arbitration awards did not suit them and they would be demanding changes when the next date for renewal came around.

Meanwhile another development took place in 1936 which vastly strengthened the position of the unions. By a referendum vote of all coast ports, Harry Bridges and a progressive slate were elected to leadership of the West Coast district of the ILA. Shortly thereafter, at the 1936 convention of the Maritime Federation, it was decided that when September 30 came around, instead of negotiating renewals or changes in the agreements separately, all the unions would present a solid front to the shipowners. All of the seven unions decided to ask amendments to the award. This precluded the possibility of the ship-owners' ignoring the demands of the seamen as they had in 1935.

It became obvious that a major showdown was impending.

The shipowners sent out circular letters to all shippers advising them to arrange to transport their goods by rail or truck after September 30 because a prolonged shut-down was going to occur. The rush of work on the docks as employers prepared for the lockout became so excessive that nearly all longshoremen on the front had to put in long hours of overtime and pay checks mounted to record highs.

Salesman I. H. McCarty of the Lake Erie Chemical Company (makers of tear gas and supplies) wrote to A. S. Ailes, vice-president of the company, informing him:

I am rushing the inventory.... Today various police departments have been asking for the first-aid sheets and inquiring if we would be able to supply enough of the new items to handle the big general strike now expected in September. From best sources they claim it is to be a lockout on the part of the corporations and a bitter battle, being worse than 1934.

Newspapers informed the public that another major strike, which had been planned the year before by communists in Moscow, was about to be launched on the Pacific Coast waterfront.

From the employers' point of view their prospects were excellent and the time was propitious. The long internal struggle within the unions was adjudged by them to be a sign of growing dissension. Likewise, the small amount of friction which had been fostered between the seamen and the longshoremen appeared all out of proportion from a distance. It seemed that this would be a spark easily fanned into a destructive blaze.

For two years a relentless propaganda campaign had been waged against Harry Bridges, the rank-and-file leaders, and the alleged "communistic" influence on the waterfront. This campaign had been extended to all sections of the public and into the ranks of the unions themselves. It was believed that an immense psychological prejudice had been built up which could be wielded to powerful advantage.

Hitherto Harry Lundeberg had been subjected to the same scorching propaganda attack as Bridges and other progressives. But now, in the interests of fostering a split, the "finger" was taken off Lundeberg. The whole force of invective was directed against Bridges, while Lundeberg was played up in a most flattering light.

Another and more important consideration from the shipowners' standpoint was the presidential election scheduled for November. Governor Landon of Kansas was running against Roosevelt on a strictly anti-New Deal platform. For a whole year in advance every propaganda medium under the influence of employers nationally had been waging a blistering campaign against the New Deal. With the election approaching, this propaganda had reached the proportions of a veritable tidal wave, and reflected as strongly against the Pacific Coast maritime unions as it did against Roosevelt.

By reading the newspapers of that period one would gather that public sentiment on a nation-wide scale was overwhelmingly against Roosevelt and the New Deal, and, by the same token, against the maritime unions. Every newspaper in San Francisco was vigorously campaigning for Landon, with the exception of the *San Francisco News*. And even the pro-Roosevelt attitude of the *News* was of a mild and unenthusiastic character. The Hearst papers were openly declaring Roosevelt to be a communist and the issues of the campaign to be "Americanism versus Communism." Simultaneously the issues on the waterfront were declared to be between Americanism and communism.

With this thunderous propaganda storm in back of them, the shipowners felt assured in the coming fight. They also believed that Landon would be elected by a landslide vote, and this would make a big difference in the government's attitude in regard to strike intervention.

There was also another consideration which seemed to weigh heavily in the shipowners' favor. The recently passed Copeland Ship Subsidy bill provided for a National Maritime Commission appointed by the President, which would have authority to determine wages, hours, and working conditions for seamen. The bill also called for a system of passports or continuous discharge books for seamen that were very similar to the ones which the seamen had burned in a huge bonfire at the close of the 1934 strike.

Ostensibly the bill was passed to curb the abuses of shipowners and to secure the rights of seamen. Nevertheless it had in it the makings of a federal dictatorship over the maritime unions, and the continuous discharge books would lend themselves readily to an effective blacklist.

The bill was prompted by the scandalous exposures of graft and misappropriations of funds by shipowners which came to light in the Senate investigation of aerial and ocean mail contracts. President Roosevelt had ordered Congress to do away with all existing forms of subsidies and to draft new legislation which would curb these abuses and safeguard the public interest. The Copeland bill was the result.

It provided that hereafter, instead of handing out subsidies in lump sums, the government would pay only an exact differential between foreign and American operating costs. Subsidy payments were to be under the strict supervision of the National Maritime Commission which was empowered to investigate the ledgers of the shipowners whenever it desired.

The maritime unions were opposed to the bill from the start. They approved of many measures to check on the shipowners and see to it that subsidies were properly expended. But too much of the bill seemed to jump right over the heads of the shipowners and land on the unions. The authority of the National Maritime Commission could be used or misused, depending on what kind of administration got in office and whether or not the shipowners' powerful Washington lobby could influence the commissioners. The ability of the national shipowning and shipbuilding interests to influence public officials had been demonstrated too well in the past. And the unions did not want their fate tied up to a political weather vane such as the commission might very well turn out to be.

With all these things apparently weighing in their favor, the employers approached the showdown with easy confidence. How much confidence is apparent in early conferences. On July 29, 1936, they served formal notice that they were dissatisfied with existing agreements and did not intend to renew them. Four or five weeks later representatives of the unions met with employers and were confronted with the demand that conditions be restored virtually to what they were prior to the 1934 strike. They wanted the men to surrender control of the hiring halls and preferential employment. They wanted the six-hour day of the longshoremen abolished and a series of penalties instituted to prevent stoppages of work and sympathy actions, such as the "hot cargo" episodes.

The demands raised by the unions were flatly rejected. These included the eight-hour day on all vessels, payment for overtime in cash instead of time off, recognized union hiring halls, and numerous other improvements. The proposition of the shipowners was that the whole matter be resubmitted to arbitration and that, in the meantime pre-1934 conditions be restored pending a new award. So far as the men were concerned this would amount to taking everything they had won in the 1934 strike and throwing it back onto a political roulette table. This would have been hazardous under any circumstances. Considering the then highly unsettled condition of national politics it would have been madness. The bitter presidential contest had churned up a state of hysteria. Men in public life were afraid even to mention the words "New Deal" for fear the next morning they would see themselves decried in the Hearst papers as "communists." It was like asking the men to open their hatches in the midst of a hurricane. They refused.

Employers promptly informed them that after September 30 hiring would be done from the pierheads instead of through union halls. This, in effect, meant a lockout of all the maritime workers on the Pacific Coast.

On September 30, at the request of the federal government, the deadline was advanced to October 15.

On October 13, two days before the time was up, the government requested both sides to continue existing awards pending investigation and arbitration. The employers agreed but the men refused.

October 15 came and went and employers still insisted that everything be thrown back into the hopper of arbitration. The men took a coastwise referendum on the matter and voted overwhelmingly that if negotiations were not productive of anything by October 29 they would strike.

At midnight, October 29, the entire maritime profession, from the captains right on down, walked off the ships and docks with the accord of a single man. What happened after that provides one of the most unusual pages in labor history.

Employers calmly tied up their ships, closed down operations, and sat back to wait until the men would be starved out.

The men established their picket lines and built small shacks at evenly spaced points up and down the Embarcadero to shelter them from wind and rain. It was a winter strike and a cold vigil. A relief committee appealed to the public for old overcoats and clothing to keep the men warm. People dug into their attics and basements and brought forth a flood of old garments.

Lincoln Steffens had just died, and his coats went to warm the backs of the pickets. The wardrobe of this famous friend of labor marched in the picket lines, where his heart and loyalty had always marched.

The men established watches and relieved each other with the same discipline and regularity to which they had been accustomed on board ship.

The Maritime Federation appointed its own police force—big, strapping men with blue armbands marked "M.F.P." They patrolled the waterfront and kept order so effectively that the regular city police were left out of the picture. Not even a drunken man was to be found the length of the front. If a seaman or longshoreman got a few too many under his belt, the MFP's would take him in custody and send him home in a car to sober up.

This vast display of discipline and competence was something that took the employers by surprise. The unions had scored the first point. A propaganda campaign had already been launched decrying the strikers as a disorderly and irresponsible mob. It appeared quite flat and foolish in the face of this orderly demonstration.

Public support to the strikers was steady and substantial from the very beginning. Organized labor had grown stronger since the 1934 strike and had won vast thousands of new sympathizers. It was immediately apparent that two years of propaganda against the maritime unions and their leadersip had fallen on deaf ears. The unions had scored point number two.

The strike committee established a Joint Publicity Committee with representatives from all maritime unions, and set up offices in Recreation Center, an abandoned warehouse which had been converted into a clubhouse, gymnasium, and sports center for the waterfront workers. A call was sent out to the public for volunteer technical aid, and soon scores of men and women were busy in every corner of the building—stenographers, journalists, artists, college students, unemployed clerks, and members of the newly organized Northern California Newspaper Guild—all people warmly sympathetic to the unions and willing to donate their efforts. A troupe of local actors even donated its talent in acting out a series of dramatized radio broadcasts four times weekly over a small station. Many times incidents which occurred on the Embarcadero in the morning were written up by volunteer writers and re-enacted over the air that very night.

This publicity corps hit first and hit hard and paced the employers' propaganda apparatus throughout the entire struggle. The unions had very little money and depended on volunteer help. The employers had almost limitless funds and employed crack press agents at top salaries. But, in a sense, the unions had the edge.

The expert publicity agents of the employers were working for money and had no particular ideals bound up with their work. They applied set and fixed, cut and dried publicity theories to the task—a bag of tricks and devices which advertising experts believe are capable of molding public opinion to any shape they choose.

But the volunteer workers on the strikers' publicity committee believed mightily in what they were doing and worked with great sincerity. There was such an unmistakable tone of honesty and conviction in all their work that no standardized publicity could compete with it. It contained warmth, humor, and imagination that made the elaborate apparatus of the employers look like a pile of moldy rubber stamps.

After proclaiming the strikers to be Bolshevik revolutionists intent upon destroying the church, the home, and the stock dividend, the highly paid publicists of the employers would run out of ideas and flounder in a vacuum.

Not so with the strikers' committee. They had endless variety to play upon. One example of the numerous handbills turned out was headed "BUY A SHIP AND MAKE YOUR FORTUNE." It read:

Why waste your time in your present line of work? Why don't you buy a Ship and make your fortune? Others have done it—right here in San Francisco. Where do they get the money? That's easy, after you learn the ropes. You can borrow it from the Government at low interest rates. Then you can make a contract with the Government to carry the mail. (This is known as ship-subsidy.) Will the contract pay? Yes, it will pay and pay and *pay!*

Fact of the matter is, you can get enough out of the contract to pay all the running expenses of your ship, so that every pound of freight and every passenger you carry gives you a clear profit. Even if you run your ship hither and yon all over the Pacific Ocean, you can't lose if you are subsidized.

Now, don't get the idea that this is a cargo of waterfront baloney. Nothing of the kind. Postmaster General Farley recently reported to the President that as near as he could figure the Government had already given out the sum of $708,618,096.06 in ship subsidies. You see!

Of course, there is a reason for the paying out of all this money from the taxpayers' pockets. It is given so that American shipowners can pay high wages to seafaring men, feed them well while at sea, give them first-class quarters aboard ship, and in general compete favorably with foreign shipowners. This is to keep the American flag flying on the high seas. Very few of the big companies pay much attention to the purposes of the ship-subsidies. . . .

The rest of the leaflet detailed the actual working out of the subsidy system in contrast to its purposes.

A neat, illustrated booklet entitled *The Maritime Crisis—What It Is and What It Isn't* was published by the San Francisco local of the ILA to sell for five cents. It read, in part:

Maritime strike! Once again, as these lines are being written, those words are blazoned in headlines across the country. Again, as in 1934, ships lie idle in the harbor. Again winches are silent, the bustle along the waterfront is stilled.

Why?

Is it because, as the shipowners would have the public believe, maritime workers are trouble-makers—men who enjoy strife for the sake of strife, men so blind that they are ready to sacrifice thousands of dollars in wages that they so sorely need merely for a little excitement? Is it because the workers are so "unreasonable" that they want everything their own way?

No honest, fair-minded citizen who is willing to look facts in the face will believe such charges. Workers do not strike for the pure joy of striking or for petty ends. The reason is very easy to understand. Workers, for the most part, live from hand to mouth—from necessity, not from choice. Unlike the shipowners, they do not have great reserves of capital piled up to tide them over a strike crisis. When work stops, they do not face a mere decrease in dividends. They face the loss of the most elementary necessities of life—food, shelter and frequently health—not only for themselves but also for their wives and children.

For this simple reason workers strike only as a last resort and only out of sheer desperation. In 1934 on the waterfront, it was that desperation that arose from unendurable conditions—conditions so bad that thousands of workers preferred to face machine guns rather than continue to endure them. In 1936, while other crafts, whose conditions were not appreciably bettered in 1934, are striking because of the same desperation which originally stirred the longshoremen to action, the situation is somewhat altered so far as the ILA itself is concerned. The desperation of the longshoremen today arises from the fact that every gain made in 1934 is now endangered by the demands of the shipowners.

The two samples of publicity shown above represent two separate types. The latter is a defensive explanation to counteract the publicity of the shipowners. The former is a direct counterattack. Both of these types were used effectively, but the greatest emphasis was thrown on the counterattack until by the end of the strike the employers were on the defensive.

Shortly before the strike twenty-six companies, including foreign operators, had been in favor of granting the demands of the men and concluding agreements. It was the persistence of three big companies —Matson, Dollar, and American Hawaiian—that prevailed over the others and forced the lockout. These were known as the "Big Three" and it was against them that the strikers threw the weight of their attack.

Sound trucks bearing huge signboards were sent through the streets announcing, "BIG THREE BLOCKS PEACE." One side of the signs was decorated with the banners of the three companies under the legend "THEIR FLAGS." The other side bore the Stars and Stripes under the legend "OUR FLAG."

Employers began to emphasize efficiency of the merchant marine and safety of lives and property at sea as a basis for their demands.

The strikers quickly pointed out that they, not the shipowners, comprised the highest existent authorities on this subject. The captains of the vessels shouldered all the practical responsibility for such matters, and the captains were on strike with the men. Soon the unions converted this argument into one of their strongest points. They demonstrated how the unions were the public's surest defense against lax regulations on vessels arising out of the shipowners' desire to save money, whereas, so far as the seamen and officers were concerned, their very lives depended on the efficiency and proper equipment. They produced reams of testimony to show that unless an officer or a seaman had a strong union to back him up, he dare not be too particular about regulations or he might lose his job. Spectacular examples were chosen. The "Morro Castle" blazed again in the public eye, and the "Vestris" went down with all its hideous loss of life. Dramatizations of scenes on sinking ships were broadcast over the radio and, all in all, the employers wished they had never brought up the subject.

The most shattering blow came when Landon was defeated by an overwhelming majority in the presidential elections. It came as an almost unnerving shock—an almost incredible setback. It meant that the newspapers of the nation, which had always been regarded as the positive force in molding public opinion, had slipped out of gear and were rattling in a vacuum.

Meanwhile the strike had spread to the East Coast seamen and it was requiring all that Joseph P. Ryan had in the way of strategy and persuasion to keep the longshoremen from going out also. In fact, the Baltimore longshoremen pulled the pants off him and sent him home in his underdrawers on the occasion of one of his rare personal appearances. These eastern unions, which had lain dormant for so long, were now demanding an equal status with the West Coast and had flared into active revolt against their conservative leaders.

Like the maritime workers in San Francisco, the warehousemen, recently organized by the ILA, were conducting major strikes.

Lee Holman, the expelled former president of the San Francisco local of the ILA, appeared on the scene again and began organizing what he called a "real American longshoremen's union." He was so roundly despised by the men on the waterfront that he dared not even show his face on the Embarcadero. He assembled an aggregation of toughs who roamed the waterfront on dark nights, waylaying and beating up union men as they came off the picket lines. Their depredations finally became so outrageous that numbers of them were arrested by the city police for assault. Feeling themselves to be licensed characters, they had begun carrying on their gangsterism openly and with very little effort at stealth. These were the only incidents of violence during the entire strike.

It was apparent that Holman had a certain amount of financial backing from some place though, at this writing, his sponsors have not yet been identified and can only be surmised. He made a particular effort to rally Negro workers and incite race riots. The unions, however, had taken special precautions against this danger. There was absolutely no discrimination against Negroes in the unions. Negroes marched in the picket lines and were seated on the strike committee. A special leaflet addressed to the Negro population was issued. In truth, the maritime unions had established new precedents of racial equality that were valued and esteemed by the Negro people.

On one occasion Holman called a meeting at the offices of the *San Francisco News-Letter Wasp*, a weekly news magazine which backed his adventures and abhorred Bridges. It was a dismal business. The longshoremen turned out with bags of stale eggs and old fruit, and the minute he showed his face bombarded him into retreat. On another occasion he held a meeting and did not appear at all, but talked through a loudspeaker from a distant point. But all this was nonsense. No matter how much the newspapers played it up, there never was the slightest prospect of success in Holman's venture, and whoever gave him financial backing was throwing away money. The most it ever amounted to was a new strategy of organizing strikebreakers into an artificial union and introducing them in this guise. As it happened, it never even reached that stage.

On December 5 the strikers planned a mass parade up Market Street. The day before the whole town had been saturated with leaflets, put out by some "mysterious" agency, which were printed in red, white, and blue type (bearing no union printer's label). They read:

S. O. S.

From: True Americans of the rank and file of the maritime industry.
To: True American citizens of the Bay area.
Here's our position.
We—the honest, hard-working Americans in the maritime industry—*want to work. We don't want to strike!*
We—the victims of Communist leaders dominating the waterfront—can't work. *We are forced to strike!*
They—the Communists—maintain Beef Squads. We must picket or *Beef Squads* will make us wish we had!
They—the Communists—are staging the Saturday parade—a "Mass Dem-

onstration" of Communism. We have to parade—*or pay fines if we don't! We need help immediately.*

You—the public—must demand that Communist leaders in marine unions agree at once to *arbitrate* this disastrous strike!

You—the public—are *victims* of this *unnecessary strike!*

We—the Americans in the American Merchant Marine—will settle the Reds. But we can't do it while *they keep us on strike!*

We—who want to work—will help. But *You*—the public—hold the balance of power. *Only public action can end this strike! Use your power! Demand arbitration! Defeat Communists!*

This was only one of the numerous similar pieces of propaganda which were circulated throughout the strike. They were almost wholly ineffective. There was too much overeagerness and hysteria in their wording, and they conformed too exactly with the shipowner's own publicity. Furthermore, whoever got them out made a fatal error which no union man would make; they left the union "bug" off. The union "bug" or label is a small device indicating that printed matter has been produced in a union shop. It must appear on all labor publicity, otherwise union men will not read it and will recognize at a glance that it is "phony."

The fact that a piece of printed matter bears a union "bug" does not necessarily constitute an endorsement of its contents. All sorts of printed matter carry the "bug"—even the publications of the Waterfront Employers. But the absence of the "bug" on an alleged labor leaflet is tantamount to absence of silk threads in the paper of a dollar bill.

The parade itself was a dramatic and entertaining spectacle that introduced new ideas. Instead of the usual procession of silent men marching by hour after hour in a show of strength, the column was punctuated by numerous floats and thousands of banners. It took two hours to go by and offered endless variety to the spectator.

At regular intervals along the line of march speakers were situated in parked cars or atop the marquees of sympathetic shops. Through amplifiers they kept up a constant explanation to the watching crowds as the parade went by. Special squads moved in and out among the spectators, handing out literature. Supplies of pamphlets and handbills were located at points a few blocks apart all the way up Market Street so that when the distributors ran out they could get new armloads without delay.

At the head of the column rode the parade marshal, a member of the Marine Cooks and Stewards Union, astride a spirited horse that had been rented from a local riding academy. Behind him followed 25,000 men, with special sections of wives and children. A union band struck up the familiar tune of "Solidarity Forever." Cheers and good-natured greetings blended the spirits of the watching crowd with those of the marchers. It was half demonstration and half carnival.

Four men carried a large sign: "Do ships pay? Ask the man who owns one!" Following behind them was an elegant town car rented from a garage. A uniformed chauffeur sat at the wheel. Up on the back of the rear seat was the burlesque figure of a shipowner—an enormously fat man with a big red nose and a silk hat, which he tipped to the spectators as he rode along puffing on a big black cigar. Over one shoulder he was holding onto a large hawser, on the end of which he was dragging a seamen with a noose around his neck. The hawser was marked "Copeland Act."

Another float bore the "Good Ship Subsidy," a rowboat in which three wildly painted pirates stood flourishing cutlasses and screaming for new subsidies. They were labeled "Matson," "Dollar," and "American Hawaiian."

A toothless seaman impersonated the famous cartoon character "Pop-Eye the Sailor Man." He roamed at large up and down the parade in the manner of a circus clown, evoking screams of delight from the children on the sidewalk.

On another float a stout longshoreman in a silk hat impersonated a shipowner with the proverbial black cigar and red nose. He sat behind an office desk and pulled a string, whereupon a wild-looking creature labeled "Lee Holman" would jump out of a garbage can and begin throwing leaflets to the spectators. When the "shipowner" relaxed the cord "Holman" would sag back into the can. The leaflets bore a mixed-up scramble of words slanting every which way: "To my dear 'friends'? Lies! Filth! Dirt! Disruption! Trash! The employers pull the string and I speak. Bla!—'Ash Can' Lee Holman, the ship-owners' puppet."

Still another float bore a complete unit of the strikers' publicity committee. Typewriters and mimeographs were operated as the truck moved along, turning out and distributing leaflets to the crowds on the curb.

From high up in office buildings shipowners watched the procession go by with considerable alarm. Some of them recognized at a glance that their cause was lost. Here was a demonstration brilliantly staged, perfectly organized, and carried out with magnificent discipline. They were discovering new depths of talent and efficiency in their employees.

It was expected that after being locked out this long the men would be restless, irritable, and quarreling among themselves. On the contrary, the strike enabled the longshoremen and seamen to fraternize on a much larger scale, and even what small dissension existed before had melted over the campfires on the picket line.

The dissension occurred, but not within the ranks of the strikers. It was the shipowners themselves who began quarreling with each other. Such abundant difference of opinion developed in their ranks that it was almost impossible for them to move as a coordinated body.

The strikers had invited the public to a mass meeting in the Civic Auditorium on the evening of December 8. The shipowners had been invited to send a speaker to present their side. Up to now the invitation had been ignored, but immediately after the huge parade it was accepted. Roger Lapham, the president of the American Hawaiian Steamship Company, was to be the employers' spokesman.

The auditorium was packed to capacity half an hour before the scheduled opening of the meeting on the evening of December 8. The seating capacity of 10,000 was filled long before that. Now all of the aisles and every conceivable bit of standing room was jammed. This was contrary to all fire regulations, but in view of the enthusiasm of the throng Fire Department officials decided to ignore rules.

Many speakers addressed the gathering, but the main speakers were Roger Lapham and Harry Bridges.

Sentiment of the audience was so emphatically one-sided that Lapham was talking into a void. Nevertheless his words were greeted with polite attention. Whenever anyone in the assemblage showed a disposition to rowdyism, the strikers themselves urged silence. Ushers for the meeting were ships' officers in full uniform.

This courteous treatment accorded Lapham was not consistent with the loud hisses and boos which had greeted employer representatives during the 1934 strike. And the difference was interesting. During most of the 1934 strike the employers had the upper hand and the men were battling against odds. Now everyone instinctively felt the situation to be reversed. There was a warm, easy confidence among the strikers and they wanted to be good sports.

In his speech Lapham said, "The shipowners have no desire to eliminate or control the hiring hall. All that they seek is the right to control hiring."

The exaggerated and strained silence was dispelled by a quick roar of laughter.

In his speech Bridges said, "All they want is control of hiring. The employers had control of hiring, much to our detriment and misery. We hope they will never get it back."

CHAPTER XXI
The Maritime Federation Wins
A Victory, Towards A National
Maritime Federation

A FTER THE DECEMBER 8 meeting it was clear to everyone that the employers had only two cards left to play. Unless they could cause the hoped-for dissension within the ranks of the strikers, or persuade the government to enforce compulsory arbitration, their cause was lost. As regards the former objective they had only one hope, and that was not a very substantial one.

Harry Lundeberg, rank-and-file leader of the sailors, still had certain fundamental differences with the Maritime Federation. Already two particular disagreements had occurred during the strike. For one thing, Lundeberg, and the syndicalist sentiment which he represented, regarded the elaborate publicity campaign as a lot of needless claptrap. They believed it to be "kowtowing to public opinion." Opposed to them were the vast majority of the men on strike who believed that labor, in its struggles, should utilize every legitimate weapon it could summon to its hand—including political action and publicity.

The other difference centered around the issue of "perishable cargo." Early in the strike employers began to raise a vigorous complaint that much valuable cargo tied up on the vessels was perishable and would be destroyed unless unloaded soon. It was emphasized also that this cargo was very much needed by the public at large. It was a small matter, really, and the cargo did not amount to much. But to certain sections of the public this appeared to be wanton destruction.

The San Francisco Strike Committee discussed the matter and decided that the surest way to silence this propaganda argument was to unload the cargo. Its quantity was so trivial that it could be accomplished in a few hours and would not harm the effectiveness of the strike one iota. Neither Lundeberg nor the sphere of influence he commanded was in sympathy with this move and opposed it hotly.

Shortly thereafter Lundeberg of the Sailors' Union and Ferguson of the Marine Firemen's Union were called into separate negotiations by the shipowners. This was an unusual procedure. Hitherto all of the unions had negotiated collectively and the ILA, realizing that its position was the strongest, had refused to negotiate at all until the other unions had been given satisfaction. One of the reasons for this was to dispel once and for all the disruptive rumor that the longshoremen were "pork chop conscious" and out to save their own necks.

Lundeberg and Ferguson, however, quickly negotiated separate agreements for their unions and also agreed to recommend immediate acceptance without modification. If such a plan were carried out it would enable shipowners to ignore the demands of other unions, in much the same manner as they had been able to ignore the seamen's demands when the longshoremen renewed their agreement in 1935.

Newspapers burst into print with news that the strike was over, despite the fact that five of the seven unions had not even been accorded negotiations yet. A general propaganda campaign was begun to stampede the men back to work. This campaign was conducted with the customary lack of skill. Newspapers even carried front-page stories announcing that Lundeberg had joined the shipowners in an attack on Bridges.

Immediately the strikers were resentful at such a proposition. They held mass meetings in all ports and, despite the insistence of Lundeberg and Ferguson, voted overwhelmingly that no union would ballot on an agreement until agreements had been negotiated by all unions.

That ended any hope of causing a split in the ranks of the strikers.

Early in January 1937 a series of minor clashes occurred when Lee Holman's men appeared on the streets on and around the Embarcadero selling copies of a little tabloid, twice-monthly newspaper, the

American Citizen. Strikers quickly accosted them and drove them out of the district.

The *American Citizen* deserves some comment. It was published across the bay in San Rafael by a Colonel Sanborn and bore the legend: "Published in order that Fascism may not become necessary to prevent Communism from becoming a reality." Like Lee Holman's organization, it was financed by sources which have not as yet been identified. But that its financing was considerable is apparent. The price was five cents per copy but little effort was made to sell it. Copies were distributed free, on occasion thrust under every door in the city. During periods like the strike the town was literally drenched in copies which were even littered through the streets for people to pick up. Although ostensibly directed against communism, its real attack was aimed against organized labor and, without any exception, it took the employers' side. Anyone who uttered the slightest liberal sentiment was immediately decried in this paper as a communist, and some of the community's most respectable citizens found themselves described in its pages as agents of Moscow. As in the case of all other similar propaganda, it rendered itself completely ineffective by its hysteria and overeagerness to incite prejudice.

The issue of December 31, 1936, which the Holman men were selling in January, bore headlines, "MEN WANTED; Where Are the Leaders of Today?" The obvious answer, of course, if anyone reasoned it out, was that they were in the ranks of the maritime unions. However, the *American Citizen* did not see it that way. The issue contained a strong plea for vigilante action against the strikers:

Spirit of 20 years ago needed to meet new menace.

Just 20 years ago violence broke forth on the waterfront of San Francisco, and the old files of the Daily Commercial News tell us how it was settled.

A mass meeting was called in the San Francisco Chamber of Commerce by a self-announced Law and Order Committee. . . .

Reading the Daily Commercial News of July 11, 1916, shows us that "there were giants in those days." At a meeting packed to the doors Mr. Koster called the men of San Francisco to action. . . .

Today we are faced with a far more sinister situation than was faced by the San Franciscans of 1916. . . .

Can we tolerate any longer our workers being used as dupes by foreign agitators, or will San Franciscans rise to the emergency and defend the city against the Muscovian attack?

Glancing over the item headings of this paper we see:

Reds boast of part in maritime strike.

Red hand shows everywhere.
Teachers warn against Reds in schools.
Reds make mockery of Christmas observance.
Bridges alien Red agitator.
Reds interfere in agreement.
Reds recruit by hunger marches.
Maritime strike is training for revolution.
Red students to plan march on Washington.
Reds demand Community Chest funds.
Reds pledge continued support of coast maritime strike.
Red domination is apparent in two months' tie-up.
Longshoremen used as Red catspaws.
S. F. faces "Soviet" control of business.

These skirmishes between pickets and Holman men were brief and not very important. They created a slight flurry in the press and then were forgotten. The main concentration of employers was now on government intervention.

Mayor Rossi was again brought into the picture and put on the air in a nation-wide broadcast urging President Roosevelt to enforce compulsory arbitration. It was spectacular but ineffective. Later on Bridges was given an opportunity to reply on a national hook-up; then Thomas G. Plant for the employers, and next Joseph Curran, then rank-and file leader of the East Coast seamen. If anything, these broadcasts strengthened the position of the unions and enabled them to bring their powerful arguments home to a national audience.

Shortly after this the employers sat down to business-like negotiations with all the unions. Tentative agreements were reached and submitted to a simultaneous referendum of all maritime workers on the West Coast. They embodied gains and improvements far beyond what had been won in the 1934 strike and were accepted by an overwhelming vote. The strike, which had lasted ninety-nine days, was ended on February 4, 1937. It was conducted with such discipline and efficiency that newspapers named it the "Streamlined Strike."

Thomas G. Plant promptly resigned as president of the Waterfront Employers' Union. The extent of the Maritime Federation victory can be judged from the following table:

What Employers Offered On September 30	*Basic Demands of the Unions*	*What the Unions Won*
GENERAL		
Arbitration	Direct negotiations	All disputes were settled by direct negotiations
INTERNATIONAL LONGSHOREMEN'S ASSOCIATION		
8-hour day	6-hour day	6-hour day
No union hiring hall	Union hiring hall	Union hiring hall
	Preferential employment	Preferential employment
SAILORS' UNION		
Optional overtime	Cash overtime pay	Cash overtime pay
No union hiring hall	Union hiring hall	Union hiring hall
Basic wage, $62.50	Basic wage, $90	$10 increase
COOKS AND STEWARDS		
Unlimited hours	8-hour day	8 hours on freighters
Optional overtime	Cash overtime pay	9 hours on passenger ships
No union hiring hall	Union hiring hall	Cash overtime pay
Previous wage scale	Wage increase	Union hiring hall
		$10 increase
RADIO OPERATORS		
Employer-controlled hiring	Preference of employment	Preference of employment
Previous wage scale	Wage increase	Wage increase
MARINE FIREMEN		
Optional overtime	Cash overtime pay	Cash overtime pay
No union hiring hall	Union hiring hall	Union hiring hall
Previous basic wage, $62.50	Basic wage, $90	$10 increase
MARINE ENGINEERS		
Employer-controlled hiring	Preferential employment	Union recognition
Previous wage scale	Wage increase	Selection of men from union hall
		$15 increase
MASTERS, MATES AND PILOTS		
Employer-controlled hiring	Preferential employment	Union recognition
Non-union masters	Wage increase	Selection of men from union hall
Previous wage scale		$15 increase

Seamen on the East Coast and Gulf had called off their strike a short while before. Bitter opposition from their top officials and the American Federation of Labor had made the going tough. Although the strike there had accomplished a lot toward strengthening the ranks of the men and developing resistance to the conservative union officials, it had never been completely effective. In calling it off, the rank-and-file strike committee issued a statement:

Our strike has been a major factor in helping defeat the union-smashing schemes of the Pacific shipowners.

Our strike has established closer unity between the East, Gulf and West coasts. We have established greater unity between the licensed and unlicensed crafts. We have helped strengthen the fight of the ILA membership against the strikebreaking, dictatorial policies of J. P. Ryan. For the first time effectively we have achieved unity between the white and Negro seamen. If we maintain the unity we have achieved in this strike then we have the beginning of a real Maritime Federation.

Greater democracy has been secured by the membership of the International Seamen's Union which has replaced its former officials with elected, progressive leaders.

The strike has encouraged hundreds, if not thousands of licensed officers to join the respective unions of their crafts.

The campaign against the Copeland and Ship Subsidy Bills has been strengthened and has forced important concessions that are in our interests.

No immediate major gains were secured when the eastern seamen called off their strike. That is, none beyond the general strengthening of their position as described above. Soon afterward, however, when the West Coast strike ended in victory, wages and working conditions of East Coast and Gulf seamen were raised to practical equality with those on the Pacific Coast. They still had no union hiring halls and remained largely under the thumbs of conservative top officials; but this much was gained.

Just prior to the ending of the Pacific Coast strike, Lundeberg and Ferguson advanced still another policy which ran contrary to the general sentiment of the Maritime Federation. They proposed continuing the strike until the government consented to revising the Copeland Act to eliminate the undesirable continuous discharge book.

The more sober rank-and-file leaders regarded such a proposition as hazardous and impractical. They didn't want the continuous discharge books any more than Lundeberg did. But already the government had been forced to postpone issuance of the books several times through mass protest of the seamen. And it was apparent that a vigorous campaign of protest in the future would be able to win a revision of the act.

Furthermore, although the East Coast seamen had put up a brave fight during the recent strike, it was clear that they had by no means developed such organized strength as existed on the West Coast. Anyone could see at a glance that they needed help and were not in a position right now to make such a fight.

Lundeberg's proposal was turned down by an almost unanimous vote of the rank and file, and a short while later a campaign of protest resulted in a revision of the Copeland Act to eliminate the undesirable features of the discharge book. Nevertheless, in the course of the dispute some friction developed. West Coast seamen refused to accept the book. East Coast seamen, much as they desired to take the same action, were not, organizationally, in a position to do so. Lundeberg took the attitude that all East Coast seamen who accepted books were "finks" and should be treated accordingly. The result was a small but unnecessary amount of conflict at a time when unity, cooperation, and understanding were prime factors.

These difficulties, however, were not enough to interrupt or damage the improved situation resulting from the strike. In summary, the effects of the ninety-nine-day struggle were:

(1) Conditions of Pacific Coast seamen were raised to practical equality with those of the longshoremen.

(2) Conditions of East Coast seamen were raised to equality with the West Coast, excepting as regards union hiring halls and rank-and-file democracy.

(3) The Maritime Federation of the Pacific had undergone its first major test and proved conclusively the importance of a unified program and policy for all unions within the maritime industry.

(4) The rank and file of the East Coast and Gulf unions had been strengthened immeasurably and had embarked upon a determined struggle to establish democracy in their organizations.

(5) Unity of program and policy had been strengthened among all crafts on the West Coast and with the workers on the East and Gulf coasts.

(6) As a result of all these things, the way was opened to begin a practical struggle toward the organization of a national maritime federation.

It cost employers over $500,000,000 to fight the 1934 strike. It cost them over $686,000,000 to fight the strike of 1936-1937. And neither of these struggles was complete in itself—neither of them comprises a separate or finished story. They are both part of the larger story, the building of a national maritime federation, which will be written in the future.

This book does not end. It comes to the end of its material and then breaks off, leaving a tangle of jagged threads. The rest of it will be written on the waterfronts of every American seaport—will be enacted by a cast of millions; and perhaps you will play some part. In any event, its influence will reach into your home and affect your life, no matter how far away from the seacoast you may live. For this is history, yet to be lived and experienced.

Peace reigns today on the Embarcadero—a restless, mistrustful peace. Already widespread struggles have taken place on the East Coast which vastly affect the unions on the Pacific. The tremendous organizational drive of the Committee for Industrial Organization, headed by John L. Lewis, is also having its effect. The Pacific Coast maritime unions are committed to the principle of industrial union-ism and are strong supporters of the CIO. Yet the maritime unions are a part of the A. F. of L., the top officials of which are at war with the CIO.*

The longshoremen have continued their "march inland" to organize the warehousemen. The result has been a bitter jurisdictional dispute with the top officials of the Teamsters' Union, who claim the warehousemen are under their jurisdiction. If this is so, then why did the teamster officials sit back for a third of a century making no effort to organize them?

In this controversy the rank-and-file teamsters are siding with the longshoremen and revolting against their reactionary officials.

Organized labor generally has made huge advances, and soon after the maritime strike the people of San Francisco repealed the anti-picketing ordinance in the civic elections. This law had been on the statutes for twenty years. Organized employers spent one million dollars to get it enacted in 1916.

A major campaign is now on to repeal the criminal syndicalism law.

The maritime unions have awakened to the fact that the gains they are making today in the economic field must be defended tomorrow in the political field. A strong sentiment toward independent political action by labor and its friends has developed and is reflected throughout the unions generally.

So much for formalized objectives and factors. Underneath them lies a warm and human goal.

During the last strike I talked with a ship's captain who, for the first time, was marching in the picket line side by side with the men.

*The Maritime Federation Convention voted to recommend all its unions take a vote on joining the CIO. Even the SUP took such a vote, but Lundeberg ignored it.

He had shipped before the mast in the days of sail. "From a boy in sail to a master in steam," was the way he characterized his career. He had been through the days of "crimps" and "shanghaiing" and brutal hardship which fiction writers have romanticized as the days of "wooden ships and iron men." But they were not "iron men." They were human beings and the rotten food gave them stomach ulcers. The dirty bunks were crawling with vermin and the dirty waterfront was crawling with "crimps" and rascals, waiting to hoodwink and fleece the seaman as soon as he stepped ashore.

This man had worked up to the captaincy of a proud sailing vessel, then went back to the fo'c'sle when steamships came in, and worked his way up all over again. He had a love of the sea that would have satisfied romanticists, but a hatred for the tragedy and suffering he had seen that would have shocked them.

He pictured the seafaring profession as it had been and as it could be. "Mothers weep," he said, "when young lads go to sea. And they think it means they are going to the dogs and will never amount to much. Well, they're going to amount to plenty. And this is just the beginning."

He envisioned turning the profession he loved into a proud and respected occupation. He wanted to see it a field in which a man could pursue a useful and constructive career, have decent security, and live like a human being instead of a social outcast. This was the goal he saw embodied in a national maritime federation. Comfort to the minds of men, and honor for their labor; freedom to live, to study, and develop without being bound and hampered by worry, adversity, and economic insecurity. He had seen thousands of men ground down and destroyed by unnecessary torments, petty greed, injustice, and brutality. He had seen enough, and now he was marching to end it. And there was a long road lying ahead.

As you close this book you leave a story unfinished. And perhaps your eyes will turn toward the waterfront, where the next chapter is being lived in flesh and blood. Tonight's newspaper may carry indications that the struggle is moving forward.

If you should chance to be a leading business executive, you may have read the brief but ominous note in Wall Street's reliable "inside information" service, the Kiplinger letter:

"There will be peace on the Pacific Coast—but it will not be a permanent peace."

THE END

[236]

POSTSCRIPT

By HARRY BRIDGES,
President, International Longshoremen's &
Warehousemen's Union, CIO

U PON FINISHING MIKE QUIN'S BOOK some might ask, "Well, what's happened since?" The answer is: the maritime workers have continued to fight, and they have not been beaten.

This story of a general strike did not begin in 1934, nor did it end when the maritime workers returned to their jobs. It goes on endlessly; tomorrow's headlines will announce a new chapter as the employers who have been forced to accept collective bargaining apply their talents to defeat the unions with phony laws and phony union officials.

The battle has not been one long dreary treadmill. A labor movement of some 3½ million in 1934 has grown to a strength of 16 million today.

We've had strikes on the waterfront since 1934, but never again have the bosses dared to shoot our men down in cold blood.

Other economic gains have been added to those secured in 1934. They add up to greater security for the men who move cargoes and sail ships. Longshoremen and seamen, once the disinherited outcasts of American industry, today enjoy wages and conditions that compare favorably with those in other industries.

The 1934 strike marked a great rebirth of American unionism. The owners of industry made an abortive but bloody attempt to crush the infant in the womb.

They did not succeed.

Today, faced with full-bodied and grown unions, the bosses have tacked and changed their course. They seek to corrupt and paralyze the unions.

To this end they have passed the Taft-Hartley Law. To this end they foster division within the labor movement, seek to dictate its policies and select its leaders through the media of propaganda and pressure. They want to tame the unions, make them meek and servile.

For one hundred years American labor unions were crushed as a regular order of business. During that century the control of unions through corrupt chiefs became something of an underground art with the bosses, but they put their emphasis on crushing the unions.

Today the bosses show their ability to keep up with the changing times. They'll still crush where they can, but they count on controlled unions as their answer.

The greatest obstacle to their design is the same obstacle that foiled them in 1934—the rank and file.

The 1934 strike is memorable because above all it demonstrated the power latent in the rank and file. The rank and file not only manned the picket lines and did the sacrificing—as it must in every strike—but it also made the big decisions and determined the strategy.

The rank and file wouldn't be bulldozed or buffaloed, browbeaten or divided, and therefore it couldn't be licked. Once it knew the score the rank and file could not be misled by any phony labor leader or panicked by any barrage of newspaper propaganda.

Ultimately the power of any union that serves as an instrumentality of the workers rests on the courage and conviction in its ranks. That is one fundamental truth that has not altered since 1934, nor will it alter in times to come.

We on the waterfront have tried to live in the light of that truth. We have viewed the test of leadership as the ability to pose the issues and alternatives in the sharpest, clearest terms so that the rank and file could exercise its judgment and render its decisions.

There are those who would confuse the issues with redbaiting, and confound the alternatives by plying prejudice and falsehood. They tried it in 1934, but their game did not work because the rank and file had its eye on the ball and would not be diverted.

We cannot afford to forget that the phony labor leaders of 1934 who marched across the pages of THE BIG STRIKE may be dead or gone, reformed or missing, but there are always new ones anxious to take their places in this seemingly endless drama.

And if any dues-payer asks, "When will it end? When can I knock off?" the only answer is, "Brother, not until we win all the way."

San Francisco
December 1949

APPENDIX

1. PROPOSED SETTLEMENT OF APRIL 3

San Francisco, April 3, 1934

1st. *Selection of Representation.* To expedite matters the Waterfront Employers' Union of San Francisco propose that they accept the International Longshoremen's Association as the representative of the majority of the longshoremen of the San Francisco Bay district. As such they will meet with the representatives of the International Longshoremen's Association for the purpose of collective bargaining. The Waterfront Employers' Union, if permitted or required by law, will recognize also the known spokesman of any other bona fide group or groups of longshoremen employed in the San Francisco Bay district. The employers commit themselves to extend to all longshoremen employed within their jurisdiction such wages and working conditions as are agreed upon between themselves and the representatives of the International Longshoremen's Association. They also commit themselves not to extend to any minor group or groups wages or working conditions more favorable than those agreed upon with the representatives of the International Longshoremen's Association.

2nd. *Collective Bargaining and Settlement of Disputes.* The Waterfront Employers' Union propose that inasmuch as the Shipping Code is, according to latest advices, shortly to be executed and as its provisions will thereafter be binding, provisions for mediation and arbitration in case of dispute can be set up in accordance with the provisions of the Code. This proposal refers to Sections 10 and 11 and the employers suggest that pending the setup of the Code machinery, the Regional Director of the Labor Board act in lieu of the Administrator and that the Pacific American Steamship Association act in lieu of the Code authority in the nomination of representatives for employee and employer.

3rd. *Dispatching Hall.* The Waterfront Employers' Union concur in the suggestion that a Dispatching Hall must be established in order to cure many of the difficulties and complaints which have arisen from the dispatching system heretofore in effect in this port, and to effectuate a more equitable distribution of the work among the men employed in the industry. Employers realize that this neither can be a hall operated solely by themselves nor can it be a hall operated solely by a labor organization. Some measure of joint representation or joint management can be worked out and the employers are confident that the employees and themselves can develop a fair and satisfactory solution.

4th. The employers again state their view that because of local differences each port's problems must be handled separately.

2. FULL-PAGE ADVERTISEMENT IN ALL PAPERS

San Francisco, Calif.
March 16, 1934

To the Longshoremen of the San Francisco Bay District:

A strike again threatens on the San Francisco waterfront. We believe the facts are not clearly understood by the men. They are as follows:

On March 5th a committee of the Employers met with a committee of the International Longshoremen's Association. This meeting was voluntarily agreed to by the Employers prior to the adoption of a Code for the industry. The meeting, therefore, was a recognition of the fact that the ILA has been selected by some of the employees (neither side knows how many), as their representative for collective bargaining.

Th Committee of the ILA demanded that the Employers of the port of San Francisco speak for the entire Pacific Coast. The Employers of this port have no authority to speak for other ports, or to commit people whom they do not represent. A number of lines call at other Pacific Coast ports which do not call at San Francisco. This was explained fully to the representatives of the ILA. The employers stand ready today, as they did on March 5, to discuss matters affecting their employees at this port.

The second demand was that the Employers sign a closed shop or exclusive employment agreement. This would mean that the Employers would bind themselves to employ only such longshoremen as are members of the ILA. The Employers advised the representatives of the ILA that they had been advised by competent legal authority that such an agreement would be clearly unlawful. The law reserves to employees "the right to organize and bargain collectively through representatives of their own choosing," and that they "shall be free from interference, restraint or coercion of employers of labor, or their agents, in the designation of such representatives." A closed shop contract, requiring all employees and all those later seeking employment, to belong to a particular union certainly would not comply with these provisions.

General Johnson, National Recovery Administrator, in his Labor Day address last year said:

"If an employer should make a contract with a particular organization to employ only members of that organization—that would in effect be a contract to interfere with his workers' freedom of choice of their representatives, or with their rights to bargain individually, and would amount to employer coercion on these matters, which is contrary to law."

These two matters, and only these two matters, were discussed at the meeting of March 5. San Francisco Bay Longshoremen are receiving wages equal to the highest paid in any port of the United States. The Employers have not refused "recognition" nor have they refused "collective bargaining."

The Employers regret that out of such a situation a strike impends which may throw out of employment men who have worked under satisfactory and harmonious conditions for the last fourteen years.

WATERFRONT EMPLOYERS' UNION

3. FULL-PAGE ADVERTISEMENT IN ALL PAPERS

Waterfront Employers' Union
Secretary's Office,
215 Market Street, Room 832
San Francisco.

To the Longshoremen of the San Francisco Bay District:

The officials of the International Longshoremen's Association state that a majority of the men in this port have voted to go on strike March 23.

The ballot on which this affirmative vote was cast submitted only one question of willingness to strike to gain recognition. Did your officials, before the ballot was issued and voting was opened, explain to you the true facts of the situation? That the employers, at their meeting with your officials on March 5, had granted recognition and had stated their willingness to meet with your representatives for the purpose of collective bargaining?

Did your officials explain to you what the actual demands were that they had submitted to your employers? That the first demand was that the employers of this port undertake to speak for all other Pacific Coast ports and to commit all employers at all other Pacific Coast ports? That the employers had explained that they could not speak for or commit people whom they did not represent, but that they were ready and willing at all times to speak for and on behalf of the employers of this port?

Did your officials explain to you that the real issue and their basic demand was that the employers agree to enter into a closed shop agreement with the International Longshoremen's Association, by which agreement the employers would be bound to employ only such longshoremen as are members of the International Longshoremen's Association, refusing employment to all men who are not members? Did your officials tell you that your employers were unable to enter into such a contract, because such a contract would be directly contrary to law?

Have your officials clearly explained to you exactly what Section 7(a) of the Recovery Act means? Have they told you that it reserves and guarantees to each employee the right to organize and bargain collectively through representatives of his own choosing? Have they told you that every official interpretation and ruling on this section definitely confirms the clear and unmistakable language used in the law, that *each* employee, each *individual* employee, has the free choice of his representative? He may choose anyone or he may represent himself. Have they told you that the same section forbids employers of labor to interfere or to coerce their employees in the free selection of their representatives? Have they told you that General Johnson, National Recovery Administrator, has ruled that closed shop contracts are equivalent to employer coercion and are contrary to law? Did your officials tell you that they did not once mention wages or working conditions at the March 5 meeting?

The strike impends on such issues. It will throw out of work thousands of men. Are the issues clear-cut enough, to your minds, to warrant the action that is threatened? It is a good thing to have some right on your side when anything so serious as a strike and all its consequences is involved. It is decidely a bad thing to strike when you have nothing but wrong on your side.

One more question, which you can answer honestly to yourselves. From the last longshore strike in 1919 until the summer of 1933, the time when your present union commenced organizing, did you have any real complaint against your employers? Were not your wages the highest paid to any longshoremen in any port of the United States, were not your working conditions as favorable, were there any *actual* abuses? Who secured these wages and working conditions for you?

Remember that if you strike, it is your own act. It is your own job and your own livelihood that you give up. The ships will be kept working.

WATERFRONT EMPLOYERS' UNION OF SAN FRANCISCO

4. PROPOSED SETTLEMENT OF MAY 28

The representatives of the Waterfront Employers of Seattle, Portland, San Francisco and Los Angeles state their respective positions as follows:

The employers at each port will accept the International Longshoremen's Association as the representative of the longshoremen employed at such port for the purpose of collective bargaining.

Committees of employers and of the International Longshoremen's Association at each of the above ports will bargain collectively. They will also formulate rules and regulations for the registration and hiring of longshoremen through hiring halls to be established at each port.

The procedure for the operation of such halls shall provide that there shall be no discrimination against any man because of membership or non-membership in a labor union.

The functions of the halls shall be confined to registration and hiring of men. The employers shall be free to select their men within those eligible and under the policies jointly determined; likewise the men shall be free to select their job; and within those principles the employers will cooperate in spreading the work.

The employers shall pay the rent of the halls and incidental expenses.

The employers shall be responsible for the registration and dispatching records and shall pay the salaries of their employees.

The International Longshoremen's Association shall maintain representatives in each hall, to see that there is no discrimination, either in registration or the hiring of any member of that Association and the International Longshoremen's Association shall pay directly the salaries of their representatives. The registration and dispatching records shall be open to the representatives of the International Longshoremen's Association at all times.

Employers agree to submit to arbitration on the facts of all existing disputes on hours and basic wages.

5. LETTER FROM INDUSTRIAL ASSOCIATION
ASSUMING AUTHORITY IN HANDLING OF STRIKE

San Francisco, California
June 13, 1934

J. W. Mailliard, Jr., President
San Francisco Chamber of Commerce
Merchant's Exchange Building
San Francisco, California

My dear Mr. Mailliard:

On behalf of the Industrial Association of San Francisco acknowledgment is made of your letter of June 12. The contents were presented to the Board of Directors and I was instructed to reply as follows:

1. The Industrial Association accepts the responsibility which you ask it to assume of determining a method of ending the intolerable conditions which are now existing in San Francisco as a result of the waterfront strike. We have been alive to the situation which has confronted this port for more than a month and have stood ready at all times to place the Industrial Association at the service of all parties involved in the controversy in the interest of the people of San Francisco as a whole.

2. We have deferred any action because of the request of the President's personal representative, Assistant Secretary of Labor Edward F. McGrady, that no steps be taken which could in any way interfere with or obstruct the course of direct negotiations which the government's representatives were attempting to guide towards a fair settlement. We agree with you, however, that the time has now come when San Francisco must protect itself from what you describe as an intolerable situation, the Federal mediators have admitted the complete failure of their efforts.

3. In this connection we think it proper to remind you of the prolonged negotiations, all culminating in failure which have marked the last three months. The history of this controversy is as follows:

4. Representatives of the employers and the International Longshoremen's Association first met with the then chairman of the Regional Labor Board on March 5, 1934. At this time, although no demands had been made on any other port by the ILA, that organization insisted on San Francisco entering into an agreement which would cover the entire coast and which, among other things, called for an exclusive closed shop contract with that union. These demands were refused on the grounds as stated by the Waterfront Employers' Union that the representatives of the local steamship operators lacked authority to bind the entire coast, and that the closed shop demand was illegal under the terms of Section 7(a) of the National Industrial Recovery Act.

5. Despite further efforts to mediate and many meetings a strike vote was taken of all Pacific Coast locals of the ILA effective March 23. A majority of all members voting favored a strike.

6. On March 22 President Roosevelt wired W. J. Lewis, District President of the ILA, urging that the strike be postponed until a fact-finding

committee could bring in a report on the matters in controversy. The ILA yielded to the President's request and the strike order was canceled. The Fact-Finding Committee consisted of the chairmen of the Pacific Coast Regional Labor Boards—J. L. Leonard of Los Angeles; Charles A. Reynolds of Seattle; and Henry F. Grady of San Francisco.

7. Commencing in San Francisco on March 28, 1934, hearings continued before the board for four days. On April 1 the recommendations of the board were presented to both sides, and on April 3 the employers presented counter proposals which the President's Board, after a thorough study recommended to the union negotiators for their acceptance. On the same day the proposals of the employers were accepted by the men.

8. A plan for a central registration and hiring hall under joint control of employers and union representatives for the purpose of limiting the men eligible to work in this port to those who had claim of seniority on the industry was proposed by the employers and accepted by the men. It was never made effective because the men could not agree on a date, after which only workers who had been employed prior to that date would have the right to register for employment. It is only within the last few months that men not experienced in longshore work in San Francisco have flocked into the city.

9. Under the provisions of the agreement of April 3, representatives of the men and of the Waterfront Employers' Union again entered into direct negotiations. These meetings were held on April 4, 5, and 6. No progress was made because of the insistence of the union's representatives that the agreement must be binding on all ports. On April 7 Chairman Grady advised the men that such a demand was in violation of the terms of the agreement of April 3.

10. On April 14 a new committee was elected by the San Francisco local and negotiations between the Waterfront Employers' Union representatives and this new committee commenced on April 16, continuing thereafter for several days.

11. At the first of these meetings employers' representatives made definite proposals for a maximum work week, a maximum work period and a minimum rest period. These were accepted by the union representatives on April 20 and became effective on the same day. Progress was made on the revision of the working rules but the conferences became deadlocked on the wage issue.

12. At the suggestion of W. J. Lewis, District President of the ILA, covering all Pacific Coast ports, the wage issue was referred to local mediation in accordance with the agreement of April 3, to settle issues which could not be settled by collective bargaining. Again the union representatives insisted that the San Francisco employers sign an agreement on wages binding on all Coast ports and companies with which they had no affiliation. The employers restated their position on negotiating for San Francisco alone and on this basis mediation was resumed. Meetings were held from April 21 through to May 5 by the executive committees of the longshoremen and employers with marked progress being made in revising the working rules and hiring conditions for this port.

13. The local mediation board, considering the matter of wages and

hours, continued meeting twice daily but no agreement could be reached. Employers then advocated resort to national mediation in accordance with the terms of the agreement of April 3 but the representatives of the men refused to consider this proposal. On May 8 the newspapers announced a strike vote by the ILA and the strike became effective in all Pacific Coast ports on the following day.

14. The next important development was the arrival in San Francisco of Edward F. McGrady, Assistant Secretary of Labor and Assistant for Labor to Recovery Administrator Hugh S. Johnson. After twenty-seven meetings with both parties in less than half as many days McGrady returned to Washington to report that he had been unable to effect a settlement. During these negotiations Joseph P. Ryan, General President of the ILA, reached San Francisco, and on May 28 an agreement was reached between the representatives of the employers, the local ILA officials and Ryan that was satisfactory to all parties. On submission of this agreement for ratification by the unions in the various coast ports it was not voted on in most of them and was turned down by a decisive majority in San Francisco.

15. The various settlements which have been proposed have not only been accepted by the representatives of the men and then repudiated because of the capricious and arbitrary attitude of the local leaders but were urged for acceptance by the Pacific Coast representatives of the federal government in charge of labor matters under NRA; by the Assistant Secretary of Labor, and, finally, by the General President of the ILA. Nevertheless, the strike still continued.

16. Picket lines were thrown across the waterfront and by threats of intimidation and violence all trucking to and from the docks was stopped. Further threats of intimidation caused the teamsters on June 7, to decline to handle any freight which had come from the waterfront. To date there have been fifty-one arrests in connection with assaults and eighty-eight miscellaneous arrests resulting directly from the strike. Only efficient police cooperation has prevented further violence.

17. We have gone into this history at some length in order that the public of San Francisco may be informed of the more than tolerant attitude of the business community and of this Association, in the face of great monetary losses to thousands of our citizens, of rapidly increasing drains on the city's relief resources. The record shows a laudable, patient effort to reach a fair solution on the part of both the employers and the conservative union leaders.

18. You yourself have succinctly stated the intolerable conditions obtaining, and the frightful losses being sustained by the business community. Certain aspects of this strike which were not touched on in your letter, but which we consider to be of paramount importance must be outlined. This is no local industrial dispute. Already its effects have worked back into the great valleys of the State where the year's crops are being prepared for harvest and shipment. The possibility of moving these fruits of the land to market is seriously threatened. Nor is this all. Our difficulty here is beginning to assume national and even international proportions. Rumblings have been heard of refusals to handle our cargoes not only on our eastern seaboard but in foreign ports as well. Ships now

departing from Pacific Coast points are threatened with complete tie-ups when they touch foreign shores.

19. The strike has had most serious aspects outside of the parties directly involved. Sailors, cooks, stewards, and other maritime workers are on strike in sympathy. You point out that workers who have no quarrel with their employers have been forced into unemployment. Should the tie-up continue thousands of other workers both here and throughout the State will be added to the ranks of the unemployed with a consequent threat to the already overburdened relief programs.

20. In assuming the responsibility for solving this situation the Industrial Association still hopes that an immediate and amicable settlement can be reached. In any event, however, the Association intends to take whatever lawful steps are necessary to protect the economic interests of this community and to restore to the people of San Francisco that security to which they are entitled.

Very truly yours,

JOHN J. FORBES,
President.

6. THE RYAN-PLANT AGREEMENT OF JUNE 16

San Francisco, California
June 16, 1934

This agreement is entered into by the Waterfront Employers of Seattle, Portland, San Francisco, and Los Angeles, each acting for itself, and the International Longshoremen's Association and its affiliated locals through its International President, and the Pacific Coast District through its officers.

GENERAL PRINCIPLES

The purpose of this agreement is to promote permanent industrial relations between employer and employee on a basis mutually satisfactory to both parties. As a condition precedent to the accomplishment of such a purpose it is recognized that responsible leadership and responsible membership must exist in both groups.

The Waterfront Employers recognize the International Longshoremen's Association as the representative of the longshoremen for the purpose of collective bargaining.

The principle of collective bargaining shall be joint and equal control of employment policies and of the management of hiring and dispatching halls.

It is mutually agreed that there shall be no discrimination against any man because of membership or non-membership in a labor union.

It is mutually agreed that the employers shall be free to select their men within those eligible and under the policies jointly determined; likewise the men shall be free to select their job.

[246]

A Labor Relations Committee, consisting of three members from the employers and three members from the Longshoremen, shall be selected at each port. The duties of these Committees shall be:

(a) To determine wages and working rules.

(b) To establish halls for the registration, hiring and dispatching of longshoremen; to determine rules and regulations for the operation of these halls, which rules must conform to the policies laid down in this agreement; to supervise the operation of these halls.

(c) To act as a Court of Appeal in case of dispute between employer and employee; to investigate and adjust any complaint of violation of the rules established for the operation of the hiring halls. In the event members of the Committee cannot agree they shall select a disinterested impartial chairman whose vote shall determine the issue.

HIRING HALLS

All longshoremen regularly employed prior to December 31, 1933, as determined by the employers' payroll, are to be registered.

Additional men are to be registered only as the need of the port may require, as determined by the Labor Relations Committee.

The qualifications for registration are to be determined by the Labor Relations Committee; applications for registration shall however be considered in order of date of application.

There shall be no discrimination in the registration of any man or in any other respect because of union or non-union affiliation.

As a means of effectuating an equitable distribution of the work, the Labor Relations Committee shall determine the maximum number of hours any man shall be permitted to work in any given period of time.

The rent and expenses of the hiring halls and the salaries of the staff shall be borne equally by the Waterfront Employers and the International Longshoremen's Association.

Each longshoreman registered at the hall who is not a member of the International Longshoremen's Association shall pay monthly to the Committee toward the support of the hall a sum equal to the pro rata share of the expense borne by each member of the International Longshoremen's Association.

The employers agree that they will not in any way endeavor to undermine the International Longshoremen's Association or induce its members to give up their membership.

The International Longshoremen's Association may discipline any of its members for violation of its rules.

The Committee may, for any cause sufficient to it, strike any man from the registration list, but he may not be otherwise dropped.

PRESENT WAGE DISPUTE

The existing dispute on hours and basic wages shall be submitted to arbitration on the facts.

There shall be no stoppage of work pending the adjustment of any dispute which may develop under this agreement, or for any other cause.

The men shall return to work on Monday, June 18, 1934. Any wage adjustment shall be retroactive to that date.

This agreement shall be binding until September 30, 1934, and shall be considered as renewed from year to year thereafter, unless either party hereto shall give written notice to the other, of their desire to have same modified, and such notice must be given at least thirty (30) days prior to the expiration of this contract. If such notice is not so given, then this agreement is to stand as renewed for the following year.

> Waterfront Employers' Union of Seattle
> By   (s) T. G. Plant
>
> Waterfront Employers' Union of San Francisco
> By   (s) T. G. Plant
>
> Waterfront Employers' Union of Portland
> By   (s) T. G. Plant
>
> Waterfront Employers' Union of Los Angeles
> By   (s) T. G. Plant
>
> International Longshoremen's Association
> By   (s) Joseph P. Ryan
>
> Pacific Coast District ILA
>   (s) J. E. Finnegan

We guarantee the observance of this agreement by the International Longshoremen's Association membership.

> (s)   Michael Casey,
>   President of Teamsters' Union of San Francisco
> (s)   John P. McLaughlin,
>   Secretary of Teamsters' Union of San Francisco
> (s)   Dave Beck,
>   President of Teamsters' Union of Seattle
> (s)   Charles A. Reynolds,
> (s)   J. L. Leonard,
>   President's Mediation Board
> (s)   Angelo J. Rossi,
>   Mayor of San Francisco

We guarantee the observance of this agreement by the Waterfront Employers' Union.

> (s)   Jno. F. Forbes,
>   Industrial Association of San Francisco

7. LETTER FROM THOMAS G. PLANT TO
INDUSTRIAL ASSOCIATION

San Francisco, California
June 18, 1934

Industrial Association of San Francisco
Alexander Building
San Francisco, California

Gentlemen:

On Saturday, June 16, 1934, a contract was executed in Mayor Rossi's office between the Waterfront Employer's Union and the International Longshoremen's Association, by its International President Joseph P. Ryan, providing for the settlement of the Longshoremen's Strike and the return to work of the longshoremen this morning, June 18.

The performance of this contract on the part of the membership of the Longshoremen's Union was guaranteed in writing at that time by the following:

Angelo J. Rossi, Mayor of San Francisco
Michael Casey, President, Teamster's Union of San Francisco
J. P. McLaughlin, Secretary, Teamsters' Union of San Francisco
Dave Beck, President, Teamsters' Union of Seattle
Charles A. Reynolds and J. L. Leonard, President's Mediation Board

The observance of the contract on the part of the Waterfront Employers' Union was guaranteed by your Association.

This agreement was in no way contingent upon ratification by the union membership. In the presence of Mayor Rossi on Thursday, June 14, 1934, Mr. Ryan, International President of the Longshoremen's Union, gave his unqualified assurance that he could make an agreement on behalf of its membership that would be effective. At the same time Mr. Michael Casey and Mr. J. P. McLaughlin, President and Secretary of the Teamsters' Union of San Francisco, and Dave Beck, President of the Seattle Teamsters' Union, stated that they would guarantee that any agreement made by Mr. Ryan would be carried out.

It was upon the faith of these assurances that Mr. Plant obtained authority from the Waterfront Employers of Seattle, Portland, San Francisco and Los Angeles to negotiate an agreement with Mr. Ryan. The agreement so negotiated is the agreement which was executed in Mayor Rossi's office on Saturday by Mr. Ryan and guaranteed by the gentlemen above mentioned.

We have now been informed that the members of the International Longshoremen's Association have refused to abide by the agreement signed by their International President but plan to continue the strike until the demands of other unions have been satisfied and to cause a general strike if possible.

The Waterfront Employers' Union has no power or jurisdiction to discuss or negotiate demands of sailors and other marine workers, its sole

[249]

authority being to handle problems of longshore labor. This has been known at all times to Mr. Ryan and as long back as May 27 Mr. McGrady, Assistant Secretary of Labor, and the Federal Mediators agreed and understood that the longshoremen's strike must be settled without reference to the demands of sailors and other marine workers.

At all times in the course of the negotiations and the execution of the agreement above mentioned, it has been understood by all parties that it was in no way contingent upon the settlement of strike demands of the sailors.

The shipowners have relied in good faith upon the integrity of the agreement executed by Mr. Ryan and guaranteed as above stated, and have already executed the necessary instructions to carry it into effect.

This immediate repudiation of an agreement made in good faith is convincing evidence that the control of the Longshoremen's Association is dominated by the radical element and Communists whose purpose is not to promote industrial peace, rather their avowed purpose is to provoke class hatred and bloodshed and to undermine the government. Further evidence of this is afforded by the fact that a majority of the committee of five selected at the longshoremen's meeting on Sunday have been active in the affairs of the Communist organizations.

It is within the power of the guarantors of the agreement to bring this strike to an end without delay and if it is made clear that longshoremen cannot expect aid or sympathy in their repudiation of the agreement the responsible longshoremen will return to work at once.

You are a party to the agreement and we request that you immediately call upon the other parties to that agreement and its guarantors to make good upon their guaranty.

Very truly yours,

Waterfront Employers' Union of San Francisco
By   T. G. PLANT, *President*

8. INDUSTRIAL ASSOCIATION TELEGRAM TO PRESIDENT ROOSEVELT

San Francisco, June 18, 1934

Honorable Franklin D. Roosevelt,
President,
White House,
Washington, D. C.

My Dear Mr. President:

Further with reference to our telegram to you of June fifteenth reporting serious waterfront labor situation in Pacific Coast ports we again beg your immediate intervention to prevent serious conflict in San Francisco and other Pacific Coast ports as result of repudiation by membership of International Longshoremen's Association of agreement signed last Saturday settling longshoremen's strike. The agreement was signed by Joseph P. Ryan, International President of the ILA and Thomas G. Plant, President of Waterfront Employers' Union of San Francisco, representing also the waterfront employers of Seattle, Portland and Los Angeles. This agreement also bore the signature of Charles A. Reynolds, Chairman of Regional Labor Board of Seattle, and J. L. Leonard, Chairman, Regional Labor Board of Los Angeles, both signing as guarantors of performance on part of membership of longshoremen's union. It also carried the signature of Angelo J. Rossi, Mayor of San Francisco; Michael Casey, President, Teamsters' Union, San Francisco; Dave Beck, President, Teamsters' Union, Seattle, all as guarantors of the observance of the agreement by the membership of ILA and the writer as President of Industrial Association as guarantor of performance by the Waterfront Employers' Union. At rump meeting, held Sunday, members of Longshoremen's Union, San Francisco, by standing vote, repudiated President Ryan's signature and voted to continue strike. We understand there is evidence in hands of Department that Communists have captured control of Longshoremen's Unions with no intention of strike settlement. We have reached crisis threatening destruction of property and serious loss of life in various ports on Pacific Coast unless you act to compel performance on the part of Longshoremen's Unions of the agreement signed by their International President. The entire business community which has been patient for more than forty days during the progress of this dispute is now insistent that this port and others on the Pacific Coast be immediately opened.

> Industrial Association of San Francisco
> John F. Forbes, *President*

WATERFRONT EMPLOYERS' UNION

President's Office
215 Market Street—Room 832
San Francisco

Mr. H. Bridges,   *June 19, 1934*
Chairman, Joint Marine Strike Committee,
Room "B"—Ferry Building,
San Francisco, California

Dear Sir:

This acknowledges receipt of and replies to your letter of June 19 in which you advise that a Joint Committee has been formed to handle negotiation for the various unions now on strike in the San Francisco Bay area, and that the Committee is now ready to enter into negotiations with our Association.

While your letter does not state the names of the various unions which your Committee represents, we understand that the International Longshoremen's Association, various unions of seafaring men, and also unions of men employed ashore such as machinists, coopers and caulkers, are included.

The Waterfront Employers' Union has no authority or jurisdiction with respect to any matters save those pertaining to longshore labor in the port of San Francisco.

It must be obvious to anyone that it has no authority or jurisdiction with respect to such trades as machinists, coopers and caulkers.

The question might arise in some minds as to whether it has authority or jurisdiction with respect to the unions of seafaring men.

The membership of the Waterfront Employers' Union is comprised of certain steamship lines serving the port of San Francisco, of foreign ownership as well as of American ownership. Contracting stevedores, or concerns whose business is limited to the loading and unloading of vessels, are also members.

The question of adjustment of demands of the unions of seafaring men affect all vessels flying the American flag, vessels trading on the Atlantic as well as on the Pacific; in fact, wherever American vessels may trade.

We think it should be apparent to anyone that a small group of vessel operators, whose offices are located in San Francisco, agents of foreign steamship companies whose vessels trade here, and of contracting stevedores who have nothing whatever to do with the management of vessels, cannot possibly have any authority or jurisdiction with respect to a matter which is so far-reaching in its scope.

Means are available in the machinery of the Federal Government for the handling of such disputes as have arisen with respect to the unions of seafaring men. On May 26 a Committee of the Pacific Coast Council of the International Longshoremen's Association presented a demand that all demands of the striking seafaring unions be met in full before the longshoremen would return to work, regardless of what settlement might be reached in the longshoremen's dispute. This question was discussed during all of May 26 and May 27 before the Assistant Secretary of Labor, Mr. Edward F. McGrady and Messrs. Reynolds, Grady and Leonard, the Regional Labor Directors for Seattle, San Francisco, and Los Angeles, respectively. Late in the afternoon of May 27 a Committee of the Pacific Coast Council of the International Longshoremen's Association was convinced that the Waterfront Employers' Union had no jurisdiction and the demand was withdrawn. The Regional Labor Directors above referred to assured the Committee of the International Longshoremen's Association that the demands of the striking unions of seafaring men would be handled through the regular channels provided by the Federal Government. The Government channels are still available and to our knowledge there are no other means through which these disputes can be handled.

We believe that our sincere desire to settle the longshoremen's strike on fair terms has been demonstrated by our execution of the agreement on June 16 with the International Longshoremen's Association, acting by its International President, Mr. Ryan. We are prepared to carry out that agreement and we cannot believe that the longshoremen of this port will permit themselves to be led into the impossible situation of demanding as a condition to the settlement of this strike that the demands of seafaring unions with which the Waterfront Employers' Union have no power or jurisdiction, be first met. Insistence upon such a demand can only mean that those leaders who persist in it have no desire to settle the strike. We cannot believe that this can be the case.

Very truly yours,

(signed) T. G. PLANT, *President*

10. TELEGRAM SENT BY THOMAS G. PLANT TO LABOR SECRETARY FRANCES PERKINS ON JUNE 21, 1934

On Saturday the Waterfront Employers' Union of San Francisco acting for itself and also by delegated authority acting for the waterfront employers of Seattle, Portland and Los Angeles, entered into an agreement with the International Longshoremen's Association through its International President, J. P. Ryan.

As proof of its complete fairness, the observance of the agreement by the longshoremen was guaranteed by Mayor Rossi of San Francisco, by Reynolds of Seattle and Leonard of Los Angeles, members of the President's Mediation Board, acting under authority from Washington, to sign the agreement, by Michael Casey, President and John C. McLaughlin, President of the Teamsters' Union of Seattle. The observance by the employers was guaranteed by the Industrial Association of San Francisco.

The agreement provided for the recognition of the International Longshoremen's Association for the purpose of collective bargaining, for non-discrimination in registration and hiring because of union or non-union affiliation, the joint and equal control and management of registration and hiring halls and equal sharing of expenses of such hiring halls, for submission to arbitration on the facts of existing disputes on hours and basic wages.

The agreement provided for the return to work on Monday, June 18, of all striking longshoremen.

On Sunday the agreement was repudiated at a mass meeting of longshoremen, dominated by communists on the grounds that it did not provide for settlement of demands of various other unions technically on strike. An ultimatum was issued that all demands of all striking unions must be met in full force before the longshoremen or any others would return to work. The unions on strike include many not even connected with shipping with respect to which it is obvious that the Waterfront Employers had no jurisdiction. Even with respect to demands of seafaring unions our association has no jurisdiction, as our membership is made up of contracting stevedores whose sole business is loading and unloading of vessels and of steamship companies serving this port, many of which are companies of foreign ownership. It is apparent that the demands of seafaring unions can only be taken up with individual companies.

All of these facts are well known to the officers of the International Longshoremen's Association, and on May 27, in the presence of the Assistant Secretary of Labor, E. F. McGrady and federal mediators, Grady, Leonard and Reynolds, the Pacific Coast Executive Committee of the ILA withdrew this demand. The renewal of the demand after the execution of the agreement on Saturday has convinced everyone that it has been renewed by radical leaders who are at present in control of the union for the sole purpose of preventing settlement of the strike and to cause its spread, if possible.

We believe that the responsible labor leadership here and the responsible membership in labor unions are entirely convinced of the fairness of the contract entered into and the press of San Francisco today all carry leading editorials requesting the men to return to work under its terms. The agreement provides that the ILA is recognized for the purpose of collective bargaining and that a joint committee composed of three of its representatives and three representatives of the employers shall meet to carry out the agreement and supervise the hiring halls and the method of registration. The agreement further provides that if these six cannot agree then a seventh is to be selected to decide the question.

We welcome your participation in the solution of these difficulties and in view of the institution of the agreement on Saturday we suggest that you join in the request that the men return to work at once and offer your good offices in connection with the carrying out of the agreement and settlement of differences which arise under it which the representatives of the ILA and of the employers cannot agree upon. In the event that the committee provided in the agreement cannot determine the question we will welcome your helpful suggestion as to the settlement of any such difference.

The most important thing at first is that commerce be started and that the men return to work, and we again repeat our earnest request to you that you ask the men to do this at once under the terms of the existing agreement, assuring them you will see that the agreement is carried out in full fairness by the employers and we will welcome your cooperation to this end.

By separate telegram we are giving you full text of the agreement executed by the Waterfront Employers' Union and by the International Longshoremen's Association through its International President.

11. ARBITRATION AWARD HANDED DOWN BY NATIONAL LONGSHOREMEN'S BOARD

In the Matter of the Arbitration between Pacific Coast District Local 38 of the International Longshoremen's Association, acting on behalf of the various Locals whose members perform longshore labor and Waterfront Employers of Seattle, Waterfront Employers of Portland, Waterfront Employers' Union of San Francisco and Marine Service Bureau of Los Angeles.

ARBITRATORS' AWARD

This award is made pursuant to agreement dated the 7th day of August, 1934, between the above named parties, which agreement is hereby referred to hereof.

Said agreement provides that the decision of the arbitrators (which shall be in writing and must be by a majority) shall constitute a series of agreements between the International Longshoremen's Association, acting on behalf of various Locals whose members perform longshore labor, first party, on the one hand, and Waterfront Employers of Seattle, a list of the members of which is attached to said agreement, marked Exhibit "A," second party, Waterfront Employers of Portland, a list of the members of which is attached to said agreement, marked Exhibit "B," third party, Waterfront Employers' Union of San Francisco, a list of the members of which is attached to said agreement, marked Exhibit "C," fourth party, and Marine Service Bureau of Los Angeles, a list of the members of which is attached to said agreement, marked Exhibit "D," fifth party, separately, on the other hand, which shall be binding upon each of said parties as aforesaid for the period to and including September 30, 1935, and which shall be considered as renewed from year to year thereafter between the respective parties unless either party to the respective agreements shall give written notice to the other of its desire to modify or terminate the same, said notice to be given at least forty (40) days prior to the expiration date. If such notice shall be given by any party other than the International Longshoremen's Association, first party, then the International Longshoremen's Association shall have fifteen (15) days thereafter within which it may give written notice of termination of all of said agreements whereon on the succeeding September 30, all of said agreement shall terminate. If such notice or notices are not so given the agreement shall be deemed to be renewed for the succeeding year.

The arbitrators decide and award as follows:

Section 1. Longshore work is all handling of cargo in its transfer from vessel to first place of rest including sorting and piling of cargo on the dock, and direct transfer of cargo from vessel to railroad car or barge and vice versa.

The following occupations are included in longshore work: Longshoremen, gang bosses, hatch tenders, winch drivers, donkey drivers, boom men, burton men, sack-turners, side runners, front men, jitney drivers, and any other person doing longshore work as defined in this section.

Section 2. Six hours shall constitute a day's work. Thirty hours shall constitute a week's work, averaged over a period of four weeks. The first six hours worked between the hours of 8 a.m. and 5 p.m. shall be designated as straight time. All work in excess of six hours between the hours of 8 a.m. and 5 p.m., and all work during meal time and between 5 p.m. and 8 a.m. on weekdays and from 5 p.m. on Saturday to 8 a.m. on Monday, and all work on legal holidays, shall be designated as overtime. Meal time shall be any one hour between 11 a.m. and 1 p.m. When men are required to work more than five consecutive hours without an opportunity to eat, they shall be paid time and one-half of the straight or overtime rate, as the case may be, for all the time worked in excess of five hours without a meal hour.

Section 3. The basic rate of pay for longshore work shall not be less than $0.95 (ninety-five cents) per hour for straight time, not less than $1.40 (one dollar and forty cents) per hour for overtime, provided, however, that for work which is now paid higher than the present basic rates, the differentials above the present basic rates shall be added to the basic rates established in this paragraph (a).

(b) For those classifications of penalty cargo for which differentials are now paid above the basic rates, the same differentials above the basic rates established by this award shall be maintained and paid;

(c) For shoveling, shoveling bones in bulk, both non-offensive and offensive, ten cents above the basic rate shall be paid in Los Angeles;

(d) For handling creosote and creosote products, green hides, and fertilizer, for which a differential of ten cents above the present basic rates is now allowed in Los Angeles to foremen, the same differential of ten cents shall also be paid in Los Angeles to men handling these commodities;

(e) For handling logs, piles and lumber which have been submerged, when loaded from water, ten cents above the basic rates established by this award shall be paid for thirty tons or over in Portland;

(f) The increases in the rates of pay established by this award shall be paid as of July 31, 1934.

Section 4. The hiring of all longshoremen shall be through halls maintained and operated jointly by the International Longshoremen's Association, the Pacific Coast District, and the respective employers' associations. The hiring and dispatching of all longshoremen shall be done through one central hiring hall in each of the ports of Seattle, Portland, San Francisco and Los Angeles, with such branch halls as the Labor Relations Committee, provided for in Section 9, shall decide. All expense of the hiring halls shall be borne one-half by the International Longshoremen's Association and one-half by the employers. Each longshoreman registered at any hiring hall who is not a member of the International Longshoremen's Association shall pay to the Labor Relations Committee toward the support of the hall a sum equal to the pro-rata share of the expense of the support of the hall paid by each member of the International Longshoremen's Association.

Section 5. The personnel for each hiring hall shall be determined and appointed by the Labor Relations Committee for the port, except that the dispatcher shall be selected by the International Longshoremen's Association.

Section 6. All longshoremen shall be dispatched without favoritism or discrimination, regardless of union or non-union membership.

Section 7. The Labor Relations Committee in Seattle, Portland and Los Angeles, where hiring halls now exist, shall decide within twenty days from the date of this award whether a hiring hall now in use shall be utilized. If in any of said ports no decision is made within such twenty days, a new hall shall be established in such port within thirty days from the date of this award.

Section. 8. The hiring and dispatching of longshoremen in all the ports covered by this award other than those mentioned in Section 4, and excepting Tacoma, shall be done as provided for the ports mentioned in Section 4; unless the Labor Relations Committee in any of such ports establishes other methods of hiring or dispatching.

Section 9. The parties shall immediately establish for each port affected by this award, a Labor Relations Committee to be composed of three representatives designated by the employers' association of that port and three representatives designated by the International Longshoremen's Association. By mutual consent the Labor Relations Committee in each port may change the number of representatives from the International Longshoremen's Association and the employers' association. In the event that such committee fails to agree on any matter, they may refer such matter for decision to any person or persons mutually acceptable to them, or they shall refer such matter, on request of either party, for decision to an arbitrator, who shall be designated by the Secretary of Labor of the United States or by any person authorized by the Secretary to designate such an arbitrator. Such arbitrator shall be paid by the International Longshoremen's Association and by the employers' association in each port. Nothing in this section shall be construed to prevent the Labor Relations Committee from agreeing upon other means of deciding matters upon which there has been disagreement.

Section 10. The duties of the Labor Relations Committee shall be:

(a) To maintain and operate the hiring hall;

(b) Within thirty days from the date of this award to prepare a list of the regular longshoremen of the port, and after such thirty days no longshoreman not on such list shall be dispatched from the hiring hall or employed by any employer while there is any man on the registered list qualified, ready and willing to do the work. No one shall be registered as a longshoreman who did not, during a period of three years immediately preceding May 9, 1934, derive his livelihood from the industry during not less than twelve months. Pending the preparation of these lists, no longshoreman who was a member of a gang or who was on any registered list or extra list between January 1, 1934, and May 9, 1934, shall be denied the opportunity of employment in the industry. The Labor Relations Committee, in registering longshoremen, may depart from this particular rule;

(c) To decide questions regarding rotation of gangs and extra men; revision of existing lists of extra men and of casuals; and the addition of new men to the industry when needed;

(d) To investigate and adjudicate all grievances and disputes relating to working conditions;

(e) To decide all grievances relating to discharges. The hearing and investigation of grievances relating to discharges shall be given preference over all other business before the committee. In case of discharge without sufficient cause, the committee may order payment for lost time or reinstatement with or without payment for lost time;

(f) To decide any other question of mutual concern relating to the industry and not covered by this award.

The Committee shall meet at any time within twenty-four hours, upon a written notice from either party stating the purpose of the meeting.

Section 11. The Labor Relations Committee for each port shall determine the organization of gangs and methods of dispatching. Subject to this provision and to the limitations of hours fixed in this award, the employers shall have the right to have dispatched to them, when available, the gangs in their opinion best qualified to do their work. Subject to the foregoing provisions gangs and men not assigned to gangs shall be so dispatched as to equalize their earnings as nearly as practicable, having regard to their qualifications for the work they are required to do. The employers shall be free to select their men within those eligible under the policies jointly determined, and the men likewise shall be free to select their jobs;

(b) The employees must perform all work as ordered by the employer. Any grievance resulting from the manner in which the work is ordered to be performed shall be dealt with as provided in Section 10;

(c) The employer shall have the right to discharge any man for incompetence, insubordination or failure to perform the work as required. If any man feels that he has been unjustly discharged, his grievance shall be dealt with as provided in Section 10;

(d) The employer shall be free, without interference or restraint from the International Longshoremen's Association, to introduce labor saving devices and to institute such methods of discharging and loading cargo as he considers best suited to the conduct of his business, provided such methods of discharging and loading are not inimical to the safety or health of the employees.

(signed)　EDWARD J. HANNA, *Chairman*
EDWARD F. McGRADY

I concur except as to the provisions of Section 3.

O. K. CUSHING

Dated this 12th day of October, 1934.
At San Francisco, California

12. "JOB ACTION" RESOLUTION ADOPTED BY THE MARITIME FEDERATION OF THE PACIFIC TO AVOID CONFUSION RESULTING FROM ILL-TIMED JOB STRIKES

Whereas, we believe and have demonstrated on numerous occasions that job action rightly used, with proper control, has been the means of gaining many concessions for the Maritime workers on the Pacific Coast; and

Whereas, inasmuch job action is and should be action taken when any group of Maritime workers desire to gain a concession without openly resorting to a strike; and

Whereas, in order to eliminate confusion and insure coordination of efforts in the best interests of all Maritime groups concerned, it is apparent that an organized method of procedure for job action be laid down by this convention, therefore, be it

Resolved, that the term "job action" shall mean only action taken by any Maritime group in attempting to gain from their employers some concessions not specifically provided for in their respective agreements or awards, and shall also mean action taken to enforce the award or agreement to the best interests of the Maritime groups concerned, or to prevent employers from violating agreements or awards, and be it further

Resolved, the job action should be confined to a job such as a ship, dock, shop or warehouse, unless otherwise agreed by the Maritime groups affected, and any Maritime group affected or liable to be affected should be notified and the issue in question be placed before them, and be it further

Resolved, that a committee of all Maritime groups affected on the job be formed on the job to consolidate action and prevent misunderstandings; such committee's authority not to exceed the constitution of the Maritime Federation of the Pacific Coast, and be it further

Resolved, that when job action reaches a point, in the opinion of the majority of the Maritime groups affected by having their members pulled off the job, and that to go further may jeopardize the Maritime Federation as a whole, the matter shall be referred where and when possible to the District Council for further action or adjustment.